Stefan Worm

Branded Component Strategi

GABLER RESEARCH

Stefan Worm

Branded Component Strategies
Ingredient Branding in B2B Markets

With a Foreword by Prof. Dr. Friedhelm W. Bliemel

GABLER

RESEARCH

Bibliographic information published by the Deutsche Nationalbibliothek
The Deutsche Nationalbibliothek lists this publication in the Deutsche Nationalbibliografie;
detailed bibliographic data are available in the Internet at http://dnb.d-nb.de.

Dissertation University of Kaiserslautern, 2009

D 386

1st Edition 2012

Editorial Office: Marta Grabowski | Anita Wilke

Gabler is a brand of Springer Fachmedien.
Springer Fachmedien is part of Springer Science+Business Media.
www.gabler.de

Coverdesign: KünkelLopka Medienentwicklung, Heidelberg
Printed on acid-free paper
Printed in Germany

ISBN 978-3-8349-1919-9

Foreword

B2B marketers are today required to master a much more comprehensive set of marketing instruments than ever before. Brand management, traditionally a domain of consumer marketing, has recently been added to the agenda of marketing managers in many B2B firms. With their imagination captured by anecdotes of successful B2B brands, B2B marketers are eager to put branding strategies in place. Yet, secured knowledge to guide marketers in the development, selection, and implementation of such strategies is scarce. In addition, brand-savvy B2B marketers are facing hard times when they try to obtain the budgets needed. The branding of components represents a domain of particular interest to many B2B suppliers. A stream of research on ingredient branding of consumer products suggests that product perceptions of end-users could be enhanced through the presence of strong component supplier brands. The shortfall of that literature is however that it stops short of looking at the impact of brand strength of suppliers for components/ingredients at the level of B2B relationships between suppliers and OEMs.

In the present study, Stefan Worm develops a theoretical framework to foster a better understanding of how branding can create competitive advantage for B2B component supplier firms. The theoretical propositions are tested using unique data from a multi-industry sample. Stefan Worm first examines to what extent strong component supplier brands affect market performance outcomes of component suppliers and which variables mediate this effect. Then he establishes a set of contingency preconditions under which strong component supplier brands generate positive market performance outcomes. Ultimately, the dissertation examines the effectiveness of various branding tools in managing component supplier brands.

The insights from this study are of potential interest to a readership in both B2B marketing practice and academia. From a practitioner's perspective, the thorough analysis of situational contingencies can help to assess whether brand building as a strategy may pay off for a particular supplier. Also, the findings can assist original equipment manufacturers in dealing with suppliers' branding initiatives. As one of the first empirical analyses of component branding, the study makes a contribution to academic research by embedding brand strength within the nomological network of buyer-supplier relationships. I thus wish that this book will be widely circulated among marketing professionals and researchers.

Prof. Dr. Friedhelm W. Bliemel

Preface

I am indebted to a number of people at TU Kaiserslautern and at Emory University who have been indispensable in completing this dissertation. First of all, I would like to thank my dissertation chair, Prof. Dr. Friedhelm Bliemel, for providing me with both the freedom and the guidance needed to successfully master this challenge. Prof. Dr. Rajendra Srivastava, through his role as external advisor, has had considerable impact on my work, and I would like to thank him for sharing his vision of marketing strategy research. I also owe big thanks to my dissertation committee members, Prof. Dr. Michael Hassemer, Prof. Dr. Stefan Roth, and Prof. Dr. Klaus J. Zink.

In addition, I would also like to thank those researchers who have indirectly contributed to this dissertation. Prof. Dr. Sundar Bharadwaj, Prof. Dr. Rod Brodie, Prof. Dr. Andreas Eggert, and Associate Prof. Dr. Jörg Henseler have been indispensable sources of inspiration and methodological expertise. My Ph.D. colleagues at the TU Kaiserslautern Marketing Department, Dr. Felix Hansen and Dr. David Zitzlsperger, have acted as great sparring partners, especially in the phase of research design and data collection. Finally I want to thank participants and faculty at the 2006 ANZMAC doctoral colloquium and the 2007 ISBM PhD Research Camp for their suggestions.

I acknowledge financial assistance that has been provided by Emory Marketing Institute, German Academic Exchange Service, Institute for the Study of Business Markets at Penn State University, and the Marketing Department at TU Kaiserslautern. Thanks for research assistance go to Jörg Broschart, Tim Zwietasch, and Lena Himbert.

Last but not least I thank my parents for the encouragement and support that they have provided throughout my educational carreer.

Dr. Stefan Worm

Summary

While researchers have placed considerable emphasis on the effectiveness of close buyer-supplier relationships, services, and customer solutions as means of adding differentiation through intangibles to business market offers, we know very little about the effectiveness of branding strategies in these settings. This study examines two research questions regarding the consequences and antecedents of component suppliers' brand strength. First, how does component supplier brand strength among original equipment manufacturers' (OEMs') customers affect the component supplier's market performance in their relationships with these OEMs, and how is such an effect contingent upon situational context factors? And secondly, which management instruments are effective in building, sustaining, and leveraging component supplier brand strength? More succinctly, this study develops and examines propositions regarding how marketing to a customer's customer influences supplier performance in business markets. This impact of component suppliers' branding in business markets is examined based on data from multiple-informants – marketing and purchasing managers – from 241 OEM firms. Findings support the expectation that strong supplier brands enhance the OEM's marketplace performance and make the supplier's components more valuable to OEMs. However, their perceptions of the value of branded components are compromised if suppliers use coercive strategies in negotiating with business customers. Higher levels of value of a supplier's branded components, as perceived by OEMs, positively affect behavioral outcomes as well as the strength of the relationship between the supplier and the OEM. A component supplier's brand strength is a more effective driver of performance for supplier industries with higher levels of competition. Also, suppliers stand to gain more from their strong brands when dealing with OEMs whose brands are weak. With regard to the antecedents of component supplier brand strength, this study finds that direct and joint communication, visibility, and – to some extent, exclusivity – represent effective brand management instruments to build, sustain, and leverage component supplier brand strength.

Brief Contents

Table of Contents

List of Figures

List of Tables

1   Introduction

1.1   Research Context

In today's globalized business markets, established component supplier firms from Germany, Europe, Japan, and the USA must resist strong competitive pressures if they want to remain successful. On the one hand, they are faced with intensifying competition from new players, especially from emerging economies in Asia, who are pushing into the world markets. On the other hand, suppliers are also under huge pressure from their own customers. Many buyers of industrial components have reduced the number of their suppliers by turning towards single sourcing or by inducing competition among a smaller set of component suppliers (Ulaga and Eggert, 2006b). The suppliers are thus forced to compete to attain and defend their positions as key suppliers. However, differentiating an offer has become increasingly difficult in business markets as many buying firms solicit bids on standardized components or require suppliers to design components to their own specifications. This results in product commoditization, i.e., similar tangible product offerings with very limited differentiation (Rangan and Bowman, 1992). Since physical product features have lost much of their power as differentiators, there is an increasing awareness of the importance of intangibles in differentiating an offer and avoiding pure price-based competition (Vargo and Lusch, 2004). Academic business market research has examined various avenues for differentiation through intangibles such as close buyer-supplier relationships (Cannon and Homburg, 2001; Ganesan, 1994; Palmatier et al., 2006), services (Fang, Palmatier, and Steenkamp, 2008; Reinartz and Ulaga, 2008), and customer solutions (Tuli, Kohli, and Bharadwaj, 2007).

However, brands, which are considered a crucial intangible asset in consumer markets, have received only limited attention from business marketing academia (Cretu and Brodie, 2007). The need for further insight in this area becomes obvious as business market managers have started to recognize the potential benefits of branding for the future performance of their businesses (Homburg, 2003, p. 1). This interest has to some extent been triggered by a few firms that have successfully pursued brand strategies in business markets, some of which are purely in business markets (e.g., IBM), while others have mixed consumer and business market backgrounds and are able to transfer some branding knowledge (e.g. Microsoft, General Electric, and Intel) (Interbrand, 2005). However, the absolute number of firms in business markets that actually pursue sound brand strategies is rather small (Homburg and Schneider, 2001, p. 605).

A major reason for this noteworthy discrepancy seems to lie in the lack of proven knowledge on the management of brands in business market settings and the firm performance outcomes resulting from those strategies. Business marketers say that they do not only lack the skills and knowledge in formulating their branding strategies, but they also have trouble convincing top management about the value of brands in order to justify brand investments and make brands an integral part of corporate strategy (Donath, 1999). Unlike most consumer goods manufacturers, many firms in business markets have traditionally viewed branding rather sceptically as a "gimmicky tactic" (Mudambi, Doyle, and Wong, 1997, p. 434) that only makes sense when dealing with buyers in consumer markets (Bendixen, Bukasa, and Abratt, 2004, p. 371; Homburg, Klarmann, and Schmitt, 2008, p. 1). Thus, without tangible proof for the impact of their brand strategy options on business performance, marketers face a tough challenge in implementing and obtaining support for successful brand strategies. Table 1 provides a summary of some questions brought up by managers in industry discussion sessions hosted by the Institute for the Study of Business Markets (ISBM) Brand Consortium. The questions fall into three broad categories: (1) the effect of brands on market performance in buyer-supplier relationships, (2) the effectiveness of the various brand management instruments, and (3) the moderating effect of situational context factors on the effectiveness of brand strategy. Against this background, there is a strong need for more detailed insight into branding in business markets.

In response to the strong need for further academic inquiry in this domain, the goal of the present study is to advance our knowledge as to how brands contribute to the performance of component suppliers in business markets.

1.2   Gap in the Literature

Branding in business markets has remained particularly under-researched though scholars have found some initial evidence for its contribution to firm performance in single industries (Aaker and Jacobson, 2001; Bendixen, Bukasa, and Abratt, 2004; Gordon, Calantone, and di Benedetto, 1993). Branding researchers have to date heavily focused on consumer-packaged goods industries while neglecting branding in business markets (Cretu and Brodie, 2007, p. 230). In addition, most of the few available studies stop short of answering the most important question, namely how brands actually create value in business markets. There have there been a few initial attempts to integrate brand-related constructs into the nomological network of business marketing, but it is only recently that academic marketing research has started a more thorough investigation of branding in business markets, partly on a broad empirical, cross-industry basis (e.g. Cretu and Brodie, 2007; Ghosh and John, forthcoming; Homburg, Klarmann, and Schmitt, 2008; Worm and Srivastava, 2009). While these studies offer initial valuable insights, many important questions still remain to be answered.

Effect of Brands on the Market Performance in Buyer-Supplier Relationships

How can suppliers make an OEM use a branded component?

How to make strong OEM brands use a branded component in the long run?

Will a component branding strategy help the supplier's sales people to be more effective?

Brand Management Instruments

How to build a brand among customers down the value chain?

Which channels should be used to communicate with indirect customers?

Does joint communication with direct customers pay off?

Effects of Situational Context Factors

When does it make sense to brand components?

When does communication directed at end-users pay off?

Source: Summarized from Donath (1999) & ISBM/BMA (2005)

Table 1: Business market managers' questions related to brand strategy

After reviewing the marketing literature, I have identified three important gaps there that impede the advancement of our theoretical understanding of brand management in business markets:

- The notion of organizational buyers as *rational decision makers* has been a key assumption of research on business marketing. The rationality assumption suggests that, due to their professionalization, organizational buying centers are able to evaluate different offers based on objective information about the products' true value (Gilliland and Johnston, 1997, p. 17). However, the existence of the

concept of "true" objective value is more than questionable. The notion that value
primarily lies in an offer's intangibles, that value cannot be objectively assessed,
and that value is not inherently embedded in an offer is a widely accepted under-
pinning of marketing theory (Vargo and Lusch, 2004, p. 10-11). If objective value does not exist, how reasonable would it be it to assume that information about
objective value is available to organizational buyers? Yet despite these inconsistencies, the rationality assumption is deeply rooted in business marketing research and it has shaped the way how marketing researchers view branding. For
example, Homburg, Klarmann, and Schmitt (2008) argue that – based on the rationality assumption – brands will have little or no effect in business markets.

- The second gap of research on branding in business markets I have identified
  concerns the *lack of integration* of the bodies of literature on buyer-supplier relationship management on the one hand and on branding on the other hand. Previous research on branding in business markets has remained largely silent on how
  branding relates to relationship marketing (e.g. Bendixen, Bukasa, and Abratt,
  2004). Since branding and relationship marketing have evolved as separate
  streams of research, academics have put forward different cause-effect chains to
  explain how firms' branding activities (e.g. Keller and Lehmann, 2003; Keller
  and Lehmann, 2006) and relationship marketing activities (e.g. Anderson and
  Mittal, 2000; Heskett et al., 1994; Rust and Chung, 2006), translate into market
  and financial performance (see Figure 1). This lack of integration is highly prob-
  lematic given that close collaboration in buyer-supplier relationships is widely
  viewed as the key to gaining competitive advantage in business markets (Dwyer,
  Schurr, and Oh, 1987; Morgan and Hunt, 1994). Thus, for research on branding
  in business markets to be relevant to practice and academia, it must provide an integrated perspective on how brand management ties in with established findings
  and practices in relationship marketing. In other words, insight is needed as to the
  linkages between the brand and relationship marketing-value chains.

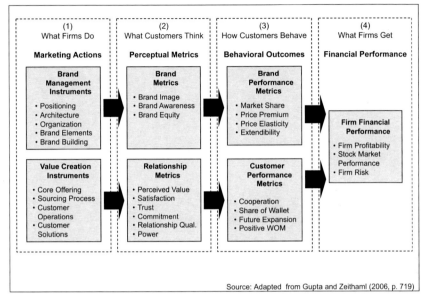

Source: Adapted from Gupta and Zeithaml (2006, p. 719)

Figure 1: Comparing the marketing-value-chains for branding versus buyer-supplier relationship
management

- As a third gap in the literature, I have identified the *focus on buyer-firm dyads* as the prevalent unit of analysis in academic marketing research. For example, Anderson, Hakansson, and Johanson (1994) have criticized the buyer-supplier relationship literature for overly simplifying the networked nature of business markets by exclusively examining dyadic relationships. In line with their criticism, other business marketing researchers have emphasized that future research on buyer-supplier relationships could better explain value creation if it also considered triadic relationships (Menon, Homburg, and Beutin, 2005, p. 5; Ulaga and Eggert, 2006b, p. 133). Parallel to the focus on buyer-seller dyads, the branding literature has usually focused solely on the end-customer as the unit of analysis. Bliemel (1987, p. 5) and Webster (2000, p. 20) have called for a more thorough analysis of branding that also accounts for the triadic relationship between suppliers, intermediaries, and customers. The only brand-related concept that includes supplier, intermediaries, and end customers is the dichotomy of push versus pull (e.g. Kotler and Keller, 2005, p. 468). However, while this concept is frequently cited in textbooks, research has failed to explore it in depth as no theoretical foundation for its systematic analysis has ever been provided (Bliemel, 1987, p. 1).

In the present study, I aim to contribute to closing these three gaps in the literature. While the gaps outlined above are very broad, I now formulate the specific research questions that are to be answered in this study.

1.3   Research Questions

One characteristic of business markets lies in the fact that customers often exist at various levels of the value chain. In Figure 2, I illustrate this reality using an example of a branded component. I focus on three consecutive levels of the value chain for General Electric (GE) branded automation components. The figure shows that the immediate buyer of GE branded automation components may be an original equipment manufacturer (OEM) of industrial machinery, for example, Liebherr. Liebherr's industrial machinery, which incorporates the GE automation components, will finally be purchased by the OEM's customer, an end-user of the machine such as a Toyota manufacturing plant. Anecdotal evidence from a handful of firms (e.g., GE, Siemens, and Cisco) suggests that component suppliers can create a competitive advantage from a branded component strategy (i.e., by systematically building and managing a brand among their OEM customers' customers). Academic marketing research, however, offers little insight as to the applicability and design of such a strategy for other firms.

The thinking inherent in the idea of a branded component somehow parallels the principle of ingredient branding in the consumer behavior literature (e.g. Desai and Keller, 2002). However, this literature is of little help in understanding a branded component strategy as it has solely focused on consumer perceptions of ingredient-branded products and ignored issues related to the corresponding buyer-supplier relationship.

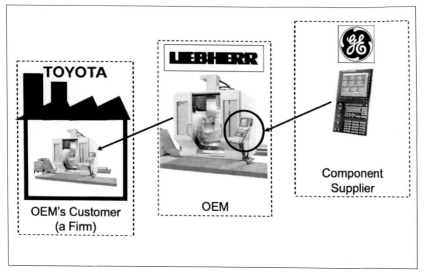

Figure 2: Example of a branded component

The present study responds to the need for a better understanding of the avenues to successfully build, sustain, and leverage component supplier brands as a means to create a competitive advantage for component suppliers in business markets and increase their firm performance. Consequently, the goal of this study research is the development and empirical test of a theoretical framework that enables the explanation and prediction of the outcomes of different suppliers' component branding strategies and activities. To guide the development and testing of the theoretical framework, I formulate two research questions for this study.

What is ultimately needed is an integrative theoretical framework linking a supplier's branding actions at the level of the OEM's customer to the market-performance outcomes of the OEM-supplier relationship. The core question that must be answered is to what extent, and in what ways, investing into building, sustaining, and leveraging a brand among OEMs' customers will actually create a significant competitive advantage for suppliers. To address this question, I draw on the theoretical framework of market-based assets. This framework provides a perspective to analyze how brands create a competitive advantage in the network of a supplier's relationships (Brodie, Glynn, and Van Durme, 2002): "the greater the value that can be generated from market-based assets for external entities, the greater their satisfaction to be involved with the firm and, as a consequence, the greater the potential value of those marketplace entities to the firm" (Srivastava, Shervani, and Fahey, 1998, p. 5). According to what is suggested by this framework, an OEM's customers' perception of the component supplier's brand would thus represent a market-based asset (Srivastava, Shervani, and Fahey, 1998). For the purpose of this study, this potential market-based asset is captured in the construct of component supplier brand strength, defined as the value that the component supplier brand adds to (or detracts from) the value that the OEM's customers perceive in the OEM's product. The above discussion leads to two research questions:

Research question one pertains to the consequences of component supplier brand strength as a potential market-based asset. Srivastava, Shervani and Fahey (1998, p. 4) suggest that the value of market-based assets is ultimately realized "in the external product marketplace," i.e., in the market performance of the supplier in its relationship with OEMs. Rather than just setting out to examine merely *if* component supplier brand strength affects market performance, this study aims at identifying the mechanism by which it does so. Thus:

1a)   How and to what extent does component supplier brand strength among the OEM's customers affect the component supplier's market performance?

Buying decisions in business markets are influenced by a complex set of situational context factors (Johnston and Lewin, 1996). It can be expected that, similar to the effectiveness of branding in business markets in general (e.g. Caspar, Hecker, and Sabel, 2002; Homburg, Klarmann, and Schmitt, 2008), the effectiveness of a branded component strategy is contingent uppon certain situational context factors. Given the high investments typically associated with building a brand, particular interest lies in examining the situations in which a branded component strategy is actually effective:

1b)   Which situational factors influence the effectiveness of component supplier brand strength among the OEM's customers in improving a component supplier's market performance?

Research question two pertains to the antecedents of component supplier brand strength as a potential market-based asset. Besides the link between the component and the market performance in the OEM-supplier relationship, discussions also at insight is needed as to the effectiveness of different approaches to managing a component brand face to the OEM's customer. Thus, the focus turns toward the variables that are under managers' control to build, sustain, and leverage the potential market-based asset of component brand strength. Thus, the second research question is:

2)   Which management instruments (or combination of management instruments) are effective in building, sustaining, and leveraging component supplier brand strength?

To answer this question, the brand management instruments that are at the hands of marketers in component supplier companies will have to be identified. Next, the effectiveness of those instruments in shaping a branded component strategy will have to be assessed.

In the next section I outline how the study is organized to answer the two research questions.

1.4   Outline of Study

The study is divided into six chapters. Chapter 1 introduces the subject area from both practical and theoretical perspectives, explains the need for research on branding in business markets, and formulates the two research questions for this study. Chapter 2 reviews the literature from the subject areas that inform the study – namely value creation in buyer-supplier-relationships, value creation through brands, and branding in business markets. In Chapter 3, I develop the theoretical framework and hypotheses put forward to answer the research questions. Subsequently, the empirical study methodology is outlined in Chapter 4, including the research design used for the cross-sectional multiple informant survey and the structural equations modeling approach used in the analysis of the data. Next, in Chapter 5, I present the results of the empirical study and compare the results obtained for the different samples. The study concludes with a discussion of its theoretical, managerial, and methodological implications, along with its limitations and the directions for future research it suggests.

2 Literature Review

This chapter reviews the relevant literature for the present study. In section 2.1, I provide on overview of the existing research on value creation in buyer-supplier relationships. In section 2.2, I then examine how brands create value. Finally, I turn to research on branding in business markets in section 2.3.

In order to enable a systematic comparison between the reported findings in the three sections of this chapter, I organize the review of the literature in each section according to the concept of the marketing value chain (cf. e.g. Gupta and Zeithaml, 2006). Marketing value chains are cause-effect chains that attempt to explain how firms' marketing actions translate into market and financial performance (e.g. Heskett, Jones, Loveman, Sasser Jr, and Schlesinger, 1994; Keller and Lehmann, 2003). The chains for branding and relationship management quite similarly consist of four building blocks (see Figure 3): (1) the firm's marketing actions, (2) perceptual metrics (3) behavioural outcomes, and (4) the firm's financial performance. It must be noted that marketing value chains are simplified abstractions of the more complex reality of a firm's marketing system. However, they have proven to be a powerful analytical approach for understanding the most important relationships among the involved constructs.

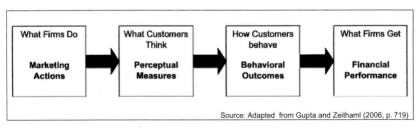

Source: Adapted from Gupta and Zeithaml (2006, p. 719)

Figure 3: The marketing value chain

Since branding and relationship marketing have evolved as separate streams of research, academics have put forward different cause-effect chains. Major differences between the brand and relationship literature emerge with regard to the metrics included in the individual blocks of the marketing-value chains. For example, the branding literature discusses marketing actions such as architecture, brand management organization, positioning, identity, brand elements, brand-building programs, secondary associations, and controlling (Keller and Lehmann, 2003), while relationship marketing research highlights the importance of relational value creation instruments (Palmatier, Dant, Grewal, and Evans, 2006; Ulaga and Eggert, 2006b). Significant differences also exist in the perceptual metrics used: brand metrics such as brand image, awareness, and equity (Keller, 1993) contrast with relationship metrics including customer-perceived value, satisfaction, trust, and commitment (Palmatier, Dant, Grewal, and Evans, 2006). With regard to the behavioral outcomes, brand performance measurement has focused on market share, price premiums, elasticities, and brand extendibility whereas customer performance is measured using customer cooperation, share of wallet, future expansion of purchases, and positive word of mouth. Research from both streams then uses similar indicators of financial performance. The following three sections elaborate on the three marketing value-chains for buyer-supplier relationship management, brand management, and brand management in business markets.

2.1   Value Creation in Buyer-Supplier Relationships

In this section, I summarize the literature in the area of value creation in buyer-supplier relationships. In doing so, I take the view that customers in business markets will not automatically prefer close buyer-supplier relationships over transactional exchanges (Gadde and Snehota, 1999, p. 2). My reasoning is based on the assumption that buying firms will only engage in close buyer-supplier relationships if they expect to receive higher value from the relational exchange than they would in a transactional exchange (Eggert, 2004, p. 5). Because there is an extensive and growing body of literature in this area, I focus only on those contributions in the literature that are of key relevance for the present study.

I start with a discussion of value creation in transactional exchanges versus close buyer-supplier relationships in section 2.1.1. The following sections are organized along the marketing value chain as adapted for buyer-supplier relationships (see Figure 4) (cf. Gupta and Zeithaml, 2006, p. 719). First, in section 2.1.2, I review the different value creation instruments in buyer-supplier relationships (i.e., the actions taken by supplier firms to create value for their customers). In section 2.1.3, I then discuss the perceptual relationship metrics, capturing how buying firms think about suppliers' offerings and their relationships with suppliers. Next, in section 2.1.4, I examine the potential behavioral outcomes that result from buyer-supplier relationships. The financial outcomes of buyer-supplier relationships are then discussed jointly with those of brands in section 2.2.5.

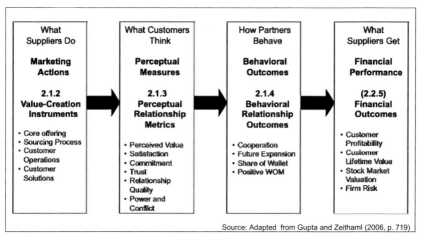

Source: Adapted from Gupta and Zeithaml (2006, p. 719)

Figure 4: Overview for section 2.1 – Value creation in buyer-supplier relationships

2.1.1 Value Creation in Transactional Exchanges versus Close Relationships

In this section I discuss to what extent the marketing discipline has undergone a paradigm shift from a focus on value creation in single transactions between companies to an emphasis on relational value creation in close buyer-supplier relationships (Vargo and Lusch, 2004). I also caution against the oversimplified view of relationships as the universal instrument in creating value for business customers (Gadde and Snehota, 1999, p. 2).

Marketing academics and practitioners alike argue that the marketing discipline has undergone a paradigm shift within the past three decades (Vargo and Lusch, 2004). An important reason for this observed shift lies in the competitive environment. The continuing global proliferation of technology and know-how, the reorganization of international economic boundaries, and the ongoing emergence of new players in world markets have changed the way value is created in today's global economy (Achrol, 1991, p. 77; Frels, Shervani, and Srivastava, 2003, p. 29): Competitive pressures have broken up formerly vertically integrated firms that controlled the entire value creation process for their product into more flexible networks of separate units and firms working closely together to create value (Anderson, Hakansson, and Johanson, 1994, p. 1;

Webster, 1992, p. 4). For example, automotive firms formerly owned the entire value chain for their product, even including steel mills and cattle farms to produce the leather. Nowadays these firms are sourcing more than 60% of a car's value from a network of suppliers (Eisenstein, 2000, p. 28). Suppliers must now rely on completely different value creation instruments: instead of providing car firms with small individual parts, the suppliers now take full responsibility for complex car components including design, testing, and quality control.

This change in economic activity has massive implications for business marketing as a discipline and an enormous impact on how buyer-supplier relationships are managed. With the increasing focus on outsourcing considerable parts of value creation, traditional governance forms such as hierarchy, power, and contracts become less effective while relational mechanisms of governance gain importance (Achrol and Kotler, 1999, p. 146; Anderson, Hakansson, and Johanson, 1994). The main focus of marketing research has thus changed from the management of discrete transactions toward the development of close and mutually beneficial relationships (Frels, Shervani, and Srivastava, 2003, p. 171). In their seminal article, Dwyer, Schurr, and Oh (1987) called for academic marketing research to focus on relational aspects of buyer-supplier behavior instead of on transactional exchanges. Their appeal has resulted in an impressive amount of publications on customer relationship management (Payne and Frow, 2005, p. 167).

Despite the growing importance of close buyer-supplier relationships, I also caution against the oversimplified view of relationships as the universal instrument in creating value for business customers (Gadde and Snehota, 1999, p. 2). Very importantly, there have been some misconceptions about the value created for customers in buyer-supplier relationships in the literature: sometimes relationships are viewed as *per se* providing customers with superior value compared to transactional exchanges (Eggert, 2004, p. 4). For example, Hougard and Bjerre (2003, p. 28) assert that:

"The value of relationships > The value of exchanges."

Relationships are, however, not a goal in themselves, they are rather a means for close interaction between buyers and suppliers in the creation of value for the customer (Flint, Woodruff, and Gardial, 1997, p. 164). Companies can use truly interactive relationships as a means to learn about their customers' needs and how best to satisfy them rather than regarding buyer-supplier relationships as a mere selling tool, (Srivastava, Shervani, and Fahey, 1999, p. 171). For example, a recent study by Ramani and Kumar (2008) demonstrates how companies can take advantage of the information gained in interactive relationships to create superior value offers for their customers and thereby improve profitability.

The need for close interaction between buyers and sellers will, however, likely differ depending on the situation. For example, if customers require customized solutions, interaction in close relationships becomes crucial in working with customers to tailor solutions to their individual needs (Oliva, 2005, p. 1; Srivastava, Shervani, and Fahey, 1999, p. 171). Contrarily, in a different situation where interaction with the supplier is not needed, customers may expect few value gains from close relationships, and a relational exchange might even come at a disadvantage. In line with this reasoning, Eggert (2004, p. 165) calls for a value-based approach to relationship marketing. He formulates the premise that business customers will only be inclined to establish and maintain close relationships with suppliers if they expect the relationship to create better value for them compared to a transactional exchange. Thus, the importance of close buyer-supplier relationships will depend on the way a supplier chooses to create value for a buyer, – i.e., on the choice of value creation instruments. In the next section I focus on the value creation instruments at business marketers' disposal.

2.1.2   Value Creation Instruments

This section provides an overview of the research on different value creation instruments in business markets. Simply stated, value creation instruments represent the actions that supplier firms can potentially take to create value for their customers. I elaborate on the four key value creation instruments discussed in the literature: value creation (1) through the core offering, (2) in the sourcing process, (3) in customer operations, and (4) through customer solutions. To fully explain what is meant by value creation, I first define customer-perceived value: customer-perceived value is the trade-off between the benefits and sacrifices of a supplier's offering as perceived by the customer firm (Eggert and Ulaga, 2000, p. 4). Value creation thus refers to adding benefits to an offer or reducing the sacrifices for the customer inherent in an offer. Since value in business markets is primarily determined by business economic use for the customer (Oliva, 2005, p. 1), value creation mainly refers to optimally supporting the buyer's own value-creating process.

Value creation instruments represent the "tool kit" of actions that supplier firms can potentially use to create value for their customers. Depending on their marketing strategies, firms will put different emphases on each instrument. Ulaga and Eggert (2006b, p. 122) identify three key value creation instruments based on an extensive study integrating qualitative and quantitative research approaches – value creation through the core offering, within the sourcing process, and at the level of the customer's operations (rows in Table 2). As can be seen from the columns in the table, each instrument can provide either benefits or sacrifices for the customer firm.

	Benefits	Sacrifices
Core offering	Product quality Delivery performance	Direct costs
Sourcing process	Service support Personal interaction	Acquisition costs Supplier's self-interest seeking
Customer operations	Supplier know-how Time-to-market	Operations costs

Source: Adapted from Ulaga and Eggert (2006b, p. 122)

Table 2: Value creation instruments in business markets

In the following paragraphs, I briefly review each of these value creation instruments:

The core offering captures those features that are viewed as a "must" for an offer (Grönroos, 1997, p. 411-412; Menon, Homburg, and Beutin, 2005, p. 5). It comprises the fundamental functional performance sought by a customer in a product to solve a specific problem (Anderson and Narus, 2004, p. 175). When sourcing product components, the core offering mainly consists of product quality, delivery performance, and direct product costs (Ulaga and Eggert, 2006b, p. 123):

• *Product quality* is defined as the extent to which a delivered product meets the customer's requirements and relates to the superiority or excellence of the product as perceived by the customer (Zeithaml, 1988, p. 4). Quality is commonly assessed by the conformity of product performance and reliability with customer specifications and by the consistency of product performance (Ulaga and Chacour, 2001). High quality (e.g., in a procured product component) is crucial because it partly determines the quality of the buyer's end-product (Homburg et al., 2005, p. 5). Although continuous improvement of quality may offer opportunities for differentiation, this strategy is becoming less viable as many suppliers today reach high quality levels and products have become increasingly interchangeable (Ulaga and Eggert, 2006b, p. 123).

- *Delivery performance* represents the second important, but often neglected, constituent of the core offering (Ulaga and Eggert, 2006b, p. 123). The first value creating aspect here is on-time delivery. Late deliveries can be detrimental if they hinder the buyer from meeting his own delivery due dates and may cause monetary losses. The second aspect is delivery flexibility, defined as the supplier's willingness to make changes to accommodate the customer's changing needs (Cannon and Homburg, 2001, p. 32; Menon, Homburg, and Beutin, 2005, p. 14). Delivery flexibility often involves short-term responses to sudden, often unanticipated customer needs – for example, peaks in demand or changes in the product mix (Cannon and Homburg, 2001, p. 32-33). Ultimately, delivery performance also becomes evident in the accuracy of delivery as this will save the buyer considerable effort in in-bound quality control (Ulaga and Eggert, 2006b, p. 123).

- *Direct cost* is the price a buying firm actually has to pay the supplier for the main product (Cannon and Homburg, 2001, p. 31; Grönroos, 1997, p. 412). Ulaga and Eggert (2005, p. 81) speculate that price has gained prominence among the cost instruments for being easy to identify. In fact, the findings of Homburg and Cannon (2001, p. 37) and Menon, Homburg, and Beutin (2005, p. 20) indicate that monetary price is of similar or even less importance compared to other cost components, perhaps because sourcing firms are aware that the cheapest supplier will likely not satisfy their business needs (Ulaga and Eggert, 2006b, p. 124).

In **the sourcing process** value can be created for the customer via the seller's service support and through communication with the seller's personnel (Ulaga and Eggert, 2006b, p. 124). The corresponding cost dimensions is acquisitions cost.

- *Service support* includes added services such as installation, training of operations staff, warranties, promotional materials, after sales service (e.g., maintenance contracts), supply of spare parts, and outsourcing activities (e.g., engineering) (Anderson and Weitz, 1992, p. 314; Homburg et al., 2005, p. 6; Menon, Homburg, and Beutin, 2005, p. 10; Ulaga and Eggert, 2005, p. 79; 2006b, p. 1124). As products in business markets become increasingly similar in their tangible attributes, differentiation through service components plays an increasingly important role (Menon, Homburg, and Beutin, 2005, p. 10) and will thus enhance the quality of a buyer-supplier relationship (Anderson and Weitz, 1992).

- *Communication* is the "formal as well as informal sharing of meaningful and timely information between firms" (Anderson and Narus, 1990, p. 44). The need for collaborative information sharing increases as buyer-supplier relationships become closer (Mohr, Fisher, and Nevin, 1996, p. 105). The content of information exchanged ranges from plans, programs, expectations, goals, and performance evaluations to frequent adjustments in specifications and schedules (Anderson and Weitz, 1992, p. 313; Ulaga and Eggert, 2006b, p. 124). Communication is often considered the "glue" that holds a relationship together as it helps to build trust by assisting in resolving disputes and by aligning perceptions and expectations (Morgan and Hunt, 1994, p. 25). For communication to enhance channel outcomes effectively it must be frequent, bidirectional, formalized, and non-coercive (Moorman, Zaltman, and Deshpande, 1992). As demonstrated by a number of empirical studies, communication in buyer-supplier relationships strongly impacts outcomes such as commitment, satisfaction, coordination, perceived benefits, relationship costs, conflict, and uncertainty (Cannon and Homburg, 2001, p. 37; Moorman, Zaltman, and Deshpande, 1992, p. 111; Morgan and Hunt, 1994, p. 30; Ulaga and Eggert, 2006b, p. 130).

- *Acquisitions costs* are costs that customers incur in acquiring and storing products from a particular supplier (Cannon and Homburg, 2001, p. 31). These include expenses for specifying the product, ordering, order handling, transportation of goods, following up with delivery delays and false deliveries, inbound inspections, and inventory management as well as the psychological costs of expected problems that will prevent the buyer from fully concentrating on other tasks and duties (Grönroos, 1997, p. 412; Menon, Homburg, and Beutin, 2005, p. 7; Noordewier, John, and Nevin, 1990, p. 82; Ulaga and Eggert, 2005, p. 313; 2006b, p. 125). As Nordewier, John, and Nevin (1990, p. 81) note, acquisition of repetitively purchased items may result in significant administrative costs caused by complicated ordering procedures. Such a recurrence makes reductions in acquisitions cost an avenue for value creation.

Customer operations represent the third instrument of value creation. Ulaga and Eggert (2006b, p. 126) identify supplier know-how and time-to-market as the two ways for suppliers to create benefits for their customers' operations. At the same time, suppliers can create value by helping the buying firm to save operations costs.

- *Supplier know-how* is defined as the buying firms' perception of the supplier's possession of competencies that are relevant to his business (Crosby, Evans, and Cowles, 1990, p. 41; Lagace, Dahlstrom, and Gassenheimer, 1991, p. 72). Access to supplier know-how can be a major driver of relationship value as specialized competencies (i.e., knowledge and skills) have become the primary unit of exchange and the source of competitive advantage in today's economies (Vargo and Lusch, 2004, p. 7). Dyer (1998) demonstrates how firms can gain competitive advantage by sharing knowledge. In fact, there are reports of major original equipment manufacturer (OEM) firms (e.g., GM, Xerox, Black & Decker, Neiman-Marcus, among others) looking to their suppliers to help them achieve competitive advantage (Ganesan, 1994, p. 1). Empirical evidence shows that know-how is a powerful antecedent of value, of relationship quality, as well as of trust in and of satisfaction with a seller (Crosby, Evans, and Cowles, 1990, 76; Lagace, Dahlstrom, and Gassenheimer, 1991, p. 44; Ulaga and Eggert, 2006b, p. 130).

- *Time to market* is another antecedent of value creation in the customer's operations. As OEM firms face increasing pressure to reduce cycle times and develop products faster, suppliers can help them better achieve their goals (Ulaga and Eggert, 2005, p. 80). This can be done, for example, by speeding up the execution of design work for the buyer's products, by improving the accuracy of prototype development, and by performing testing and validation tasks for the buyer (Ulaga and Eggert, 2006b, p. 126-27).

- *Operations* costs are incurred in the buying firm's day-to-day operation of its business and comprise expenses for research and development, manufacturing and downtime, and internal coordination (Cannon and Homburg, 2001, p. 31). For example, the suppliers can make suggestions about how to save money in the production process, design the component to better fit the customer's internal processes, or improve tooling and warranty costs (Ulaga and Eggert, 2006b, p. 127). Empirical studies show that reductions in the customer's operations costs represent a crucial antecedent of customer value (Cannon and Homburg, 2001; Menon, Homburg, and Beutin, 2005; Ulaga and Eggert, 2006b).

Faced with intense global competition, some suppliers who formerly sold stand-alone products in business markets are combining the value creation instruments outlined by Ulaga and Eggert (2006b) and therefore increasingly turn towards *customer solutions* in an attempt to better differentiate their offers (Court, French, and Knudsen, 2007). Customer solutions have been defined as a set of relational buyer-supplier processes aimed at defining customer requirements, customizing and integrating products, deploying them, and providing post-deployment support (Tuli, Kohli, and Bharadwaj, 2007). For example, BASF offers to operate a car manufacturer's entire paint shop and charges per painted car. While there are examples of successful transition to a customer solutions strategy, it must be noted that many manufacturing companies struggle to offer profitable solutions (Johansson, Krishnamurthy, and Schlissberg, 2003; Stanley and Wojcik, 2005), a consideration that exemplifies the suggestion that close relationships are only beneficial in certain situations. For example, researchers have suggested that, for a solutions strategy to be successful, suppliers must reach a critical sales ratio of solutions to sales (Fang, Palmatier, and Steenkamp, 2008), suppliers and customers must expose certain organizational characteristics, and suppliers must embrace a customer-focused view of solutions (Tuli, Kohli, and Bharadwaj, 2007).

Yet despite the advances that have been made in recent years by research on value creation instruments in buyer-supplier relationships, some important questions remain open. Note that value-based relationship marketing is very much based on what Prahalad and Ramasway (2004) refer to as co-creation of value,, in which buyer and supplier are viewed as creating superior value for the buyer's customer jointly in the relationship (cf. Lusch and Vargo, 2006, p. 284; Vargo and Lusch, 2004, p. 10-11). Existing research does not, however, fully account for the triadic nature of co-creation. While most examples of value creation in buyer-supplier situations involve more than two parties, most studies only examine dyadic buyer-supplier relationships as an isolated phenomenon. Future research on buyer-supplier relationships could better account for the networked nature of value creation if it considered the triadic relationships of supplier, intermediary, and end customer (Menon, Homburg, and Beutin, 2005, p. 5; Ulaga and Eggert, 2006b, p. 133).

2.1.3   Perceptual Relationship Metrics

In this section I provide an overview of the most important perceptual relationship metrics from the buyer-supplier relationship management literature and how they relate to each other. Perceptual customer metrics capture "what customers think" about a supplier's offerings or the relationship with a supplier (Gupta and Zeithaml, 2006). I also contrast the different perspectives in the literature as to the relative importance of perceptual metrics. Because perceptual metrics are abstract, unobservable constructs, they must be obtained directly from the customer through surveys. In the relationship value-chain, perceptual customer metrics are crucial because they mediate the effect of firm actions on the customer's behavioral outcomes: supplier firms can indirectly control perceptual customer metrics through their actions, and perceptual measures will in turn affect behavioral outcomes. In other words, perceptual relationship metrics represent what is referred to as the "black box" in stimulus-organism-response (SOR) models (Kotler, Keller, and Bliemel, 2007, p. 276-78). The literature suggests a plethora of relational constructs that mediate the effects of relationship value on outcomes (cf. Palmatier, Dant, Grewal, and Evans, 2006, p. 139). In the following paragraphs I cover the metrics most frequently discussed in the literature: customer-perceived value, satisfaction, commitment, trust, relationship quality, as well as power and conflict.

Customer-perceived value takes a central role in the academic discussion of perceptual relationship metrics. Although the literature offers a diverse set of definitions, consensus has been achieved that customer-perceived value involves some trade-off between what the customer gets (e.g., quality, service, utility) and what he or she gives up to acquire and use the product (price, effort, other sacrifices) (Kotler, Keller, and Bliemel, 2007, p. 45; Parasuraman and Grewal, 2000, p. 169; Woodruff, 1997, p. 141; Zeithaml, 1988, p. 14). In this study I define customer-perceived value as resulting from the trade-off between the benefits that customers receive in a product and the sacrifices they make to acquire the product (Kotler, Keller, and Bliemel, 2007, p. 45; Parasuraman and Grewal, 2000, p. 169; Woodruff, 1997, p. 141; Zeithaml, 1988, p. 14). In other words, given that businesses primarily purchase products as input for their own value-creating activities (Vargo and Lusch, 2004), customer-perceived value in business markets is determined by business economic use for the customer (Oliva, 2005, p. 1). Note that the creation of customer-perceived value does not necessarily require a close relationship to exist. However, it must be assumed that, for a relationship to exist, there will most likely need to be customer-perceived value (Eggert, 2004, p. 4). In this respect, customer-perceived value is different from commitment, which requires a relationship to exist. Thus, customer-perceived value represents a relationship antecedent while other perceptual relationship metrics (e.g., commitment, trust, and reputation) characterize the relationship itself and its outcomes (Ulaga and Eggert, 2006a).

Commitment, the second perceptual relationship metric discussed here, is commonly defined as the enduring desire to maintain a valued relationship (Moorman, Zaltman, and Deshpande, 1992, p. 316). Commitment to a relationship thus builds up if one exchange partner believes that an ongoing relationship with another partner is so important as to warrant the maximum efforts at maintaining it (Morgan and Hunt, 1994, p. 23). However, commitment goes beyond a simple, positive evaluation of the other party based on currently received value in the relationship as it implies a long-term orientation (Anderson and Weitz, 1989, p. 19). Based on the belief that the relationship is stable, commitment develops to the extent that the parties are willing to make short-term sacrifices to maintain the relationship (Jap and Ganesan, 2000, p. 229). One party's actual commitment thus depends on the perception of the other party's commitment (Anderson and Weitz, 1989, p. 20).

The third perceptual relationship metric, *trust*, is related to commitment. It is defined as a party's confidence in an exchange partner's reliability and integrity (Morgan and Hunt, 1994, p. 23) or "the willingness to rely on an exchange partner in whom one has confidence" (Moorman, Zaltman, and Deshpande, 1992, p. 82). Trust is conceptualized in the literature as consisting of up to three facets – competence, benevolence, and determination to solve the partner's problems (Doney and Cannon, 1997, p. 36; Sirdeshmukh, Singh, and Sabol, 2002, p. 17). Competence refers to the objective ability to perform as promised (Sirdeshmukh, Singh, and Sabol, 2002, p. 17). Benevolence results from the belief that the trusted party is reliable and has high integrity – i.e., the customer's interest is placed ahead of self-interest (Morgan and Hunt, 1994, p. 23; Sirdeshmukh, Singh, and Sabol, 2002, p. 18). Ultimately, the determination to solve the partner's problems, as evidenced in the anticipation and timely resolution of problems that arise, has been suggested as a third facet (Sirdeshmukh, Singh, and Sabol, 2002, p. 18). Trust has also been conceptualized as one of the components of relationship quality (Moorman, Zaltman, and Deshpande, 1992, p. 315).

Many researchers have studied *satisfaction* with the buyer as a perceptual relationship metric (e.g. Crosby, Evans, and Cowles, 1990; Reynolds and Beatty, 1999). Satisfaction reflects a partner's comparative judgments resulting from a product's perceived performance (or perceived value) in relation to his or her expectations (i.e., prior to purchase) (Kotler, Keller, and Bliemel, 2007, p. 48). Anderson and Narus (1990, p. 46) hold that satisfaction will lead to the long-term continuation of relationships because it allows the prediction of the partner's future behavior, which gives an indication that their definition of satisfaction is broader and actually taps aspects of trust. Some research examines the interaction between satisfaction with the salesperson and satisfaction with the company (Reynolds and Beatty, 1999). While some studies focus on satisfaction as the sole key mediator, other researchers have suggested that, along with commitment and trust, relationship satisfaction forms a complex measure of relationship quality (Palmatier, Dant, Grewal, and Evans, 2006, p. 139). Relationship quality is briefly outlined in the following paragraph.

Relationship quality, the fourth perceptual relationship metric, is defined as the overall assessment of the strength of a relationship (De Wulf, Odekerken-Schröder, and Iacobucci, 2001). Relationship quality is commonly conceptualized as a higher-order construct consisting of varying dimensions reflecting the constructs of commitment, trust, and satisfaction (Crosby, Evans, and Cowles, 1990, p. 70; De Wulf, Odekerken-Schröder, and Iacobucci, 2001, p. 36; Kumar, Scheer, and Steenkamp, 1995, p. 55).

There is no agreement in the literature as to which of the constructs represents the central relational mediator (Palmatier, Dant, Grewal, and Evans, 2006, p. 139). For example, Berry (1996, p. 42) favors "trust as the single most powerful relationship marketing tool." Morgan and Hunt (1994, p. 23), on the other hand, claim that commitment is the "essential ingredient for successful long-term relationships." Others again prefer the complex construct of relationship quality over unidimensional constructs as mediators (De Wulf, Odekerken-Schröder, and Iacobucci, 2001, p. 36). In this respect, controversy exists with regard to the relevance of backward-looking metrics such as satisfaction versus forward-looking metrics, especially customer-perceived value.

Customer satisfaction management, paired with quality management techniques on the operational side, has been a popular approach to building and sustaining buyer-supplier relationships in the 1980's and 1990's (Woodruff, 1997, p. 137). These practices were based on the conception of a relationship as a continued, repeat purchase: if a seller satisfies the customers' expectations, they will come back and buy again, and so forth. From this perspective, customer relationships are solely a means to sell, deliver, and service the product (Srivastava, Shervani, and Fahey, 1999, p. 171). However, customers may be satisfied and still switch to another supplier (Jones and Sasser, 1995). This is because they may be satisfied with their past purchases from a supplier, but their changing needs may still be better served by a competitor (Flint, Woodruff, and Gardial, 1997, p. 164). Customer satisfaction management alone is thus unable to serve as a basis to maintain long-term buyer-supplier relationships because it reinforces the firm's internal orientation through its sole focus on producing consistent quality.

In response to the shortcomings of the customer satisfaction approach discussed above, researchers have turned towards customer-perceived value as the key driver for profitable, long-term buyer-supplier relationships (e.g. Anderson and Narus, 1998; Flint, Woodruff, and Gardial, 1997; Grönroos, 1997). Customer value is related to satisfaction, which can be defined as the perceived discrepancy between expected and perceived value (Kotler, Keller, and Bliemel, 2007, p. 48), but it is conceptually different in that it is forward-looking and puts the customer first in the process. Customer satisfaction management applies after the product has been engineered, manufactured, delivered, and used. Contrarily, the customer-value approach first examines the benefits that the customer could be looking for in a product and then aims at creating a superior value proposition. This outlook has led to value management being nowadays considered "the cornerstone to business market management" (Anderson and Narus, 2004, p. 4)

As mentioned earlier, criticism has been leveled that research on buyer-supplier relationship management implicitly focuses too much on the positive aspects of relationships while neglecting their downsides (Eggert, 2004). In response to this criticism, I suggest that conflict and power be included as the kind of additional perceptual relationship metrics that capture the less desirable aspects of relationships. Conflict and power are discussed in the marketing channel literature, but they have received little attention in the buyer-supplier relationship management literature. In the next paragraph I take a closer look at those two constructs.

Conflict in a relationship is commonly defined as a situation in which one relationship partner perceives another partner to be engaged in behavior that is preventing or impeding him from achieving his goals (Gaski, 1984, p. 11). There are two dimensions of conflict: frequency and intensity (Lusch, 1976, p. 383). A history of frequent or intense relationship conflicts can signal that the partners are not committed to the relationship. Thus, absence of conflict makes it easier to trust in the other party (Anderson and Weitz, 1989, p. 22).

Supplier power is the ability of the supplier to influence the behavior of the buyer (Hunt and Nevin, 1974, p. 186). Importantly, power does not refer to the objective, but rather to the potential influence or control as perceived by either of the two parties (Hunt and Nevin, 1974, p. 188). Power is viewed as a function of dependence (El-Ansary and Stern, 1972, p. 47), or, in other words, the second party's need to maintain the relationship with the first party in order to access resources crucial for achieving desired goals (Frazier and Rody, 1991, p. 53; Gundlach and Cadotte, 1994, p. 517). The literature differentiates between coercive and non-coercive power strategies (Hunt and Nevin, 1974, p. 188). Coercive strategies can be distinguished from non-coercive strategies in that they involve potential negative consequences such as punishment, threat, demands, or negative normative statements, whereas noncoercive strategies reference consequences for compliance (Gundlach and Cadotte, 1994p. 517; Hunt and Nevin, 1974, p 188). Research shows that power in a buyer-supplier relationship should be balanced for better relationship quality (Gundlach and Cadotte, 1994; Hibbard, Kumar, and Stern, 2001).

Having reviewed the key perceptual relationship outcomes, I now turn to the behavioral outcomes of buyer-supplier relationships.

2.1.4   Behavioral Relationship Outcomes

This section provides an overview of the behavioral outcomes of buyer-supplier relationships, i.e., the effects of perceptual relationship metrics on how relationship partners behave. Prior research has examined the behavioral outcomes of relationship value and of the relational mediators at various levels including dyadic, customer focused, and supplier-focused outcomes (Palmatier, Dant, Grewal, and Evans, 2006, p. 137). Dyadic outcomes, such as cooperation, relate to the behavior of both buyer and supplier. Customer focused outcomes include for example, expectation of continuity, word of mouth, or loyalty, and how the buyer behaves. Supplier-focused outcomes are measured at the level of the supplier (e.g., the supplier's objective business performance) (Palmatier, Dant, Grewal, and Evans, 2006, p. 137). These outcomes are now discussed individually.

Cooperation occurs if two or more parties work together to achieve mutual goals (Anderson and Narus, 1990, p. 45). Cooperation is based on the assumption that joint outcomes will exceed what the partners would achieve when acting by themselves (Anderson and Narus, 1990, p. 45). Effective cooperation within a firm's network of relationships will promote effective competition among networks (Morgan and Hunt, 1994, p. 26). Relationship commitment leads to more intense cooperation in several ways. First, committed parties will regard cooperation as an opportunity to make the relationship work in the long run (Morgan and Hunt, 1994, p. 26). Second, the perception that the other party is committed to the relationship makes relationship partners more confident that the other party will perform its cooperation activities faithfully so as not to put the future of the relationship at risk (Heide and John, 1990, p. 26). Similarly, trust positively affects the parties' inclination to engage in collaborative action as it reduces the perceived risks of short-run inequities and future opportunistic behavior that come with it (Heide and John, 1990, p. 26; Morgan and Hunt, 1994, p. 26). Cooperation is also held to affect other relationship outcomes; it can lead to higher sales, for example (Homburg, Kuester, Beutin, and Menon, 2005, p. 8).

Expectation of continuity represents the first buyer-focused relationship outcome. It is defined as the customer's intention to maintain the relationship in the future, including the likelihood of continued purchases (Palmatier, Dant, Grewal, and Evans, 2006). Empirical evidence suggests that trust has a strong effect on expectations of continuity (Crosby, Evans, and Cowles, 1990, p. 70; Doney and Cannon, 1997, p. 45). Also, higher levels of trust and commitment significantly reduce a buyer's propensity to discontinue the relationship because terminating a stable relationship makes little economic sense (Morgan and Hunt, 1994, p. 26).

The second buyer-focused outcome is *loyalty*, consisting of attitudinal and behavioral loyalty. Attitudinal loyalty is defined as the "deeply held intention to re-buy or re-patronize a preferred product or service" (Kotler and Keller, 2006, p. 143) and is conceptually close to relationship commitment. The intention to expand the share of purchases from a certain supplier in a product category represents an indicator of behavioral loyalty (Sirdeshmukh, Singh, and Sabol, 2002, p. 20). Behavioral loyalty is evidenced by the buying firm's actual behavior in the relationship (De Wulf, Odekerken-

Schröder, and Iacobucci, 2001, p. 37). Repeat purchase and share of wallet are common performance measures in consumer marketing environments. However, share of wallet, i.e., the actual volume for a product sourced through a particular supplier, must also be considered a key measure in business markets where various suppliers for one component often compete for a larger share of a buyer's business for that component (Ulaga, Eggert, and Schultz, 2006). Relationship commitment is held to affect loyalty because customers who are committed to a relationship may act loyal to remain consistent with their commitment (De Wulf, Odekerken-Schröder, and Iacobucci, 2001, p. 37). Empirical studies show that many of the perceptual relationship metrics affect attitudinal and behavioral loyalty.

Word of mouth, the third buyer-focused outcome, is defined as informal communication between a customer and other potential customers (Hennig-Thurau, Gwinner, and Gremler, 2002, p. 231-32). Since personal communication is viewed as a more reliable source than non-personal information, word of mouth is a very powerful tool and probably the oldest mechanism by which attitudes are developed, shaped, and spread (Hennig-Thurau, Gwinner, and Gremler, 2002, p. 232; Reynolds and Beatty, 1999, p. 16). The reasoning that relationships displaying high levels of trust, commitment, and satisfaction lead to customer advocacy and increased word of mouth has been confirmed in a number of studies (e.g. Hennig-Thurau, Gwinner, and Gremler, 2002, p. 240; Reynolds and Beatty, 1999, p. 22).

From the perspective of the supplier, the *supplier's objective performance* is probably the most important relationship outcome (Palmatier, Dant, Grewal, and Evans, 2006, p. 140). Performance at the level of the supplier can be measured in terms of actual sales or share of wallet (Doney and Cannon, 1997, p. 45; Palmatier, Dant, Grewal, and Evans, 2006, p. 106; Ulaga, Eggert, and Schultz, 2006, p. 4). While some studies (Doney and Cannon, 1997; Siguaw, Simpson, and Baker, 1998; Ulaga, Eggert, and Schultz, 2006) have confirmed the effect of relationship value and relational mediators on the supplier's objective performance, other findings indicate that the effectiveness of relationship quality in driving supplier performance may depend on context, thus supporting the proposition that close buyer-supplier relationships only matter depending on context (Crosby, Evans, and Cowles, 1990, p. 76).

Having reviewed the literature on value creation in buyer-supplier relationships in the context of the relationship-value chain, I now turn to the review of the brand literature.

2.2   How Brands Create Value

In response to strong practitioner interest, branding has received considerable attention from marketing academia throughout the past two decades. Following Aaker's (1991) book and special issues of the International Journal of Research in Marketing (Barwise, 1993) and the Journal of Marketing Research (Shocker, Srivastava, and Ruekert, 1994), the marketing discipline has experienced a plethora of publications on branding. It is now widely recognized that brands represent major drivers of a firm's market performance and financial success (see the brand value chain in Figure 5) (Srivastava, Shervani, and Fahey, 1998).

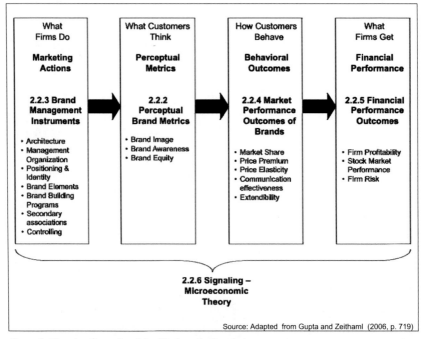

Figure 5: Overview for section 2.2 – The brand value chain

Even in the 2000's, strong interest from both academics and practitioners persists as the Marketing Science Institute (MSI) ranks branding as a top research priority (McAlister, 2005) and three out of the top five most frequently downloaded MSI Working Papers deal with brand-related issues (MSI, 2007). Given the vast amount of publications on the topic, the present review concentrates on the literatures that are of key relevance for the present study.

This section is organized as follows: In section 2.2.1 I define the key brand-related concepts. In an attempt to give the best possible overview of the current state of the literature, I organize the remainder of this section along the marketing value chain for brands depicted in Figure 5, also referred to as brand value chain (Keller and Lehmann, 2003). Section 2.2.2 discusses the key perceptual brand metrics – awareness, image, and equity. I then take a look, in section 2.2.3, at the brand management instruments used by managers. Next, sections 2.2.4 and 2.2.5, respectively, cover the behavioral and financial outcomes of brands. Finally, section 2.2.6 takes up a different but complementary point of view by illustrating how brands are seen from the perspective of microeconomic theory.

2.2.1   Key Definitions

First, I provide definitions of the key brand-related terms. The extensive use of the term "brand" in business practice and marketing research has given rise to a varied array of meanings (Kotler, Keller, and Bliemel, 2007, p. 509). Keller (2008), for example, tries to account for the ambiguity of the word by differentiating between "brand" and "Brand" throughout the book. As Stern (2006, p. 217) speculates, brand "researchers may be studying different things with the same name, the same thing with different names or a combination of the two. This is in sharp contrast with science theorists' calls for the use of unambiguous and "refined" terminology in scientific language systems. Hempel (1970, p. 664) describes the refinement process that an ordinary language term must undergo as the reduction of "the limitations, ambiguities, and inconsistencies of [its] ordinary usage by propounding a reinterpretation intended to enhance the clarity and precision of [its] meanings as well as its ability to function in hypotheses with explanatory and predictive force." In line with these recommendations, the present section develops clear, unambiguous definitions for the key terminology in the *brand* literature.

Both the word *brand* and the phenomenon commonly referred to as *brand* existed long before the term originally entered the marketing discipline in 1922 (Stern, 2006, p. 217). The word "brand" is derived from an old Germanic word meaning "to burn" and describes the act of making different owner's livestock distinguishable by means of burn marks (Keller, 2008, p. 2). The brand phenomenon itself has existed for a very long time. For example, roman manufacturers of bricks placed their identifying symbol on their product. Similarly, medieval guilds required craftspeople to put trademarks on their products as an indicator of quality (Kotler, Keller, and Bliemel, 2007, p. 520). Since the term *brand* entered the marketing discipline, it has constantly taken on new meanings and has been combined in phrases such as brand reputation, brand commitment, or branding power (Stern, 2006, p. 218).

I used a linguistic framework developed by Stern (2006, p. 221), illustrated in Table 3, in the process of refining and defining the meaning of key brand-related terminology. Each term is defined and classified according to four semantic dimensions: nature, function, locus, and valence. Nature describes whether the term *brand* is used in its literal sense or metaphorically. The term can either be used as a noun or a verb, and thus branding terms can take both the function of an entity or process, respectively (Stern, 2006, p. 218). Locus expresses whether the term describes an entity or process in the real world or in the mind of customers and companies. Ultimately, the dimension of valence examines if the term can take up positive and negative meanings in the marketing literature.

Term	Definition	Nature	Function	Locus	Valence
brand (noun)	Name, term, sign, symbol, or design, or a combination of them, intended to identify the goods and services of one seller or group of sellers, to differentiate them from those of the competitors, and to act as a carrier of associations (Kotler, Keller, and Bliemel, 2007, p. 509)	Literal	Entity	World	Positive
to brand (verb)	The process of differentiating a product from those of competitors through the use of a name, term, sign, symbol, or design, or a combination of them.	Literal	Process	World	Positive
brand or brand image	The meaning assigned to the brand by customers as reflected by associations linked to a brand in customer memory (Keller, 2003, p. 3)	Metaphoric	Entity	Mind	Positive or Negative
brand equity	The value added to or detracted from a product by the brand associations either from the seller's or customer's perspective (adapted from Aaker, 1991, p. 15; Farquhar, 1990, p. 7; Keller, 1993, p. 2)	Metaphoric	Entity	Mind	Positive or negative
brand management	The organizational process of planning, implementing and controlling marketing programs to build, nurture, and leverage brand image and equity	Integrative	Process	World and Mind	Positive

Source: Adapted from Stern (2006)

Table 3: Definition and linguistic classification of key brand-related terms

The noun *brand* is frequently used interchangeably with the term *product* in management literature and practice (e.g., by referring to a branded product or a branded line of products as a brand (Kotler, Keller, and Bliemel, 2007, p. 509). In an effort to avoid any ambiguity, I embrace the purely literal definition of the term *brand* as it is heralded by Kotler, Keller, and Bliemel (2007, p. 509) and the American Marketing Association:

A brand is a "name, term, sign, symbol, or design, or a combination of them, intended to identify the goods and services of one seller or group of sellers and to differentiate them from those of the competitors" Brands act as carriers of associations.

As a noun, *brand* therefore reflects the literal meaning of the word "brand" as it can be derived from its historic origins as discussed above. It relates to an entity in the real world, namely the combination of elements a firm uses to make its products recognizable and identifiable. Analogously, the word can also come as a verb: *to brand* describes the process of making a seller's products recognizable and identifiable through a certain combination of elements.   In the marketing literature, both noun and verb have a positive valence.

Besides its literal meaning, the noun *brand* can also convey metaphorical meaning. The term "brand image" mirrors the conception that most products are of a mixed tangible/intangible nature and that the feelings, ideas, and attitudes linked to brands in customer memory affect purchase behavior (Dobni and Zinkhan, 1990, p. 110). Brand image consequently denotes an entity in the customer's mind that is defined as follows (Keller, 1993, p. 3):

Brand image is the meaning assigned to the brand by customers as reflected by associations linked to a brand in customer memory

Quite frequently, researchers refer to brand image by just using the noun "brand". This short form is tolerable if it is possible to easily infer from the context that the term "brand" is used in its metaphorical rather than literal sense. For example, when stating that a customer "likes brand X," it is clear that reference is made to the image of the brand.

Depending on context, brand image can have positive as well as negative connotations. For example, customers may find a brand's image favorable or unfavorable. Brand image will be discussed in more detail in the following section (2.2.2).

"Brand equity" represents a second, widely used term that mirrors the metaphorical usage of brand. Brand equity is often confused or used interchangeably with brand image. However, it is distinct in meaning: while brand image refers to the associations about a brand stored in customer memory, brand equity reflects the incremental effect caused by those brand associations (Barwise, 1993, p. 94). Definitions of brand equity abound, but the ones used most frequently come from Aaker (1991, p. 15) and Keller (1993, p. 2).

Aaker (1991, p. 15) defines brand equity as "a set of brand assets and brand liabilities linked to a brand, its name and symbol, that add to or detract from the value provided by a product or service to a firm/ and or to that firm's customers." There are three strong points to this definition:

- It highlights that brand equity can alternatively be analyzed from a customer or a firm perspective (Ailawadi, Neslin, and Lehmann, 2003, p. 1)

- It indicates that brand equity can be both positive and negative

- It emphasizes the nature of brand equity as a firm asset that creates value.

However, Aaker's (1991, p. 15) definition is too broad in that "a set of assets and liabilities linked to a brand" comprises more than just brand image and awareness effects. For example, the definition would include value from a brand's patent rights or geographical distribution in the brand equity construct. Although these factors can be highly relevant in marketing, it appears worthwhile to differentiate them from brand equity in the development and testing of theoretical frameworks. Keller's (1993, p. 2) definition explicitly limits the scope of brand equity to effects of brand knowledge while at the same time missing the notion of value creation. He defines brand equity as "the differential effect of brand knowledge on consumer response to the marketing of the brand". For the purpose of the present study, I therefore define brand equity as follows:

Brand equity is the value added to or detracted from a product by brand knowledge and can either be seen from the seller's or from the customer's perspective.

The term "brand management", finally, is of an integrative nature in that it deals with brand both in the literal and metaphoric sense. The brand manager controls the brand's appearance in the real world through brand-related marketing activities, thereby shaping the associations linked to the brand in the consumer's mind:

Brand Management is the organizational process of planning, implementing, and controlling marketing programs to build, nurture, and leverage brand image and equity.

The discussion in this section served to define and distinguish key concepts in the brand literature. The concepts of brand image, brand equity, and brand management and the relationships among these concepts are illustrated and elaborated on in more detail in the following sections.

2.2.2   Perceptual Brand Metrics

In this section I take a closer look at the three key perceptual brand metrics: brand awareness, brand image, and brand equity. Perceptual brand metrics have received considerable interest in the consumer behavior literature (e.g. Keller, 2001, p. 3; Leone et al., 2006, p. 125).

Brand awareness and brand image both form part of *brand knowledge*, which reflects the associations and knowledge structures about a brand in a customer's memory. Brand knowledge acts as a source of brand equity by linking a customer's past experiences with the branded offering to the value that a customer perceives in the firm's current products, thereby determining market performance (Kotler, Keller, and Bliemel, 2007, p. 509). Note that depending on context and on the specific content of brand knowledge, its effect on value perceptions and market performance can be both positive and negative.

Most conceptualizations of brand knowledge are based on the assumption that customer memory is organized as an associative network (Eysenck, 1999, p. 87). Associative models regard memory as consisting of a set of nodes connected by relational links. Activation of a node in long-term memory depends on the information being processed in long-term memory and the strength of the association between the node activated in working memory and the target node (Janiszewski and Van Osselaer, 2000, p. 332). These relational links are established and strengthened when a person processes information that associates nodes in some meaningful way. Whenever a person thinks or hears about a concept, such as a brand name, the corresponding node is activated and activation spreads to closely related nodes, such as nodes that concern brand knowledge (cf. Eysenck, 1999, p. 87).

Keller's (1993) conceptualization of brand knowledge is widely used to understand how customers store brand-related information in an associative network. As displayed in Figure 6, Keller distinguishes two main dimensions – brand awareness and brand image.

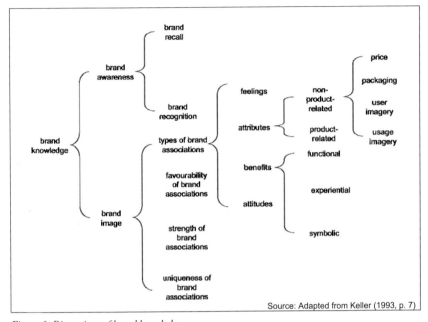

Figure 6: Dimensions of brand knowledge

Brand awareness refers to the customer's ability to identify the brand under different conditions and can be thought of as the strength of the brand node in memory. Basically, the level of brand awareness expresses the likelihood that a customer will come up with a brand name when given a cue (Keller, 2008, p. 54). Researchers commonly differentiate between two forms of brand awareness based on the type of the cue:

- *Recognition* (or aided recall) is the customer's ability to confirm prior exposure to the brand when given the brand name, logo, or symbol as a cue,

- *Unaided recall* relates to the ability to name the brand when cued with a product category or need (Keller, 1993, p. 3).

The effects of brand awareness discussed in the literature are threefold (Keller, 2008, p. 54):

- First, brand awareness is a prerequisite for the formation and learning of brand-related associations that make up brand image.

- Second, higher levels of brand awareness increase the likelihood that the brand will be in the customer's evoked consideration set in a purchase situation (Baker et al., 1986, p. 637).

- Third, customers may use brand awareness as a choice heuristic even though they lack any other knowledge about the brand, especially in situations of low involvement (Hoyer and Brown, 1990, p. 141).

Brand image has been an important concept in behavioral research since the 1950s (Dobni and Zinkhan, 1990, p. 110). It describes the perceptions about a brand as reflected by the brand associations held in customer memory. As illustrated by Figure 7, brand image associations can relate to the performance characteristics of a brand's products, usage imagery, judgments, feelings, and relational states captured in resonance. Importantly, some of these brand image associations relate to the product, but they only become part of the actual product if it is branded. For example, if a brand with an image of "high quality" launches a new product, customers will initially assume that the product is of high quality regardless of its actual quality.

Now I briefly review the theoretical foundations of the brand image concept from the perspective of cognitive psychology. In an associative network model of the customer mind, associations can be thought of as informational nodes connected to the brand node (Keller, 1993, p. 3). Brand associations vary by their type, favorability, strength, and uniqueness (cf. Keller, 2008, p. 56):

- The *type of association* describes the content of information stored in customer memory. Brand associations can vary in their level of abstraction depending on how much the information is aggregated (Alba and Hutchinson, 1987, p. 415). Figure 7 shows an example of how brand associations on different levels of abstraction can be organized in a hierarchy (Keller 2008, p. 8-16). As discussed earlier, brand awareness (labeled here brand salience) is the prerequisite for any association to be established. At the basic level, the hierarchy distinguishes two categories of associations in customer's minds: performance-related associations that refer to the more tangible aspects of a product and brand-related imagery, such as a brand's values or user imagery. At the intermediate level of abstraction, performance attributes (e.g., reliability) are subsumed under more general judgments about the brand (e.g., quality). Similarly, the customer may associate feelings (e.g., security) that are abstractions of brand imagery (e.g., user imagery). At the highest level of abstraction, referred to as resonance, the customer thinks and feels about the brand as one does about a relationship partner (Fournier, 1998), as indicated by brand associations like attitudinal loyalty and attachment. In support of this view, Chaudhuri and Holbrook (2001) find that relational constructs such as brand trust and affect better explain attitudinal and behavioral brand loyalty than lower-level brand attributes. This perspective has led to the development of personality-like typologies of brand associations such as Aaker's (1997) brand personality scale. Alternatively, brand associations could also be categorized into attributes, benefits, attitudes, and feelings (Keller, 1993, p. 4).

- Brand associations also differ in their *favorability*. Only if the brand associations help create value for the customer (i.e., if they provide a significant benefit to the customer or reduce the perceived sacrifice) will they positively affect behavior.

- Depending on the *strength of association* between an attribute and a brand node, attributes will be retrieved faster when a brand node is activated. Strength of association depends on how it is encoded and stored in memory. For example, if intensive processing is required, it will create stronger associations.

- Ultimately, brand associations are characterized by their *uniqueness* in comparison to other brands. For example, a car brand's strong association with "safety" might be less effective if other car brands have similar associations. Contrarily, creating strong brand associations of "fuel efficiency" might work better if this association has more uniqueness in the corresponding industry. If a brand takes a unique position in customers' minds, this will create a compelling reason for buying that brand.

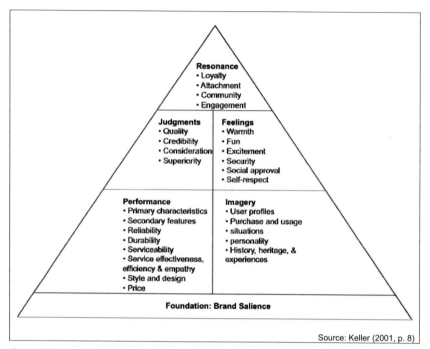

Figure 7: Types of brand associations

I now briefly examine the third perceptual brand metric, brand equity. Brand equity has been defined earlier in this chapter as the value added to or detracted from a product by brand knowledge. Value is defined here as the "consumer's utility overall assessment of the utility of a product based on perceptions of what is received and what is given" (Zeithaml, 1988, p. 14). This definition implicitly recognizes that value is inherently subjective in nature – i.e., instead of embedding value in products, the firm can only make value propositions and value is only created when the customer uses the product (Vargo and Lusch, 2004, p. 11).

An important question is how brand equity is determined by brand image and elements of the marketing-mix. The attributes of a value proposition can be dichotomized into intrinsic and extrinsic attributes (Olson and Jacobi, 1972, p. 167f.). Intrinsic attributes relate to a product's objective physical attributes, as they can, for example, be obtained from expert ratings (Zeithaml, 1988, p. 6). Extrinsic cues are product-related but not part of the physical product – such as the objective price, brand associations, advertising, or the appearance of a firm's employees (Jacoby, Olson, and Haddock, 1971, p. 570; Zeithaml, 1988, p. 6). Figure 8 displays a simplified, basic conceptual model developed from a review of the literature illustrating how an offer's brand, product, and price work together as antecedents of perceived value and brand equity.

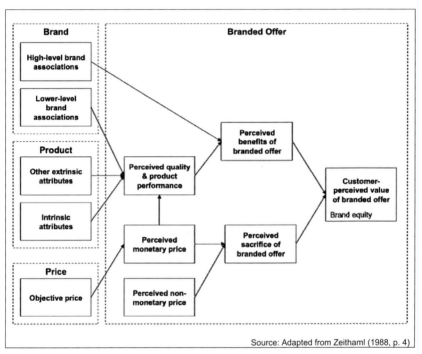

Figure 8: Linking brand image and selected marketing mix variables to brand equity

The objective price affects the perceived monetary price, but is not always equal to it as the customer may not accurately remember the price information or just remember the price as "cheap" or "expensive" (Zeithaml, 1988, p. 10). Besides the perceived monetary price, perceived sacrifice is driven by perceived non-monetary components such as time, energy, and psychological effort (Kotler, Keller, and Bliemel, 2007, p. 45). Customers judge perceived quality from cues such as lower-level brand associations, other non-brand extrinsic attributes, and intrinsic attributes. Lower-level brand attributes cause product performance perception biases in that customers may perceive a high-quality brand's product to be of higher quality compared to a physically identical product from a low-quality brand (Srinivasan, Chan Su, and Dae Ryun, 2005, p. 1439). Also, perceived price has been shown to act as a quality cue in that higher prices lead to the perception of better quality (Dodds and Monroe, 1985; Dodds, Monroe, and Grewal, 1991; Jacoby, Olson, and Haddock, 1971). Increases in perceived quality add to the perceived benefits of the product (Zeithaml, 1988, p. 4). Higher-level brand associations directly lead to perceived benefits without affecting perceptions of attributes (Srinivasan, Chan Su, and Dae Ryun, 2005, p. 1439). For example, the association of the *Apple IPod* with modern, urban life can give the customer a social benefit. The model also illustrates what brand equity is and what makes it such an elusive concept. Brand equity, signified by the shaded area, is the incremental value that can be attributed to the brand-related cues. This means that brand equity must be calculated as the total effects of the higher and lower level brand associations on the customer-perceived value of the branded offer from but cannot be directly measured.

After having established the perceptual brand metrics that differentiate strong brands from weak brands, I now turn to the brand management instruments that act as antecedents of how customers perceive brands.

2.2.3   Brand Management Instruments

In this section, I review the brand management instruments that are in the hands of marketers to build, maintain, and leverage brands. Brand management is the management of brand associations (Kotler, Keller, and Bliemel, 2007, p. 510). Brand management instruments are thus "marketing actions" by seller firms aimed at creating brand awareness and shaping the image of the brand in customers' minds. The brand management process depicted in Figure 9 groups the instruments into three consecutive stages in a recurring cyclic process: planning, implementation, and control (see Aaker, 1991; Keller, 2008 for alternative management processes). It is important to note that brand management does not occur in isolation from a firm's other marketing activities. Consequently, some of the brand management instruments, like product strategy, are general marketing tools with a strong impact on brand associations while others – brand architecture, for example – are exclusively brand-related.

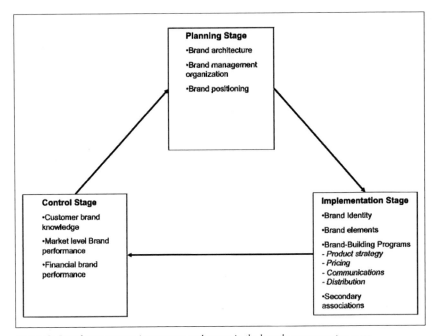

Figure 9: Brand management instruments and stages in the brand management process

As part of the planning stage, marketers have to decide on brand architecture, set up the brand management organization, develop brand positioning, and carve the brand identity.

Brand architecture relates to both the firm's brand portfolio and the branding of the individual product as it describes the hierarchy and type of brands, respectively. The brand hierarchy is the major parameter of brand architecture (cf. Laforet and Saunders, 1994, 67-68; Rao, Agarwal, and Dahlhoff, 2004, p. 127):

- *Corporate dominant branding (branded house):* The corporate brand name dominantly endorses all of the firm's products. The corporate brand then assumes the function of an "assortment brand" (Kotler, Keller, and Bliemel, 2007, p. 530).

- *Mixed branding:* A firm's various business units are dominantly endorsed by different "assortment brands" (Kotler, Keller, and Bliemel, 2007, p. 530). An example for this would be Beiersdorf selling Nivea and Tesa branded product lines. One of the "assortment brands" can be the corporate brand, as it is the case with The Coca-Cola Company selling Coke and Fanta lines of branded soft drinks. In the past decade, this approach has become increasingly popular among consumer-packaged goods companies (Laforet and Saunders, 2005, p. 319) as a result of their brand acquisition strategies.

- *Separate brands (house of brands)*: Products are dominantly branded with separate brands, also called "monobrands" (Kotler, Keller, and Bliemel, 2007, p. 530). The firm's corporate name is not featured dominantly on the products. This strategy is pursued, for example, by Procter and Gamble.

- *Complex brand architectures*: Firms may also opt for combinations of the above strategies. For example, Volkswagen combines the corporate brand name with separate individual brands for products as in "Volkswagen Passat." The corporate brand then takes the role of an "orientation brand" (Kotler, Keller, and Bliemel, 2007, p. 530-531)

A firm's actual brand hierarchy is determined by various factors including corporate history, business philosophy, centralization, strategy, markets served, segmentation, and product range (Laforet and Saunders, 1999). Consequently, competitors in the same industry very often employ different approaches (Kotler, Keller, and Bliemel, 2007, p. 530; Laforet and Saunders, 1999, p. 69). The marketing advantages of corporate dominant branding include economies of scale in marketing, decreases in the overall cost of advertising, lower brand building cost, lower cost of new product introduction, and better extendibility of brands (Laforet and Saunders, 1999, p. 53-54; Rao, Agarwal, and Dahlhoff, 2004, p. 128). Conversely, firms may benefit from separate brands strategies through better extendibility into some product categories, larger share of shelf space, limited risk of cannibalization, better customization of products to different customer groups, avoidance of channel conflict, and reduced damage from negative publicity (Aaker and Joachimsthaler, 2000b, p. 11; Laforet and Saunders, 1999, p. 53-54; Rao, Agarwal, and Dahlhoff, 2004, p. 128). For example, the dominance of the corporate brand strategy has been shown to affect the relationship between corporate image and product attitudes and thus determines the effectiveness of corporate social responsibility programs (Berens, van Riel, and van Bruggen, 2005). In addition, Rao, Agarwal, and Dahlhoff (2004) found that corporate dominant branding enables better communication with the stock market, thereby positively impacting a company's valuations by the stock markets. When pursuing a separate brand strategy, corporate perceptions of the stock market can be driven only by a small subset of the actual brand portfolio (Varadarajan, DeFanti, and Busch, 2006, p. 196). Mixed branding strategies combine some of the advantages and disadvantages of the corporate and separate branding approaches. There seems to be some consent in the literature that the decision on "the right" brand architecture largely depends on a firm's situational and contextual factors (Joachimsthaler and Pfeiffer, 2004, p. 733f.)

Brand Management organization. Many companies in the consumer-packaged goods industry have adopted the so-called brand manager system to deal with the multitude of brand and products in their portfolios (see Buell, 1975; Low and Fullerton, 1994 for a detailed discussion). The brand manager system was developed to overcome the weaknesses of previously used functional marketing organization (Panigyrakis and Veloutsou, 2000, p. 165-166). The brand manager is held accountable for the brand, which is considered a major driver of brand management success (Aaker and Joachimsthaler, 2000a, p. 26). Compared to the product manager system, which is commonly used in companies serving business markets, the brand manager focuses more on customer-facing aspects related to brand building, i.e., marketing and advertising, and less on technical aspects of the product (Kotler, Keller, and Bliemel, 2007, p. 1148). The idea underlying the system is that of a brand manager who coordinates the work of the firm's functional areas and acts in the brand's best interest (Kotler and Keller, 2006, p. 699). One major downside of the system lies in the focus on promoting short-term performance (Kotler and Keller, 2006, p. 700), a concentration, which fails to incentivize managers to build long-term brand equity. The challenge in the development of a brand-management organization therefore lies in supporting a long-term orientation (Esch, 2003, p. 55f.). In addition to these structural aspects of a brand-management organization, firm culture is regarded as having a strong impact on brand success (Esch, 2004, p. 774f.): (1) the entire organization should "live the brand" (Aaker and Joachimsthaler, 2000a, p. 26; Esch, 2004, p. 775) and (2) top management should be supportive of the brand (Esch, 2003, p. 56f.).

Brand positioning is the act of designing the brand's "image so that it occupies a distinct and valued space in the target customers' mind" (Keller, 2008, p. 98). In their classic research, Gardner and Levy (1955, p. 36f) conclude that for a brand to be successful in the long run, marketers must develop a clear positioning right from the start (see also Park, Jaworski, and MacInnis, 1986, p. 135). According to Keller, Sternthal, and Tybout (2002, p. 82), the selection of the appropriate frame of reference is the starting point for any positioning strategy – i.e., the company must find out in which segments or against which brands it wants to compete. Analogously to the conceptualization of brand knowledge discussed earlier in this chapter, positioning can be based on criteria at different levels of abstraction such as product attributes, features, or benefits. Since consumers will most likely categorize brands according to the benefits they offer, the positioning should clearly differentiate the brand from its close competitors (Esch, 2003, p. 124; Meffert and Buhrmann, 2002, p. 78; Park, Jaworski, and MacInnis, 1986, p. 137). As a prerequisite, a criterion considered for positioning should have the potential to improve customer-perceived value in the product category in question by providing perceived benefits or lowering perceived costs. In a consumer marketing context, benefits can be functional, social, affective, epistemic, aesthetic, hedonic, situational, or holistic (Lai, 1995, p. 381-382). The perceived cost component involves monetary cost, time cost, risk, and human energy cost (Lai, 1995, p. 385). Generally speaking, criteria for positioning a brand should satisfy each of the following criteria (Esch, 2001, p. 235; Kotler, Keller, and Bliemel, 2007, p. 404):

- Relevance

- Distinctiveness

- Superiority

- Communicability

- Inimitability

- Added value

However, Carpenter, Glazer, and Nakamoto (1994) demonstrate that marketers can also achieve differentiation with meaningless criteria. Park, Jaworski, and McInnis (1986, p. 136) suggest that positioning will be more effective when it is only based on a limited number of criteria and one core benefit. Keller and colleagues' point of parity and points of difference positioning concept claims that, in addition to establishing points of difference that differentiate a brand from its competitors, marketers should position it as performing sufficiently compared to competing brands on criteria called points of parity (Keller, Sternthal, and Tybout, 2002, p. 82). Points of parity are basic requirements that must be met for a brand to be considered a noteworthy player in a certain market. Once brand positioning has been established, it should be held constant over time to deliver a consistent image to customers (Aaker, 1996, p. 218).

As part of the **implementation stage**, brand managers carve out a brand identity, select brand elements, develop the appropriate marketing-mix to establish the desired brand image and create secondary associations with external entities.

Brand identity is an operational form of the brand promise defined in the positioning and is mainly a tool of internal marketing communication (Keller, 1999, p. 43). Brand identities guide the implementation process and make sure that the brand promise is strictly adhered to in the design of the marketing-mix. In essence, the brand identity conveys to the employees of the firm 'what the brand should be like' and how it wants to be perceived by its customers (Keller, 2008, p. 122-123).

Brand elements – i.e., the brand name, term, sign, symbol, or design—are at the heart of the definition of the brand. Accordingly, the basic function of brand elements is to enable customers to identify a brand and distinguish a brand's products from those of competitors (Keller, 2008, p. 140). However, the tasks performed by brand elements go far beyond their basic function. The literature identifies the following key criteria for selecting brand elements (Esch and Langner, 2001, p. 442f.; Keller, 2008, p. 140; Kotler, Keller, and Bliemel, 2007, p. 423; Robertson, 1989, p. 61f.):

- Conveyance of brand benefits and support of the desired brand image

- Memorability, recognizability, and ease of pronunciation

- Likability and aesthetics

- Transferability to brand extensions

- Legal protectability

Given this large number of criteria that must be met on the one hand and the importance of the brand element for a brand's success, researchers have suggested various structured procedures to guide the selection procedure (see e.g. Collins, 1977; Kohli and LaBahn, 1997; Robertson, 1989).

Brand-building programs are designed to establish brand awareness and craft and to maintain favorable, strong, and unique brand associations in the customer's mind (Keller, 1993). These can utilize any instrument of the marketing-mix that has the potential to affect the customers' brand knowledge – product policy, pricing, communications, and distribution (Yoo, Donthu, and Lee, 2000). Research indicates that the key to effective brand building lies in the consistency of a brand's actions both over time and across the instruments of the marketing-mix: customers perceived brand credibility, brand quality and the value of a brand's products more favorably if the brand conveyed a consistent image (Erdem and Swait, 1998, p. 142; Erdem, Swait, and Valenzuela, 2006, p. 45-47). Consequently, to convey a consistent impression of the brand, marketing academics have voiced calls for an organizationally embedded view of marketing as the starting point for any business activity (Srivastava, Shervani, and Fahey, 1999, p. 168). I now briefly examine how each of the marketing-mix instruments affects brand image:

- The customer's **direct experiences** with the brand's products and other customer's reports of their direct experiences are considered the most powerful driver of brand image (Keller, 1993, p. 10; Kotler, Keller, and Bliemel, 2007, p. 511; Shocker, Srivastava, and Ruekert, 1994, p. 155). This priority is in line with more recent findings in marketing that emphasize the importance of interactivity in the creation of value, also referred to as "co-creation" (Prahalad and Ramaswamy, 2000, p. 84; Vargo and Lusch, 2004). Customer experiences can be created through any interaction with the product, the employees, or support services and can be sensory, affective, social, bodily, and intellectual in nature (Zarantonello, Schmitt, and Brakus, 2007, p. 475). Probably the worst scenario from a brand-building perspective occurs if the firm's actual value creation process could not deliver on the brand promise spread through marketing communications. This is why, from a brand-building perspective, the product development and supply chain management processes are equally important as the customer management process (Srivastava, Shervani, and Fahey, 1999, p. 170).

- **Marketing communications** is another powerful brand-building instrument in the marketing mix, but it is less effective than direct experience (Kotler, Keller, and Bliemel, 2007, p. 511). Communications can be used complementary to the product policy by explaining the benefits of a branded product's quality and by conveying the brand image attributes to customers (Keller, 1993, p. 10). Substantive empirical evidence suggests that advertising spending increases brand equity and its antecedents (cf. Boulding, Lee, and Staelin, 1994; Simon and Sullivan, 1993; Yoo, Donthu, and Lee, 2000). Also, advertising strategy and execution impact brand image and awareness (Burton, Andrews, and Netemeyer, 2000; Percy and Rossiter, 1992). At the same time, sales promotions, which are also considered marketing communications, convey a low-quality brand image and therefore erode brand image and equity (Boulding, Lee, and Staelin, 1994; Yoo, Donthu, and Lee, 2000).

- Customers use **price** as an indicator of product quality, benefits, and value, especially if they have no prior experience with the branded offering and if quality can hardly be inferred from intrinsic cues (Bliemel, 1984; Dodds, Monroe, and Grewal, 1991, p. 308; Zeithaml, 1988, p. 4). The level of a brand's price is directly linked to perceptions of quality which is an important constituent of brand image (Rao and Monroe, 1989, p. 355). Also, higher-priced brands are regarded as less vulnerable to competitive price cuts (Yoo, Donthu, and Lee, 2000, p. 198). For their brand to be credible and consistent, marketers must price their product to mirror the intended positioning.

- There are several ways how **distribution** can be used to build brand equity. First, a brand can associate itself with retailers that have a good image. Selling through stores with good reputations has been shown to increase a brand's quality perceptions (Dodds, Monroe, and Grewal, 1991, p. 307; Yoo, Donthu, and Lee, 2000, p. 205). This strategy will likely come with exclusive or selective distribution to highlight the cooperation between retailer(s) and manufacturer (Yoo, Donthu, and Lee, 2000, p. 199). The way a brand's products are displayed at the retail store also affect brand perceptions (Buchanan, Simmons, and Bickart, 1999). Alternatively, distribution intensity can also be a brand-quality signal as customers infer that something that is widely available must be good.

In addition to the traditional instruments of the marketing-mix, marketers can create **secondary associations** with external entities to build brand image (Keller, 2003, p. 595). The rationale behind this is that it may be faster, more efficient, or more effective to "borrow" an image from some other entity (Rao, Qu, and Ruekert, 1999, p.

259). If the brand and the external entity have some basic fit (Simonin and Ruth, 1998, p. 33), the external entity carries relevant associations, and those relevant associations are transferable in a meaningful manner, associations linked to the external entity will affect brand knowledge and vice versa (Keller, 2003, p. 597). The literature mainly discusses four types of external sources of associations:

- Celebrity endorsements have been shown to affect brand image. The selection of a suitable celebrity and the integration into marketing communications seem to be the most important success factors with this strategy (e.g. Seno and Lukas, 2007)

- Country-of-origin effects occur when customers transfer country-specific associations to a firm's products (Nagashima, 1970; Nagashima, 1977). Research shows that the country-of-origin effect impacts both brand image and brand equity (Lin and Kao, 2004; Yasin, Noor, and Mohamad, 2007).

- Sponsorship of public events can lead to transfer of feelings and attributes to the brand (Kotler and Keller, 2006, p. 592).

- Co-branding is the pairing of two or more distinct brands on one product (Levin and Davis, 1996, p. 296). The external brand can either come as branded ingredient, as a branded complementary product, or as some other brand (Samu, Krishnan, and Smith, 1999, p. 57). Research shows that co-branding affects (1) brand image perceptions of the joint brand, (2) the brand image of the partner brands, (3) the extendibility of the partner brands, and (4) customer acceptance of competitors' counter-extensions (Desai and Keller, 2002; Kumar, 2005; Park, Jun, and Shocker, 1996; Simonin and Ruth, 1998; Worm and Van Durme, 2006). However, caution is warranted because borrowing brand association from another brand does not necessarily build associations for the company's own brand (Desai and Keller, 2002; Janiszewski and Van Osselaer, 2000).

During the stage of **brand controlling**, marketers monitor the performance of the brand and the branded product to (1) guide marketing strategy and tactical decisions, (2) evaluate the effectiveness of marketing decisions, (3) track the brand's health compared with that of competitors, and (4) to assign a financial value to the brand for accounting purposes (MSI, 1999). Since brand equity can hardly be directly measured and no single measure exists that can satisfy all these purposes, researchers have developed three different approaches to evaluate brand equity (Ailawadi, Neslin, and Lehmann, 2003, p. 1-2):

- *Customer mind-set* measures assess brand knowledge as the source of brand equity – i.e., awareness, attitudes, attachments, and loyalty in customer's minds (Keller, 1993, p. 12).

- *Product-market outcome* measures are based on the assumption that brand equity is reflected in a brand's products' marketplace performance (Ailawadi, Neslin, and Lehmann, 2003, p. 2).

- *Financial market measures* judge the value of the brand from its value at the stock market – e.g., from the price that is paid for a brand during acquisitions (Mahajan, Rao, and Srivastava, 1994).

Altogether, brand-controlling instruments provide opportunities for the marketing function to demonstrate the contribution of brand-building investments and their impact on long-term firm performance, and thereby justify the importance of marketing at top-management levels (Doyle, 2000).

This section provided an overview of the most important instruments that managers can use to build and shape their brands (i.e., the antecedents of brand strength). In the next section, I take a look at the behavioral consequences that firms can derive from strong brands.

2.2.4   Market Performance Outcomes of Brands
This section focuses on the market performance outcomes that result from the perceptual brand metrics discussed in section 2.2.2. In other words, I examine how customer perceptions of brand awareness, brand image, and brand equity translate into "how customers behave." Market performance encompasses the consequences of customer behavior that are considered desirable by firms (Keller, 2001, p. 25-26; Srivastava, Shervani, and Fahey, 1998, p. 8). Market performance has also been defined as the effectiveness of a firm's marketing activities (Homburg and Pflesser, 2000, p. 452). Branding research primarily draws on market share, price premium, price elasticity, advertising effectiveness, and the extendibility of brands as measures of market per-

formance (Keller and Lehmann, 2006; Rust et al., 2004). In the next paragraphs I briefly review these outcomes and how they are affected by perceptual brand metrics.

Figure 10 illustrates the market share premium and price premium earned by products of strong brands over products of weaker brands according to perceptual brand. The *market share* – based on unit sales – captures how well a firm's branded offering performs in the marketplace relative to its major competitors (Kotler, Keller, and Bliemel, 2007, p. 1185-87). In Figure 10, unit sales are plotted against the corresponding *price* levels in price-demand functions for a strong brand's product versus a weak brand's product (cf. Kotler, Keller, and Bliemel, 2007, p. 594).

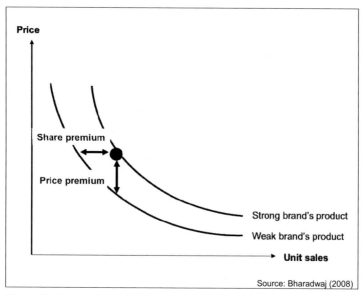

Figure 10: Price premium and share premium as behavioral outcomes of brands

The arrows in the figure symbolize the share premium and price premium for a given price or a given market share, respectively:

- *Share premium:* When both the strong brand's product and the weak brand's product sell at the same price, the strong brand's product can command a share premium over the weak brand's product (see Figure 10) (Bharadwaj, 2008).

- *Price premium:* For the strong and the weak brand to reach the same number of unit sales in a given period, the strong brand can command a price premium over the weak brand (see Figure 10). In fact, a large number of empirical studies confirm that stronger brands can command larger price premiums (e.g, Agrawal, 1996; Park and Srinivasan, 1994; Simon, 1979).

Ailawadi, Lehmann, and Neslin (2002; 2003) criticize that neither the price premium nor the share premium alone capture the conditions for increased market performance. They propose using the revenue premium, calculated by multiplying a brand's sales for the product with the price premium earned over an equivalent private label product as a more adequate measure of a brand's market performance outcomes (Ailawadi, Neslin, and Lehmann, 2003, p. 4).

In addition to the ability to command a price premium or a share premium over their weaker competitors, price elasticity is frequently mentioned as a market performance outcome of strong brands (Keller, 1993, p. 9). If brands are strong on perceptual brand metrics, they can benefit from lower *price elasticity* of demand (Krishnamurthi and Raj, 1991; Sivakumar and Raj, 1997). As visualized in Figure 11, the strong brand can be expected to sacrifice less unit sales volume than the weak brand when the price is raised by an incremental unit.

Advertising effectiveness is another frequently cited market performance outcome of strong brands (Keller, 1993). Empirical findings support the expectation that customers with more positive levels on perceptual brand metrics are more receptive to marketing communication from that brand and will be more sensitive to increases in advertising intensity (Raj, 1982).

Finally, branding researchers have devoted considerable attention to customer *acceptance of brand extensions* as a behavioral outcome of strong performance on perceptual brand metrics (see Voelckner and Sattler, 2006 for an overview). During recent years, it has become increasingly popular in marketing practice to use a current brand name to enter a completely different product class (Aaker and Keller, 1990, p. 27; Park and Srinivasan, 1994, p. 271). The potential behavioral advantages of extending a strong brand include lower start-up and maintenance costs, higher sales, reduced risk of failure, and increased efficiency of marketing communication.

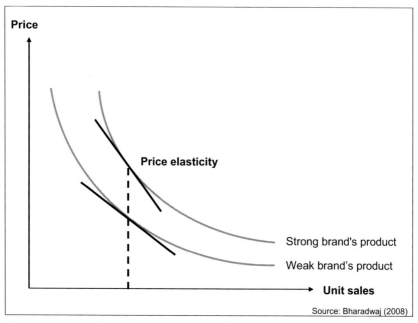

Figure 11: Price elasticity as a behavioral outcome of brands

The major finding in this section is that perceptual brand metrics (i.e., brand image, awareness, and brand equity) affect the ways customers behave about a brand in the marketplace with regard to market share, price premium, price elasticity, advertising effectiveness, and the extendibility of brands. In the following section I examine how the market performance outcomes of a branded product derived from strong customer perceptions of a brand translate into the financial performance of the firm.

2.2.5   Financial Performance Outcomes

This section draws on the resource-based view of the firm to outline how perceptual brand metrics, relationship metrics, and market performance impact the financial performance outcomes of a firm. Financial performance is assessed from firm profitability, stock market performance, and stock risk. This perspective demonstrates "what firms get" in exchange for the investments in building their brand(s). The section is organized as follows: first, I make the case to better link perceptual and behavioral marketing performance metrics to firm financial performance. Subsequently, I outline how brands and customer relationships can be viewed as market-based assets and how they contribute to firm financial performance.

There is a paradox in how marketing is viewed in the boardroom. Although market strategy is seen as the key driver enabling companies to create value and compete successfully in the marketplace, marketers are losing influence at the top management level (Brodie, Glynn, and Van Durme, 2002, p. 5; Doyle, 2000, p. 300). The basic reason for this is evident from the fact that common marketing performance metrics such as sales, market share, brand awareness, customer attitudes, repeat buying, and customer satisfaction do not fit with the financially-oriented language of top management (Doyle, 2000, p. 300; Srivastava and Reibstein, 2005, p. 86). Marketers consequently have to provide a translation of marketing performance measures into financial measures – most essentially, shareholder value – to make their achievements more appreciated (Srivastava and Reibstein, 2005, p. 86) and thus obtain adequate funding (Aaker and Jacobson, 1994).

The award-winning framework of market-based assets by Srivastava, Shervani, and Fahey (1998) draws on the resource-based view of the firm (cf. Hunt and Morgan, 1995) to establish a link between marketing and the net present value of cash flows and hence shareholder value. The resource-based view argues that the key to sustained competitive advantage in the marketplace lies in a firm's resources (Barney, 1991). This view differs from the approach of industrial organization economics (e.g. Porter, 1980; Porter, 1985b) that puts firm performance down to environmental conditions, for example in the "five forces" model (Conner, 1991). The origins of the resource-based view go back to pioneering work by Schumpeter (1934) and Penrose (1959). Resource-based thinking was then first discussed in the strategic management literature (Barney, 1986; Wernerfelt, 1984) before Hunt and Morgan (1995) introduced the concept to the marketing discipline. Since then, resource-based thinking has increasingly affected marketing theory, as demonstrated recently in Vargo and Lusch's (2004; 2006) often-cited article on the paradigm shift towards a service-dominant logic of marketing which also follows a resource-based view baseline argumentation.

Firm resources are also referred to as "assets" in the more financially oriented terminology of market-based assets. An asset can be defined "as any physical, organizational, or human attribute that enables the firm to generate and implement strategies that improve its efficiency and effectiveness in the marketplace" (Hunt and Morgan, 1995,

p. 6; Srivastava, Shervani, and Fahey, 1998, p. 4). The strategy literature suggests evaluating an asset's ability to contribute to sustainable competitive advantage based on the following four tests (Barney, 1991, p. 102; Bharadwaj, Varadarajan, and Fahy, 1993, p. 84; Srivastava, Shervani, and Fahey, 1998, p. 4; Srivastava, Shervani, and Fahey, 1999, p. 789):

- *Convertibility:* the firm can use the asset to exploit an opportunity or neutralize a threat

- *Rarity:* the asset is not possessed by the firm's rivals

- *Inimitability:* it is difficult for rivals to imitate the asset

- *Substitutability:* perfect substitutes for the asset are not available to competitors

- *Durability:* the firm can sustain the asset over time

A firm's assets thus comprise both tangibles such as plant, equipment, and inventory as well as intangibles such as skills, customer relationships, brands, specialized knowledge, and intellectual property. Intangible resources are increasingly recognized as the key drivers of sustainable competitive advantage in the marketplace and shareholder value by marketing academics and practitioners (Lusch and Harvey, 1994, p. 101f; Vargo and Lusch, 2004, p. 2-4). For example, more than 70% of the financial market value of the Fortune 500 stems from intangible assets (Capraro and Srivastava, 1997). From a corporate strategy perspective, marketing expenses should consequently create, build, and nurture intangible assets that generate future cash flows with a positive net present value (Doyle, 2000, p. 302). Srivastava, Shervani, and Fahey (1998) conclude that the intangible assets created by marketing activity are market-based assets (i.e., assets that result from the commingling of the firm with marketplace entities such as customers, channels, suppliers, and competitors). They differentiate two related types of market-based based assets (Srivastava, Shervani, and Fahey, 1998, p. 4-5; Srivastava, Shervani, and Fahey, 1999, p. 779-780):

- *Relational market-based assets* represent outcomes of the relationship with a firm's external stakeholders, including distributors, retailers, end customers, and other strategic partners. These assets are based on reputation and trust. For example, brand equity may be the result of superior product quality or advertising and channel equity may be the result of long-term successful business relationships.

- *Intellectual market-based assets* lie in the "knowledge that a firm possesses about the environment, such as the emerging and potential state of market conditions and the entities in it, including competitors, customers, channels, suppliers [...]" (Srivastava, Shervani, and Fahey, 1998, p. 5). For example, a market orientation (Srivastava, Shervani, and Fahey, 1998) may help to generate such assets.

There is broad agreement in the literature that brands or brand equity can be considered relational market-based assets because they reflect the trusting relationship between a company and its customers (Barney, 1991, p. 115; Day and Wensley, 1988, p. 3; Doyle, 2000, p. 302; Hunt and Morgan, 1995, p. 10; Wernerfelt, 1984, p. 174). Figure 12 shows how brands and other market-based assets, such as relationships, create shareholder value (Srivastava, Shervani, and Fahey, 1998, p. 5-14):

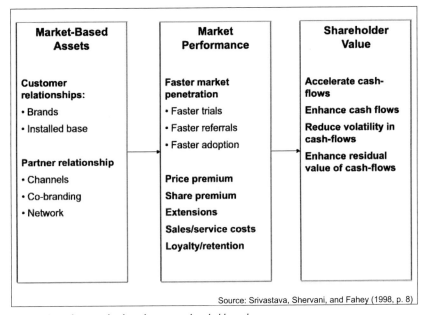

Figure 12: Linking market-based assets to shareholder value

First, the greater the value generated by market-based assets displayed in the first column, the greater their satisfaction and willingness to be involved with the firm and thus the more value the firm can gain from collaborating with these marketplace entities. For example, a manufacturer's brand equity among end customers enables relationships between manufacturer and resellers (Webster Jr, 2004; Worm et al., 2007).

Following this reasoning, the firm can reap the following benefits from market-based assets shown in the second column:

- Lowers costs: Knowledge of channels and customers lowers sales and service costs

- Attain price premium: brand and channel equity add to customer perceived value

- Generate competitive barriers: customer loyalty and switching costs help retain customers

- Provide a competitive edge by making resources more productive (satisfied customers are more responsive to marketing efforts)

- Provide managers with options: faster penetration of innovations through brand category extensions

The more a firm's market-based assets satisfy the resource-based tests, the more they lead to sustainable competitive advantage and increased market-performance for the firm (Srivastava, Shervani, and Fahey, 1998, p. 5). The benefits provided by brands are more sustainable because they satisfy the resource-based tests discussed above. The reputation and trust for a brand usually results from a specific company history that may make it unique, inimitable, and hard to substitute by other means such as warranties (Barney, 1991). This notion is also implicit in the uniqueness of brand associations previously discussed in section 2.2.2. Also, the competitive advantage from a brand can be sustained in the long-term with good brand management as demonstrated by Golder (2000) in his historical analysis of category-leading brands.

Third, as indicated in the third column, the company can leverage or tap the market-based assets in several ways to improve the net present value of cash flows (Srivastava, Shervani, and Fahey, 1998, p. 5). According to the value-planning approach by Rappaport (1983), the value of any strategy is ultimately driven by four value drivers: (1) acceleration of cash-flows, (2) increase in the level of cash flows, (3) reduction of risk associated with cash flows (i.e. vulnerability and volatility), and (4) increase in the residual value of the business (Kim, Mahajan, and Srivastava, 1995). Srivastava, Shervani and Fahey (1998, p. 8-14) then demonstrate that brands and other market-based assets positively impact these value drivers, thereby enabling firms to achieve gains in shareholder value.

This view of brands as a key strategic driver of shareholder value is strongly supported by a number of empirical studies. In a longitudinal study, Aaker and Jakobson (1994) find that increases in a firm's perceived quality, a major component of brand image, lead to higher stock market valuations of the company. In line with this, brand equity was found to make up for up to 30% of the value of a company in merger/acquisition situations (Mahajan, Rao, and Srivastava, 1994). Also, changes in brand attitudes for high-technology firms have been shown to lead to analogous changes in stock returns (Aaker and Jacobson, 2001). A recent study by Madden, Fehle, and Fournier (2006) demonstrates that strong brands do not only deliver greater stock return, on average, but also do so with less risk.

There are two major lessons learned from this strategic view on brands and relationships as market-based assests: first, marketers should design their branding strategies and activities to optimally build, sustain, and leverage brands as market-based assets; and, second, marketers should develop adequate metrics that illustrate the financial impact of those investments to top management (Rust, Ambler, Carpenter, Kumar, and Srivastava, 2004).

2.2.6   *Brands as Signals – The Perspective of Microeconomic Theory*

In this section I summarize the perspective of microeconomic theory on brands as signals. Signaling is presented here because it provides additional insights on branding that complement those obtained from the discussion of the brand value chain discussed in sections 2.2.2-2.2.5. This section is organized as follows: First I briefly outline the theoretical background of signals in information economics. Next, I explain how brands can act as signals of unobservable quality.

Information economics, a more recent extension of traditional microeconomic theory, provides an alternative perspective on brands (Kirmani and Rao, 2000). The behavioral view of brands as discussed in section 2.2.2 is rooted in cognitive psychology and analyzes the customer's cognitive processes. However, buyer behavior does not account for the interaction between buyers and sellers in the marketplace (Erdem and Swait, 1998, p. 132). The perspective of signaling theory in information economics demonstrates why brands are efficient marketplace signals for both buyers and sellers.

Information economics theory is different from traditional microeconomic theory in that it explicitly recognizes that imperfect information prevails in most markets. In his classic article "The Market for Lemons", Akerlof (1970) illustrates the consequences of imperfect information on the market for used cars. In his account, there is information asymmetry because car sellers know more about the particular car's condition than potential buyers. Buyers are unable to judge the quality before purchase and consequently worry that they are being cheated. Therefore, buyers are only willing to pay low prices for used cars. The low price in turn provides no incentive for sellers of high-quality used cars that consequently leave the market.

The extent of potential information asymmetry depends on the difficulty of quality evaluation: it exists primarily in markets for experience and credence goods and is less present with search goods (Rao and Ruekert, 1994, p. 88). Experience goods are products whose quality cannot be observed prior to purchase (e.g., cars). The quality of credence goods can not be observed at all (e.g., legal consulting) (Kotler and Keller, 2006, p. 404; Kotler, Keller, and Bliemel, 2007, p. 551). Unfortunately, academic marketing research is largely silent on the determinants of different products' difficulty of quality evaluation.

Imperfect information potentially results in the following information asymmetries between buyer and seller (Kirmani and Rao, 2000, p. 67; Woratschek and Roth, 2004, p. 352):

- *Hidden characteristics* occur if the seller hides the true characteristics of the product or his true skills, qualifications, and abilities in delivering the product from the buyer.

- *Hidden intention* is present if the seller hides his true intention to opportunistically exploit the buyer (hold-up) once the deal has been closed.

- *Hidden action* means that the seller will not act in the buyer's best interest after the deal has been closed because the buyer is unable to monitor his actions.

According to information economics, subjects in a market can use two types of mechanisms to overcome situations of information asymmetry: (1) the seller can actively send a signal to credibly convey the characteristics of his offer, or (2) the buyer can actively collect information on the seller (Woratschek and Roth, 2004, p. 365-357).

The rationale underlying the signaling mechanism is that sellers provide a signal of a certain quality level that makes it impossible for them to cheat without incurring major economic losses (Wernerfelt, 1988, p. 458). Warranties are a popular example of marketplace signals: offering a good warranty for a product only makes sense for a seller when the product is actually high quality. If the product was poor quality, offering a warranty would be foolish because of the high warranty fulfillment cost (Rao and Ruekert, 1994, p. 89).

A considerable stream of research has investigated the ability of brands to act as signals of unobservable quality. According to the signaling perspective, brands that falsely claim high quality will forfeit: (1) past investments in brand equity and (2) future profits that accrue to a strong brand (Rao, Qu, and Ruekert, 1999). A brand's quality promises are therefore likely to be true. Woratschek and Roth (2004, p. 358f.) draw on theoretical considerations to conclude that brands can serve as signals of product quality for both goods and services to reduce the perceived risk of hidden characteristics, hidden intentions, and hidden action. Conceptual and empirical research has studied various aspects of signaling quality with brands and demonstrated the relevance of signaling as a complementary theoretical approach:

- Shapiro (1982; Shapiro, 1983) examines the conditions that must be met for brands to act as efficient signals.

- Wernerfelt (1988) and Montgomery and Wernerfelt (1988) find that an umbrella branding strategy can signal new product quality by putting future revenues from both the established and new product at stake.

- Rao, Qu, and Ruekert (1999) and Rao and Ruekert (1994) investigate how a brand ally can credibly signal quality

- In two empirical studies, Erdem and Swait (1998) and Erdem, Swait and Valenzuela (2006) find that the consistency, credibility, and clarity of a brand are the key drivers of the value added to the product by the brand signal. Further results show that the effectiveness of brand signals is higher for collectivist and high uncertainty-avoidance countries.

In sum, the microeconomic view of brands as signals makes two important contributions to this study. First, I draw on signaling in the conceptualization of what makes a strong brand in Chapter 3. Second, signaling provides a more general perspective on the conditions that must be met for branding to occur in a market. The important finding here is that greater information asymmetries between buyers and sellers increase the likelihood that brands can be effective and efficient signals. As information asymmetries equally exist in consumer as well as in business markets, this finding lends support to the initial proposition that brands also matter in business markets. The next section analyzes the existent research on brands in business markets.

2.3   Branding in Business Markets

This section provides an extensive overview of the findings on branding in business markets that have been achieved so far and indicates some gaps for further investigation. The vast majority of scholarly research on brands focuses on consumer marketing, and only a very limited body of publications examines branding in a business market setting (Cretu and Brodie, 2007, p. 230). The fact that only a handful of those studies have appeared in higher-ranked journals indicates that research in this area is still at an exploratory stage.

Importantly, the key issue for research on branding in business markets does not lie in the question whether firms should place a brand name or symbol on their products – most products already have brand names (Kotler, Keller, and Bliemel, 2007, p. 520). The important issue is rather if branding should be an integral part of a business market strategy and how brands can be systematically managed in this setting. The two questions that business marketers need to ask with regard to their marketing strategies can be summarized as follows:

1) What is the firm performance impact of brands' strong performance with regard to perceptual brand metrics, e.g., brand image, brand awareness, and brand equity?

2) Which management instruments can business market managers use to systematically manage perceptual brand metrics?

In this section I attempt to answer these questions from a review of previous research. Similar to the preceding section, the literature review is organized according to the framework of the brand value chain shown in Figure 13 (Gupta and Zeithaml, 2006).

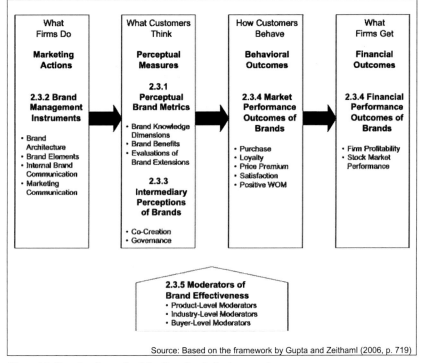

Figure 13: Overview for section 2.3 – Branding in business markets

The first step in answering the questions is to conceptualize perceptual brand metrics. Consequently, I start with an examination of proposed conceptualizations of perceptual brand metrics for business market settings in section 2.3.1. Next, in section 2.3.2, I discuss the brand management instruments available to firms in business markets, (i.e. the antecedents of perceptual brand metrics). Following that, section 2.3.3 investigates the role of brand perceptions by intermediaries in the value chain. Section 2.3.4 then examines the market performance outcomes and financial performance implications of perceptual brand metrics. To account for the large heterogeneity of different business markets, I conclude with an examination of the moderators of brand effectiveness in business markets in section 2.3.5.

2.3.1   Perceptual Brand Metrics

This section gives an overview of the diverse set of perceptual brand metrics that have been suggested by the literature (see Table 4). First, I focus on brand knowledge dimensions before I turn to the benefits for buyers of the branded product derived from brand knowledge. Similarly to conceptualizations of brand knowledge in consumer markets, brand knowledge in business markets is held to consist of brand awareness and brand image (Webster and Keller, 2004, p. 389). There is, however, some consent that the image component is relatively more important in business markets since low involvement buying situations where awareness is used as a shortcut to judge quality are less likely to occur in organizational buying. In fact, only the studies by Hutton (1997) and Homburg, Klarmann, and Schmitt (2008) report that brand awareness has an effect. Brand image seems to exist at two levels of abstraction:

- *Higher-level brand image associations* reflect relational and intellectual brand image associations such as trustworthiness, credibility, stability, reputation, skillfulness, and innovation.

- *Lower-level brand image associations*: are related to the performance of a firm's market offering on (1) functional attributes (e.g., quality, reliability, usability, upgradeability, durability, maintainability, compatibility) and (2) service & solution (e.g., technical support, problem solving, know-how transfer, delivery, flexibility).

Some of the studies (e.g. Kuhn, Frank, and Pope, 2008) mix up product-related brand image associations and actual properties of the product. Future research could benefit from a clearer distinction between the two.

Also, no empirical research has investigated the relative importance of the different types and levels of associations. Product-related intangible attributes are likely more successful than non-product related symbolic attributes (e.g., prestige and lifestyle) common in consumer settings (Webster and Keller, 2004, p. 396). It is suggested that service-related associations work better to differentiate commoditized products than associations related to functional superiority (Webster and Keller, 2004, p. 392). It is, however, less evident if firms in differentiated capital goods markets should emphasize functional associations or service-related associations (Srivastava, 2006). Research is also silent on how the importance of those associations depends on factors such as role in the buying center, buying stage, and stage in the product life cycle (Mudambi, Doyle, and Wong, 1997, p. 436). An unresolved issue of further interest would be the importance of different associations in emerging market countries where the business environment is dramatically different in socioeconomic, demographic, cultural, and regulative terms (cf. Burgess and Steenkamp, 2006, p. 338).

To summarize the previous paragraphs, the strength of a brand is – quite similarly to consumer settings – determined by the type, strength, and uniqueness of brand image associations. When it comes to the benefits potentially created for organizational buyers by brand image associations (see the right-hand column in Table 4), risk reduction is the most frequent mention in the literature. Although perceived risk is obviously highly important in a branding context (Erdem and Swait, 1998), the research on value creation in business markets discussed earlier in this literature review (e.g. Ulaga and Eggert, 2006b) suggests that value for buyers in business markets can potentially also be created on other dimensions than risk reduction.

Publication	Study	Product	Suggested Brand Knowledge Dimensions	Benefits that Buyers of Branded Products Derive from Brand Knowledge
Kuhn, Alpert, & Pope (2008)	Qualitative interviews with buyers	Waste tracking technology	Associations of… • Product performance • Proven technology • User profiles • Credibility • Innovativeness • Service support • Continuity	
Homburg, Klarmann, & Schmitt (2008)	Survey among suppliers	Industrial products	• Brand awareness • Associations of brand liking	
Russell-Benett, McColl-Kennedy, & Cote (2007)	Survey among buyers	advertising media	• Attitudinal loyalty associations	
Cretu & Brodie 2006	Survey of small firms	Hair shampoo	Associations of… • Product performance • Good company reputation	
Van Riel, Mortanges, & Streukens (2005)	Survey of a firm's customers	chemicals	Associations of… • Product image • Company image	

Webster & Keller (2004)	Conceptual		Associations of…
			• Functional product performance
			• Firm characteristics:
			  - Trustworthiness
			  - Reliability
			  - Credibility
			  - Expertise
			  - Delivery
			  - Service
			• Installed base
			• (Emotional associations)
			• Awareness
				• Perceived risk reduction:
				  - Performance risk
				  - Psychological risk
				• Consensus in buying-center

Lynch & De Chernatony (2004)	Conceptual		• Functional associations
			• Emotional associations:
			  - Trust
			  - Image
			  - Reputation
				• Piece of mind
				• Perceived security
				• Prestige

Bendixen, Bukasa, & Abratt (2003)	Conjoint study & survey among buyers	Circuit breaker panels	Associations of… • Quality • Reliability • Performance	• Perceived risk and uncertainty reduction

Caspar, Hecker, & Sabel (2002)	Survey among industrial buyers	20 product categories	Associations of…
			• Country of origin
			• Trust
			• Continuity
				• Information efficiency:
				  - Information gathering
				  - Decision effort
				• Perceived risk reduction
				  - Performance risk
				  - Personal risk
				  - Future compatibility risk
				• Symbolic benefit:
				  - Employee prestige
				  - Reputation transfer to buying firm

Table 4: Brand knowledge dimensions and brand benefits in business markets (cont. on next page)

Publication	Study	Product	Suggested Brand Knowledge Dimensions	Benefits that Buyers of Branded Products Derive from Brand Knowledge
Aaker & Jacobson (2001)	Survey of Corporate Buyers & Stock Market Data	Computer hardware & software	• Brand attitude associations	
Michell, King, & Reast (2001)	Survey among selling firms	Industrial products	Associations of… • Quality • Reliability • Performance • Service	• Confidence in purchase decision • Demonstrate company commitment
Berry (2000)	Case study among 250 employees from 14 firms	Consumer services	• Associations of brand meaning • Brand awareness	• Perceived risk reduction - Monetary - Social - Safety
Shaw, Giglierano, & Kallis (1989)	Focus groups & survey among buyers	Mainframe computers operating systems	Associations of… • Functional attributes • Intangible attributes - Credibility - Problem solution - Service support - Future upgradeability	• Reduce perceived risk • Avoid uncertainty
Hutton (1997)	Survey of industrial buyers	Computers, copiers, fax, disks	• Brand familiarity	•
Mudambi, Doyle, & Wong (1997)	Qualitative interviews with industrial buyers and sellers	Precision bearings	Associations of… • Product quality • Firm reliability • Technical support • Firm expertise • Internationality and market leadership	• Perceived failure risk reduction: - Safety - Recall/warranty - Downtime • Perceived supply risk
Cordon & Calantone (1993)	Experiment involving industrial buyers	Electrical breakers	• Quality associations	

Table 4: Brand knowledge dimensions and brand benefits in business markets (continued)

For example, brands can make it easier to reach consensus among members of the buying center or just save the buying firm the effort of going through the time-consuming process of evaluating a seller's qualification (Caspar, Hecker, and Sabel, 2002, p. 24; Webster and Keller, 2004, p. 395). Brands can also provide symbolic benefits when buying firms expect brand associations to transfer to employees (e.g., prestigious company cars) or to the firm's own market offering (e.g., renewed component suppliers) (Caspar, Hecker, and Sabel, 2002, p. 27).

The paucity of substantive empirical research on brand knowledge and brand benefits limits firms' ability to design and implement branding strategies in business markets. In order to systematically manage and exploit the benefits of branding in business markets, marketers need an idea of the brand associations they want to create and the benefits they want to evoke with the brand among their customers. Consequently, these issues are of high relevance and should be addressed in future studies.

2.3.2   Brand Management Instruments

Existing research examines the use and effectiveness of a number of brand management instruments in business markets. As mentioned earlier, brand management instruments are the actions that firms can take to build their customers' perceptions about the brand. The instruments presented here are a subset of the instruments that have been discussed earlier in this chapter in section 2.2. However, this subset is far from complete as only a few instruments have so far been studied in a business marketing context. Table 5 provides an overview of the instruments mentioned in the literature: brand architecture, brand elements, brand building programs, internal brand communication, and marketing communications.

For the majority of firms in business markets, *brand architecture* is different from consumer markets in that the corporate name acts as the primary brand name (i.e., a branded house architecture) (Webster and Keller, 2004, p. 397). In the light of the crucial importance of interaction and co-creation in business markets (cf. Ramani and Kumar, 2008; Srivastava, Shervani, and Fahey, 1999) this strategy makes sense because buyers primarily interact and have relationships with the company, not with the product (Bendixen, Bukasa, and Abratt, 2004, p. 372; Webster and Keller, 2004, p. 397). Along similar lines, buyers were found to have better awareness and stronger associations for corporate brands compared to sub-brands at the product level (Kuhn, Frank, and Pope, 2008, p. 45). On the one hand, the challenge is thus posed for marketers to establish consistency among an extensive line of products that is often marketed under the company brand (Gordon, Calantone, and di Benedetto, 1993, p. 7). On the other hand, the complexity of brand management is reduced (Homburg, 2003, p. 2).

Research demonstrates that *brand elements* (discussed in more detail in section 2.2.3) in business markets should be recognizable, supportive of the intended brand meaning, and should demonstrate continuity (Richter, 2007, p. 146), thus mirroring the findings in a consumer context. There is, however, some evidence that slogans and names are less effective in conveying brand meaning (Kuhn, Frank, and Pope, 2008, p. 45). Although there is more to a strong brand than brand elements (Mudambi, Doyle, and Wong, 1997, p. 444), a structured approach to developing brand elements is recommended (Shipley and Howard, 1993).

Brand building programs: Brand image is affected at any point of contact between the customer and the branded offering. While advertising can establish awareness for a brand, personal experiences with the brand's products represent the main source of brand image (Berry, 2000, p. 129). Given the high rate of interaction and cooperation between buyers and sellers in business markets, effective brand building requires high consistency in a brand's actions (Webster and Keller, 2004, p. 390). The importance of an integrated management of value-creating processes (Srivastava, Shervani, and Fahey, 1999) in order to align brand promise, brand value, and operations should thus be highlighted.

Consistency can be promoted through *internal brand communication*, frequently discussed as a tool to align organizational behavior with the intended brand image (Berry, 2000, 134; Homburg, 2003, p. 3; Webster and Keller, 2004, p. 398). As Berry (2000, p. 134) puts it, employees must live the brand because "values cannot be faked" in a service encounter. There is a need for research that further develops and evaluates managerial approaches to achieve consistency. For example, future research could address how organizational structures and instruments (i.e., metrics) should be designed to optimally support and control the company brand.

There are several *marketing communication* channels for companies in business markets to communicate with (potential) customers. In general, marketers in business markets should think beyond traditional one-way marketing communications such as advertising (Bendixen, Bukasa, and Abratt, 2004, p. 379) and emphasize instruments that better account for the relational nature of buyer-supplier relationships. Frequently mentioned communications channels to interact with buyers include sales representatives, hotlines and on-call services, training of technical personnel, trade shows, and technical conferences (Abratt, 1986, p. 296; Bendixen, Bukasa, and Abratt, 2004, p. 379; Lynch, 2004, p. 410; Mudambi, Doyle, and Wong, 1997, p. 443). Recent research shows that buyers in business markets increasingly turn towards the company web site as the primary point of interaction with the supplier. Such research suggests that an interactive web site tailored towards the customer featuring detailed information on product specifications, supplier service, ordering information, and a helpful support section is crucial to any communications strategy.

Besides company-controlled communication, the perception of a brand is also shaped by *external communication* through customer word of mouth, communication by distributors and intermediaries, and publicity. Word of mouth is powerful in business markets as buyers have been found to actively seek other users' experiences with a supplier firm when evaluating a brand (Kuhn, Frank, and Pope, 2008, p. 49). Distributors and other intermediaries also affect customers' brand perceptions in either positive or negative ways as they may be responsible for passing on product and sales literature, setting up product demonstrations, and servicing the product (Gordon, Calantone, and di Benedetto, 1993, p. 8-9). Manufacturers may want to gain from association with certain intermediaries through selective or exclusive arrangements (Gordon, Calantone, and di Benedetto, 1993, p. 8).

In summary, few substantial insights have been generated about the use and effectiveness of various brand management instruments in business markets. Insights from the few empirical studies are constrained to certain industries or only test a small subset of instruments.

Publication	Study	Product	Insights / Propositions regarding Brand Management Instruments
Kuhn, Alpert, & Pope (2008)	Qualitative interviews with buyers	Waste tracking technology	Qualitative insights: • Branded house architecture used more frequently • Slogans ineffective • Importance of word of mouth and references • Impact of company personnel
Homburg (2003); Richter (2007)	Survey among sellers	Industrial products	Instruments identified as effective: • Positioning • Brand architecture • Brand elements • Brand internalization

Webster & Keller (2004)	Conceptual		Propositions:
			• Branded house architecture used more frequently
			• Every point of contact should contribute to a consistent brand image:
			  - Internal brand communication
			  - Focus on customer relationships/interaction
			  - Consistency in the marketing-mix

Lynch & De Chernatony (2004)	Conceptual		Proposed instruments: • Personal selling • Advertising • Trade shows • Internal brand communications • Sales force training

Bendixen, Bukasa, & Abratt (2004)	Conjoint study & survey among buyers	Circuit breaker panels	Instruments identified as effective:
			• Branded house architecture favored
			• Preferred information sources:
			  - Technical consultants
			  - Sales representatives
			  - Conferences

Aaker & Jacobson (2001)	Survey of Corporate Buyers & Stock Market Data	Computer hardware & software	Instruments identified as effective: • Dramatic innovations positively affect brand attitudes • Product problems and legal actions have a negative effect • Advertising shows no effect

Berry (2000)	Case study among 250 employees from 14 firms	Consumer services	Proposed instruments::
			• Marketing communication builds brand awareness
			• Word of mouth and publicity
			• Manage experiences as major driver of brand image:
			  - Consistency
			  - Achieve superior performance and results
			  - Internal branding
			  - Firms should live core values

Mudambi, Doyle, & Wong (1997)	Qualitative interviews with industrial buyers and sellers	Precision bearings	Instruments identified as effective: • Brand name selection • History of high quality • Clarity and comprehensiveness of catalogs • Hotlines & on-call service • Training of technical personnel
Cordon & Calantone (1993)	Experiment involving industrial buyers	Electrical breakers	Proposed instruments: • Consistency of products marketed under the same brand • Partner with and support distributors to gain cooperation in shaping brand image • Exclusive or selective distribution • Different distributors for differently positioned product lines • Special sales force that visits customers directly
Shipley & Howard (1993)	Survey among sellers	Industrial products	Instruments identified as effective: • Brand naming strategy
Abratt (1986)	Survey among buyers	Laboratory instru-mentation	Instruments identified as effective: • Sales representatives • Exhibitions/ trade shows • Conferences • Direct mail

Table 5: Brand management instruments in business markets

2.3.3   Intermediary Perceptions

In this section I introduce intermediary perceptions of branded products as an additional block of perceptual brand metrics in the brand value chain. Intermediary perceptions capture how intermediaries in the value chain perceive a supplier's branded offer and/or the relationship with that supplier. In other words, intermediary perceptions mirror "what resellers or original equipment manufacturers think" about a branded offer. The reason for including intermediary perceptions in the brand value chain is that they are suggested to act as mediators of the effect of perceptual brand metrics at the end-customer level on market and financial performance.

To date, marketing academia and practice have to a large extent taken a dyadic perspective on value creation through brands. This perspective has resulted in a focus on perceptual brand metrics for a single customer group: Consumer marketers, on the one hand, have analyzed brands as a link between the manufacturer of a branded product and its end-user. On the other hand, research in business markets focuses on the dyad of sellers and their immediate customers. There is, however, a growing recognition that the scope of branding goes beyond the dyadic relationship perspective that dominates the branding literature (see Table 6). I suggest that, from a triadic perspective, perceptual brand metrics at the end customer level will be related to perceptions of the component suppliers' offering at the intermediary level. The literature takes two theoretical approaches to explaining this effect of perceptual brand metrics – co-creation of value and relationship governance. I review both of these two approaches in the subsequent paragraphs.

First, I discuss the co-creation approach. Webster (2000, p. 20) suggests taking both a business and a consumer-marketing perspective and concludes that brands should be analyzed in the context of a three-way relationship between manufacturers, intermediaries, and end-users. The theoretical framework of market-based assets by Srivastava, Shervani, and Fahey (1998) provides a perspective to analyze how brands, which are essentially market-based assets, create value in the network of relationships between a product's manufacturer, its resellers, and end customers: "The greater the value that can be generated from market-based assets for external entities, the greater their satisfaction and willingness to be involved with the firm and, as a consequence, the greater the potential value" of the brand to the firm. The value of the triadic relationship for any of the three players thus depends on the quality and strength between the other two (Anderson and Narus, 2004; Webster, 2000, p. 20). This interdependence implies that, for a manufacturer's branding strategy to create a sustainable competitive advantage, it must create value for both resellers and end-users. Since value in business markets is determined by business economic use for the direct customer (Oliva, 2005), marketing intermediaries will see value in the brand if it helps them to improve their business and deliver better value to their own customer base. This co-creation oriented view of brands is in line with the evolving service-dominant logic of the firm (cf. Vargo and Lusch, 2004), but is also radically different from the traditional conception that regarded brands as a means of coercive power over intermediaries (see e.g. McCarthy, Shapiro, and Perreault, 1986).

Some publications on branding in business markets acknowledge that a brand's strength among end-customers yields benefits for intermediaries and thus affect the relationship with intermediaries (Caspar, Hecker, and Sabel, 2002, p. 27; Lynch, 2004, p. 408; Mudambi, Doyle, and Wong, 1997, p. 444; Webster and Keller, 2004, p. 397). Only recently, however, researchers have started to investigate this issue in more detail. Glynn, Motion, and Brodie (2007) find that end-customer brand equity affects grocery retailers' satisfaction with the manufacturer. In a similar vein, end user brand equity for industrial machinery adds to the value perceived by retailers (Worm, Hansen, Peters, and Zitzlsperger, 2007).

Now I turn to the relationship governance perspective. Ghosh and John (forthcoming) take a relationship governance perspective to answer the question why some original equipment manufacturers (OEMs) and their suppliers have branded component arrangements while others do not. Importantly, the dependent variable in this study mirrors the contractual specification within a given buyer-supplier relationship, not the choice of supplier. Consequently, under a branded component arrangement, the OEM and the supplier are mutually bound to make the component supplier brand visible to end customers. The findings indicate that OEMs are more likely to pursue branded component (as opposed to white-box) arrangements with a supplier if the supplier brand has better differentiation capability. The differentiation that a branded component arrangement adds to the OEM's product creates dependence by the OEM to counterbalance specific relationship investments on the supplier's side. The resulting balance of power in the relationship reduces conflict in the relationship.

Publication	Study	Product	Findings Regarding Relationship between Perceptual Brand Metrics at End-Customer Level and Intermediary Perceptions
Gosh & John (forthcoming)	Survey of OEM firms	Machinery and electronics	• OEM firms are more likely to use a branded component arrangements (as opposed to a white-box component) when the component brand differentiates their own product • Branded component arrangements act as a safeguards to protect specific supplier investment • Selection of the "wrong" contract leads to opportunistic behavior in the relationship
Worm et al. (2007)	Survey among retailers	industrial equipment	• End customer brand equity to affects retailer-perceived benefits of a product
Glynn, Motion, & Brodie (2007)	Qualitative interviews with retailers	Consumer packaged goods	• End-customer brand equity enhances manufacturer-reseller relationships outcomes

Anderson & Narus (2004)	Conceptual		• Marketplace equity results from an interplay of:
			  - Brand equity (value to end-user added by supplier's brand)
			  - Channel equity (value to reseller added by supplier's brand)
			  - Reseller equity (value to end-customer added by reseller)

Webster & Keller (2004)	Conceptual		• Firms' purchases are guided by their own value-creating strategy • Brand should consequently support direct customers in delivering superior value to their own customers • Strong brand among end users enables management of strategic partner relationships in firm's value network
Lynch & De Chernatony (2004)	Conceptual		• Strong B2B brands create ties with channel intermediaries
Caspar, Hecker, & Sabel (2002)	Survey among industrial buyers	20 product categories	• Expect a marketing benefit through reputation transfer from supplier brand, do however not directly test for this effect
Webster (2000)	Conceptual		• Value is created in a three-way relationship between manufacturers, resellers, and end users • Manufacturer's brands represent valuable asset for resellers, can enhance reseller profitability
Hutton (1997)	Survey of industrial buyers	Computers, copiers, fax, disks	• Who owns the customer? Discussion of loyalty to supplier brand versus loyalty towards intermediary
Mudambi, Doyle, & Wong (1997)	Qualitative interviews with industrial buyers and sellers	Precision bearings	• Expect that buyers chose high reputation supplier brand to increase acceptance of their products
Gordon & Calantone (1993)	Experiment involving industrial buyers	Electrical breakers	• Suggest direct contact with end-users (e.g. sales force) to supplement indirect contact through intermediaries

Table 6: Intermediary perceptions as a consequence of perceptual brand metrics

In this respect, it is interesting to know in which situations intermediaries are most likely to embrace a branded component arrangement. Ghosh and John (forthcoming) conclude that OEM firms that are relatively larger compared to the supplier are less inclined towards branded component arrangements. Also, fragmentation in the supplier's industry reduces the inclination of OEM's to favor branded components while OEM's specific investments, number of potential OEMs, and importance of component showed no significant effect.

In summary, while the relevance of perceptual brand metrics at the end customer level for intermediary perceptions of a branded offer has received some attention in a retailing context, we know only very little about this issue in a buyer-supplier relationship context. The questions whether and how perceptual brand metrics at the end-customer level actually affect intermediaries' evaluations and choice of suppliers' offerings thus remains open for further research. It would be particularly interesting to examine this effect for different types of supply chains (e.g., pure business market supply chains vs. supply chains for consumer markets). Finally, research should develop measures of each partner's contributed share of benefits as perceived by the end customer.

2.3.4 Market & Financial Performance Outcomes of Brands

The most important question, from a managerial perspective, is to what extent perceptual brand metrics enhance the performance of firms in business markets. In this section I present some existing evidence that perceptual brand metrics positively affect customer reactions towards a business market firm's branded offering, the firm's market and financial performance, as well as customer acceptance of brand extensions. Table 7 provides an overview of this research.

First, I report findings on market performance implications. Gordon, Calantone, and di Benedetto (1993, p. 13) conduct an experiment in which they compare industrial buyer's attitudes towards and purchase intentions for an unbranded versus a branded version of otherwise identical products. Their finding that product perceptions and customer behavior are strongly affected by brands in a business market setting parallels simlar findings in consumer markets.

More recent studies lend further support to this finding by examining the impact of perceptual brand metrics on market performance in business market settings. Not only do brands affect customer choice, they also enable a price premium of up to 12-26% over less respected or unknown brands' products (Bendixen, Bukasa, and Abratt, 2004; Homburg, Jensen, and Richter, 2006; Homburg, Klarmann, and Schmitt, 2008;

Hutton, 1997). Other findings indicate that positive performance on perceptual brand metrics leads to better relationship outcomes such as loyalty, share of wallet, expectations of continuity, and expansion of purchases (Cretu and Brodie, 2007; Russell-Bennett, McColl-Kennedy, and Coote, 2007; van Riel, Mortanges, and Streukens, 2005). Also, positive performance on perceptual brand metrics can lead to word of mouth (Cretu and Brodie, 2007; van Riel, Mortanges, and Streukens, 2005).

In sum, compared to the amount and sophistication of the theoretical development and testing of the outcomes of perceptual brand metrics in consumer markets, research on brands in business markets still seems to be at a very early stage.

Second, I present results from the single available study regarding financial performance outcomes. Aaker and Jacobson (2001) combine longitudinal brand image measurements with a time-series of stock market data to confirm that positive performance on perceptual brand metrics actually enhances computer software and hardware manufacturers' stock returns.

Third, I review existing studies on brand extension acceptance. Table 8 displays a summary of the research on brand extensions in business market settings. While brand extension research in consumer markets typically uses experimental designs (cf. Aaker and Keller, 1990; Bottomley and Doyle, 1996; Keller and Aaker, 1992; Sunde and Brodie, 1993), only the study by Gordon, Calantone, and di Benedetto (1993, p. 14) goes beyond a survey design. The main finding from the studies is that there is potential for brand extension strategy in business markets (Bendixen, Bukasa, and Abratt, 2004; Gordon, Calantone, and di Benedetto, 1993; Hutton, 1997). Yet, despite the considerable value of this insight, more guidance would be needed concerning the actual design and implementation of brand extension strategies. In a fashion similar to the multitude of brand extension success factors that have been examined in consumer markets (see Voelckner and Sattler, 2006 for a detailed overview), future research could investigate the drivers and consequences of brand extension success in business markets.

Publication	Study	Product	Performance Outcome Measure Affected by Perceptual Brand Metrics
Homburg, Klarmann, & Schmitt (2008)	Survey among selling firms	Industrial products	• Purchase volume • Price premium
Richter (2007)	Survey among sellers	Industrial products	• Market performance • Financial performance
Russell-Benett, McColl-Kennedy, & Cote (2007)	Survey among buyers	Advertising media	• Behavioral loyalty (share of wallet)

Cretu & Brodie (2006)	Survey of small firms	Hair shampoo	• Attitudinal loyalty
			  - Word of mouth
			  - Expansion of purchases

Van Riel, Mortanges, & Streukens (2005)	Survey of a firm's customers	Chemicals	• Attitudinal loyalty
			  - Satisfaction
			  - Word of mouth
			  - Expectation of continuity

Webster & Keller (2004)	Conceptual		• Support from partners in value chain • Marketing efficiency and effectiveness
Bendixen, Bukasa, & Abratt (2003)	Conjoint study & survey among buyers	Circuit breaker panels	• Price premium of 14-26% over unknown brand
Homburg, Jensen, & Richter (2006)	Conjoint study	Industrial products	• Purchase decision (8 %)
Aaker & Jacobson (2001)	Survey of Corporate Buyers & Stock Market Data	Computer hardware & software	• Stock market return
Michell, King, & Reast (2001)	Survey among selling firms	Industrial products	• Market position (suggested)
Hutton (1997)	Survey of industrial buyers	Computers, copiers, fax, disks	• 12-18% price premium • Word of mouth
Cordon & Calantone (1993)	Experiment involving industrial buyers	Electrical breakers	• Purchase likelihood

Table 7: Performance outcomes of brand metrics in business markets

Publication	Study	Product	Finding related to Customer Evaluation of Brand Extensions
Webster & Keller (2004)	Conceptual		• Opportunity for brand category extensions
Bendixen, Bukasa, & Abratt (2003)	Conjoint study & survey among buyers	Circuit breaker panels	• Higher brand equity leads to more favorable evaluations of category extensions
Aaker & Jacobson (2001)	Survey of Corporate Buyers & Stock Market Data	Computer hardware & software	• Advertising for extension products favorably affects brand attitudes
Hutton (1997)	Survey of industrial buyers	Computers, copiers, fax, disks	• High brand attitude leads to greater likelihood to include brand extension in consideration set
Cordon & Calantone (1993)	Experiment involving industrial buyers	Electrical breakers	• Brand extension strategy strongly affects the evaluation and acceptance of line extensions.

Table 8: Brand extension research in business markets

Srivastava (2006) outlines some avenues for future research on brand extensions and the ability of brands to accelerate market penetration rates. Research could, for example, examine branding strategies for collaborative moves into adjacent markets (i.e., when two firms form a joint venture to create a novel product offering). The brand extension options would then be to use one of the single brands for the joint product, use both brands together, or introduce a new brand. Another issue worth investigating is the link between brands and adoption rates. The theoretical framework of market-based assets suggests that brands enable fast adoption rates (i.e., a time premium) for innovations (Srivastava, Shervani, and Fahey, 1998, p. 8). Firms could leverage faster adoption rates in two ways: (1) enter first and accelerate adoption early to take the first mover advantage, or (2) enter late to avoid risk and use the brand to "take over" the market. Research would be needed to inform the selection of the adequate strategy in this case.

2.3.5   Moderators of Brand Effectiveness

The literature discusses a wide array of factors that determine the effectiveness of branding strategies in a specific situation. Brand effectiveness is defined as the strength of the effect of perceptual brand metrics on market performance and financial performance. The stronger the effect, the higher the brand effectiveness. Table 9 displays a compilation of the findings from previous research. The moderators that influence the effectiveness of brands in gaining competitive advantage fall into three groups: product-related factors, industry-level factors, and buyer-related factors.

Product-related moderators are difficulty of product evaluation, potential loss, and interactivity of the value creation process.

- *Difficulty of quality evaluation* describes the ability of the buyer to judge the quality of the product prior to purchase (Kotler and Keller, 2005, p. 404). A product with high difficulty of quality evaluation would be high in credence and experience qualities (Kotler, Keller, and Bliemel, 2007, p. 551). Difficulty of quality evaluation for a product is suggested to be higher for *technically complex products* that are hard to understand for the buying firm (Aaker and Jacobson, 2001; Homburg, Klarmann, and Schmitt, 2008; Hutton, 1997; Richter, 2007). It is also suggested that in the presence of high *technological dynamic*, buyers may find it hard or even impossible to rationally evaluate a product so they are likely more inclined to take their decision based on brand reputation (Aaker and Jacobson, 2001; Homburg, Klarmann, and Schmitt, 2008; Richter, 2007). One study suggests that larger amounts of *quality differences* between competing offers for a certain product make it more challenging for customers to judge quality (Caspar, Hecker, and Sabel, 2002, p. 35). The theoretical underpinnings of this finding are, however, questionable as quality differences could also facilitate product evaluations if they were observable. To conclude, if buyers find it difficult to evaluate the quality of a product for the above mentioned reasons, the importance of perceptual brand metrics as a cue for (good) quality increases and perceptual brand metrics will likely have a stronger effect on market performance.

- *Potential loss* captures the potential negative consequences that could arise if the buyer makes a wrong purchase decision. Potential loss increases if the purchased product is of higher importance (Homburg, Klarmann, and Schmitt, 2008, p. 109; Richter, 2007) for the company and thus if malfunctioning could severely harm the buyer's profitability, productivity, or reputation. Potential loss is also perceived as being higher for products in the early stage of their life cycle as the technology still needs to be improved (Kuhn, Frank, and Pope, 2008, p. 49). Uncertainty about the future development of technology in a product field increases the potential loss associated with buying technology that may be obsolete tomorrow or does not comply with future technological standards. Similarly, product system purchases decisions that make it costly for a firm to switch to another supplier in the future create potential loss for the buyer (Caspar, Hecker, and Sabel, 2002, p. 32). Brands create a bond between buyers and sellers that reduces the potential loss perceived by buyers (Erdem and Swait, 1998, p. 142). Brands with positive performance on perceptual brand metrics are thus more effective for products categories that comprise high potential loss for the buying firm.

- *Interactivity of value creation* is defined as the extent to which the buyer and supplier need to interact in the creation and delivery of value in the product (Kotler, Keller, and Bliemel, 2007, p. 552-53). Service-intensive products, for example, may require buyer and supplier to work together continuously throughout a product's entire life cycle and to form a maintenance contract. Another driver of interactivity is customization of the product (Caspar, Hecker, and Sabel, 2002). Customized solutions represent a set of customer-supplier relational processes (Tuli, Kohli, and Bharadwaj, 2007) and therefore imply interactivity by definition. The more interactively value is created for a customer, the more intangible it is, the more sources exist for variability in quality, and the more the value delivery process will take place post-purchase (Kotler and Keller, 2005, p. 406). Again, the perceptual brand metrics can act as a signal of constant quality, thereby providing a safeguard that suppliers will stick to their promises in their post-purchase interactions with the buying firm (Erdem and Swait, 1998; Erdem, Swait, and Valenzuela, 2006). This measure implies that brands will be more successful in business markets for products with high interactivity of value creation.

Two *industry-level moderators* that influence brand effectiveness in business markets can be found in the literature: competitive intensity and market fragmentation.

- *Competitive intensity* captures the level of competition faced by sellers in an industry (Jaworski and Kohli, 1993, p. 57). In situations of low competition (e.g., in a monopolistic situation), even a poor, undifferentiated product can be successful because buyers may have no choice (Jaworski and Kohli, 1993). With higher levels of competitive intensity, however, the additional differentiation provided by the perceptual brand metrics to buyers may be crucial in attaining a competitive advantage (Richter, 2007, p. 102). Interestingly, this conclusion may appear counterintuitive at first sight. One might mistakenly reason that, facing high levels of competitive intensity, competitors will be ready to brand their products as well, thereby reducing the relative competitive advantage gained from the brand. However, building on the discussion of market-based assets in section 2.2, I argue that, because perceptual brand metrics fulfill the resource-based tests of rarity, inimitability, and substitutability, competitors will unlikely be able to mimic a successful brand (Srivastava, Shervani, and Fahey, 1998, p. 789). Thus, I argue that competitive intensity will positively moderate the effect of (positive) perceptual brand metrics on market and financial performance, and my argument is congruent with the marketing strategy literature (e.g. Bharadwaj, Varadarajan, and Fahy, 1993).

- The *fragmentation* of an industry is closely related to competitive intensity. It is defined as the number of different brands or manufacturers selling a specific product. The more competing brands there are, the higher the potential for high competitive intensity and the more difficult it will be to break through the clutter. Thus, the differentiation that results from high performance on perceptual brand metrics is even more valuable when there are many competitors. Contrastingly, Caspar, Hecker, and Sabel (2002, p. 35) conclude that the less fragmented a market is, the greater the potential to implement effective branding strategies. Their theoretical reasoning is, however, flawed because they mix up the effort required to build a brand with brand effectiveness.

There are three groups of *buyer-related moderators* affecting brand effectiveness in business markets – characteristics of the buying center, buyer sophistication, and buyer motivation.

- *Buying center characteristics* lie in the heterogeneity and size of the buying center. Heterogeneity reflects the differences between the members of the buying center in terms of functional background, education, goals, expertise, and information (Richter, 2007, p. 113). The size of the buying center is determined by the number of persons it generally comprises. It can be assumed that the greater the heterogeneity and the larger the size of the buying center, the more complex the decision process and the more difficult it will be to reach consensus among its members. Research suggests that brand associations and trust can function as tools to overcome problems of size and heterogeneity in a buying center to reach faster and easier decisions (Caspar, Hecker, and Sabel, 2002, p. 34; Richter, 2007, p. 113; Webster and Keller, 2004, p. 46). Positive perceptual brand metrics will thus be more effective with large and heterogeneous buying centers (Homburg, Klarmann, and Schmitt, 2008). This view is in line the finding that organizational buyers tend to select reputable supplier brands more often if a product has high potential for conflict within the buying center (Lehmann and O'Shaughnessy, 1974, p. 37).

- *Buyer sophistication* is the second buyer-related factor. It is defined as the expertise of the buying organization with the product. One antecedent of sophistication is novelty of purchase, reflecting the buying situation (i.e., a new task, modified rebuy, or straight rebuy) that the buyer is in (cf. e.g. Kotler and Keller, 2005, p. 212). The second driver of sophistication is the actual experience of the buying organization with the type of product. Research findings indicate that the more sophisticated a buying firm (i.e., the less novel the buying task and the greater the experience) the less likely buyers will feel the risk of making a wrong purchase decision and thus the less effective will be the result of positive perceptual brand metrics (Homburg, Klarmann, and Schmitt, 2008; Richter, 2007). Note that, while positive perceptual brand metrics are held to be more efficient with less sophisticated buyers, building a brand among this group of buyers may require more effort as they lack direct experience with the product by definition. This means that a brand extension strategy is especially beneficial when selling a new product category to existing customers who have experiences with the brand but lack experience with the product.

- *Buyer motivation* represents the third characteristic of buyers mentioned in the literature. For example, if the buying firm incentivizes their buyers to buy at a low price, they will overemphasize price as a buying criterion and thus the brand will be a less powerful tool (Caspar, Hecker, and Sabel, 2002, p. 34). Another example is the buyers or the buying firm's uncertainty avoidance (Webster and Keller, 2004, p. 395). Brands have been demonstrated to be more effective with high uncertainty avoidance customers (Erdem, Swait, and Valenzuela, 2006, p. 34).

The conclusion that can be drawn from the review of the moderators of brand effectiveness is that investing in branding only makes sense if certain conditions are met. If empirical support has been found for a moderator, this is indicated by an asterix in the right-hand column of Table 9. However, the research on moderators of brand effectiveness is still at a very early stage as some of the studies do not use state-of-the art empirical methods. Also, some inconsistencies in theoretical argumentation have been identified in this section. This highlights the need for further theoretical and empirical advancement in this area.

Finally, I would like to briefly formulate the key insight obtained from the review of the literature. Branding and relationship marketing have evolved as separate streams of research. A major challenge for research on brand management in business markets lies in integrating branding with buyer-supplier relationship marketing. Close collaboration in buyer-supplier relationships is widely viewed as the key to gaining competitive advantage in business markets (Dwyer, Schurr, and Oh, 1987; Morgan and Hunt, 1994). Thus, for research on branding in business markets to be relevant to both practice and academia, it must provide an integrated perspective on how brand management ties in with established findings and practices in buyer-supplier relationship marketing. However, as branding and relationship marketing have emerged as two distinct streams of research, we know very little about the linkages between these two areas (Leone, Rao, Keller, Luo, McAlister, and Srivastava, 2006). Even previous research on branding in business markets has remained largely silent on how branding relates to relationship marketing (e.g. Bendixen, Bukasa, and Abratt, 2004).

Publication	Study	Product	Moderators of Brand Effectiveness
Kuhn, Alpert, & Pope (2008)	Qualitative interviews with buyers	Waste tracking technology	• Heterogeneity of buying center • Early stage of life cycle
Homburg, Klarmann, & Schmitt (2008)	Survey among selling firms	Industrial products	• Product complexity* • Technological dynamic* • Product importance* • Buying center size*
Richter (2007)	Survey among sellers	Industrial products	• Technological dynamic* • Competitive intensity* • Complexity of offer* • Novelty of purchase* • Importance of purchase* • Buying center size* • Quality focus • Manufacturer firm size
Bengtsson & Servais (2005)	Case study	Construction supplies	• Technological uncertainty
Homburg, Jensen, & Richter (2006)	Conjoint study	Industrial products	• Importance of purchase* • Buyer's experience with product*
Van Riel, Mortanges, & Streukens (2005)	Survey of a firm's customers	Chemicals	• On-line purchases • High-risk situations
Webster & Keller (2004)	Conceptual		• Complexity of buying process • Size and scope of buying center • Risk avoidance
Caspar, Hecker, & Sabel (2002)	Survey among industrial buyers	20 product categories	• Low fragmentation of market* • Low complexity of buying process* • Complexity of buying center* • Quality differences between brands* • Visibility of brands to employees and public*
Aaker & Jacobson (2001)	Survey of Corporate Buyers & Stock Market Data	Computer hardware & software	• Difficulty of evaluating a technically complex product • Technological change
Michell, King, & Reast (2001)	Survey among selling firms	Industrial products	• Complex decision making • Incomplete information
Hutton 1997	Survey of industrial buyers	Computers, copiers, fax, disks	• High perceived risk* • Service-intensity of product* • Product complexity* • High information cost*
Mudambi, Doyle, & Wong (1997)	Qualitative interviews with industrial buyers and sellers	Precision bearings	• Early buying phase, inclusion in consideration set
Lehmann & O'Shaughnessy (1974)	Scenario experiment involving buyers	Industrial products	• High potential for disagreement in buying center*

*Empirically supported

Table 9: Moderators of brand effectiveness

3 Theoretical Framework

In this chapter I develop the theoretical framework to address the two research questions in this study. In section 3.1, I briefly outline the approach used in the development and refinement of the theoretical framework. Next follows the theoretical framework for research question one in section 3.2. The chapter concludes with the theoretical framework for Research question two in section 3.3. Figure 14 illustrates the research context for the two theoretical frameworks by placing them along the brand-value chain for a branded component. The brand value chain links suppliers' brand management actions to their financial performance via both unobservable customer metrics and observable customer metrics. Framework one establishes a causal chain of effects between what OEM's customers think of a component supplier brand and how the OEM behaves in the relationship with the supplier. Framework two, in contrast, focuses on how marketing actions by the supplier affect what OEMs' customers think about the supplier brand.

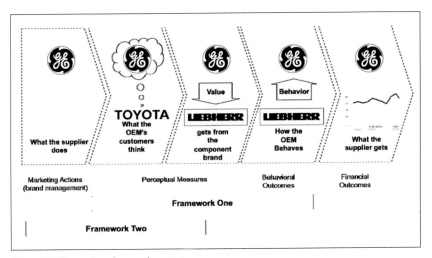

Figure 14: Illustration of research context

3.1 Approach

Developing the present study's theoretical outlook involved an iterative interplay between deductive testing and inductive reasoning (cf. Zaltmann, LeMasters, and Heffring, 1982, p. 100). The deductive approach starts with a set of concepts and proposi-

tions and deduces that, if those propositions are true, certain observable events will occur. This approach aims at gradually eliminating invalid propositions. Conversely, the
starting point for inductive theorizing is data. The researcher looks at patterns in the
data and develops a tentative theory from those observations.

Many researchers today claim that those approaches are not mutually exclusive. Box
(1976, p. 791) remarks that "science is a means whereby learning is achieved, not by
mere theoretical speculations on the one hand, nor by the undirected accumulation of
practical facts on the other, but rather by a motivated iteration between theory and
practice." Figure 15 illustrates this iteration between theory and practice. A researcher
may induce an initial tentative theory from matters of fact. Deductions from this tentative theoretical framework may be at odds with certain known facts. Based on this potential discrepancy, the researcher will then modify the theoretical framework. Subsequent testing of deductions made from the modified theoretical framework may reveal
other inconsistencies, and so forth (see Figure 15).

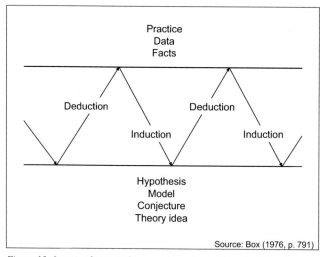

Figure 15: Iteration between theory and practice in theoretical development

The data used for inductive testing in the early stages of developing a theoretical
framework for the present study was primarily based on the observation of firms pursuing branded component strategies, including successful as well as unsuccessful examples. The deductive generation of propositions drew from the existing bodies of li-

terature on brands and business markets. The tentative theoretical framework was then discussed, at a practitioners' conference focusing on branding in business markets, with marketing managers and consultants who were experts in the field of component branding. Insights from this pre-testing of the tentative theoretical framework with real-life data triggered a process of further refinement of the theory.

3.2 Research Question One: Brand Strength of Component Suppliers as a Driver of Their Market Performance

In this section I develop the theoretical framework for research question one. I examine how component supplier brand strength among the OEM's customers affects the supplier's market performance. I also analyze the situational factors that moderate the effectiveness of a strong component supplier brand. In order to guide the discussion and development of the theoretical framework, a conceptual model identifying the key constructs included in the study is provided in Figure 16. As shown in the figure, the framework falls into three major blocks. The first block is discussed in section 3.2.1. This block captures what the OEM's customers think about the component supplier brand. It conceptualizes the construct of component supplier brand strength. The second block is described in section 3.2.2. Here, I examine the ways in which component supplier brand strength affects the perceived value of what the OEM gets when buying from a certain component supplier. In the following two sections I discuss the third block, which incorporates the behavioral outcomes. In section 3.2.3 I analyze the consequences of an OEM's valuations of branded components on the relationship between OEM and suppliers. Subsequently, I focus on the impact of an OEM's value perceptions of branded components on the market performance of the supplier in the relationship with the OEM in section 3.2.4. I conclude with an examination of the moderating effects of situational context factors in section 3.2.5.

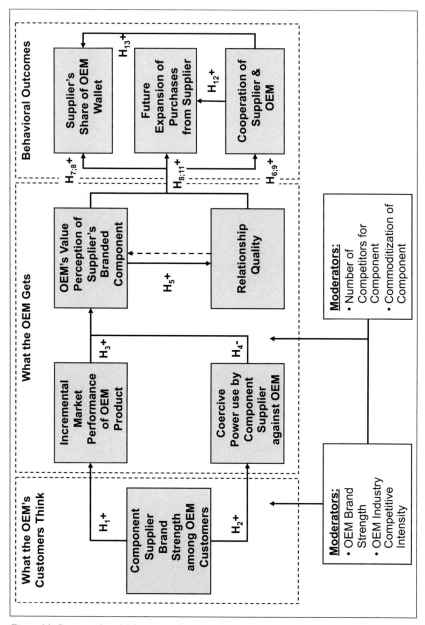

Figure 16: Conceptual model for research question one

3.2.1   Conceptualizing Component Supplier Brand Strength

As pointed out in the preceding review of the literature, the co-creation of value has emerged as the new paradigm for successful management of customer relationships and the key to competitive advantage (Lusch and Vargo, 2006, p. 284; Vargo and Lusch, 2004, p. 10-11). When applied to a business-marketing context, the co-creation of value entails generating superior value propositions for both the end user and the customer. The implication of value co-creation for component suppliers involves designing their brand management efforts to optimally support the OEM's value creation activities. A corresponding idea of value co-creation through brands has been implicit in discussions of ingredient branding in the consumer behavior literature (Desai and Keller, 2002; Park, Jun, and Shocker, 1996; Rao, Qu, and Ruekert, 1999; Simonin and Ruth, 1998; Worm and Van Durme, 2006). Ingredient branding research shows that an ingredient or component brand can add value to a product.

Proceeding from the above discussion, I conclude that a supplier brand that adds value to the OEM product will be fundamental for a component branding strategy that has the potential to drive the supplier's business performance. In this section, I conceptualize component supplier brand strength.

Component supplier brand strength is defined, from the end customers' perspective, as the value that the component supplier's brand adds to (or detracts from) the OEM's product. Value is defined here as a trade-off between benefits and sacrifices. From reviewing the literature I conclude that there are four major, interrelated avenues for brands to create value for customers: improving perceived quality, reducing perceived risk, saving information costs, and enabling easier decisions at the buying center.

- First, the consumer behavior literature demonstrates that attribute perception biases caused by brand associations can lead to better perceptions of product quality (Srinivasan, Chan Su, and Dae Ryun, 2005, p. 1439; Zeithaml, 1988, p. 4). Similarly, microeconomic signaling theory suggests that brands can act as marketplace signals of quality in situations of imperfect information (Montgomery and Wernerfelt, 1992; Wernerfelt, 1988).

- Second, brands and the associations linked to brands in customers' minds have also been shown to reduce the perceived risk arising from the customer's uncertainty about product attributes (Erdem and Swait, 1998, p. 138-142).

- Third, the more perceived risk a purchase involves, the greater the need for detailed information about the product. Trust in a brand can thus create value for customers by reducing the costs of information gathering and processing (Erdem and Swait, 1998, p. 138; Erdem, Swait, and Valenzuela, 2006, p. 38).

- The fourth facet is especially relevant in a business marketing context in which purchasing decisions are often made in complex buying centers (Webster and Keller, 2004, p. 46). Compared to other product information, like technical specifications or financial contract details, the information provided by a brand and the associations linked to brands are more likely meaningful to all members of the buying center, thereby enabling faster and easier joint decisions. In other words, the brand helps to prevent and resolve conflicts in the buying center. This view is supported by Lehmann and O'Shaughnessy (1974, p. 37), who find that organizational buyers favor well-reputed suppliers more strongly if there is potential for disagreement in the buying center.

In the following sections, I establish a causal chain of effects to explain how component supplier brand strength impacts the supplier's business performance.

3.2.2   Impact of Component Supplier Brand Strength on OEMs' Perceptions

The first two hypotheses pertain to the immediate consequences of component supplier brand strength: the incremental market performance of OEM products and the use of coercive power by the supplier.

Market performance reflects the consequences of customer behavior that are considered desirable by firms (Srivastava, Shervani, and Fahey, 1998) and has been defined as the effectiveness of an organization's marketing activities (Homburg and Pflesser, 2000, p. 452). I define incremental market performance as the effectiveness of the supplier brand in driving the market performance of the OEM product. In other words: how much better will the OEM's product perform in the marketplace (i.e., among OEM customers) if the component supplier brand is used? Widespread consensus exists in the marketing literature that customer-perceived value might be the most important driver of market performance (Parasuraman, 1997; Woodruff, 1997). Customer-perceived value is held to positively impact a broad array of market performance outcomes, for example, customer satisfaction (Woodruff, 1997, p. 143), customer loyalty (Parasuraman and Grewal, 2000, p. 170), purchase behavior (Zeithaml, 1988, p. 4), repeat purchases, and relationship quality (Grönroos, 1997, p. 25). By definition, a strong component supplier brand enhances the value a customer perceives in the OEM product, resulting in higher market performance. In the language of resource-advantage theory, the strength of a component supplier's brand represents a market-based asset that provides a competitive advantage to an OEM that uses the branded component. The above discussion suggests that:

H_1:   The higher the component supplier brand strength, the higher will be the incremental market performance of the OEM product.

Coercive power used by suppliers represents the second immediate consequence of value added to an OEM product. It captures the perceived propensity of the supplier to use his brand as a source of power to make the OEM accept unreasonable or unfavorable contractual conditions. Power refers to the perceived ability of the supplier to influence the behavior of the OEM (Hunt and Nevin, 1974, p. 186). Coercive power is different from noncoercive power in that it involves potential negative consequences such as punishment, threat, demands, or negative normative statements (Gundlach and Cadotte, 1994, p. 517; Hunt and Nevin, 1974, p. 188). The ability to exercise power is a consequence of dependence–for example, the OEM needs to maintain a relationship with the component supplier in order to access important resources (e.g. the component brand) that are crucial for achieving desired goals (El-Ansary and Stern, 1972, p. 188; Frazier and Rody, 1991, p. 53). The OEM's dependence will thus be larger if the supplier brand adds more value to his product, especially if there is not another supplier's strong brand as a substitute. The greater the dependence of the OEM, the more likely the supplier will exercise coercive power (by negotiating hard to raise prices, etc.). The formal and testable hypothesis is:

H_2:   The higher the component supplier brand strength, the more likely the supplier will make use of coercive power.

The following two hypotheses examine how OEM's value perception of the branded component is affected by the incremental market performance of OEM product and the use of coercive power by the supplier, respectively. Customer-perceived value results from the trade-off between the benefits customers receive from a product and the sacrifices they make to acquire the product (Kotler, Keller, and Bliemel, 2007, p. 45; Parasuraman and Grewal, 2000, p. 169; Woodruff, 1997, p. 141; Zeithaml, 1988, p. 14).

Since businesses primarily purchase products as input for their own value-creating activities (Vargo and Lusch, 2004), value in business markets is determined by business economic use for the customer (Oliva, 2005, p. 1). A component brand's ability to improve the market performance of the OEM product adds to the business economic use of acquiring the component from the supplier. The practice of "inject[ing] high value into the customer's own value-creating processes" (Ravald and Grönroos, 1996, p. 27) increases the perceived benefits for the OEM. Conversely, the potential disruptions in the OEM's value creation process that arise from coercive power by the supplier represent a risk that increases the sacrifices of buying from the supplier. Stated formally:

H$_3$:   The greater the incremental market performance of the OEM product attributable to the component brand, the greater the value the OEM perceives in the branded component.

H$_4$:   The more the supplier makes use of coercive power, the less value the OEM perceives in the branded component.

3.2.3   Impact of OEMs' Value Perceptions of Branded Components on OEM-Supplier Relationships

The next hypothesis pertains to the effects of the OEM's value perception of the branded component on the OEM-supplier relationship – more precisely, on relationship quality. Relationship quality is defined as the overall assessment of the strength of the relationship between the OEM and the supplier (De Wulf, Odekerken-Schröder, and Iacobucci, 2001, p. 36). Building on the extant literature (Crosby, Evans, and Cowles, 1990, p. 70; De Wulf, Odekerken-Schröder, and Iacobucci, 2001, p. 36; Kumar, Scheer, and Steenkamp, 1995, p. 55), I choose to conceptualize relationship quality as reflected in the trust of the supplier and in the OEM's commitment to the relationship with the supplier. Trust is defined as the OEM's confidence in the supplier's reliability and integrity (Morgan and Hunt, 1994, p. 23). Closely related to trust is the commitment to the relationship, i.e., the enduring desire to maintain a valued relationship (Moorman, Zaltman, and Deshpande, 1992, p. 316). As discussed earlier, a firm's suppliers may be crucial to the firm's ability to deliver value to its own customers (Webster, 1991, p. 28). It consequently makes sense for OEMs to commit themselves to establishing, developing, and maintaining relationships with suppliers that deliver high value (Morgan and Hunt, 1994, p. 24-25). Also, if a supplier consistently delivers high value over time, the OEM cultivates trust in the supplier. This tendency leads to the following testable hypothesis:

H_5:   The higher the OEM's value perception of the branded component, the better the relationship quality.

This hypothesis implies that causality flows from the perceived value of the branded component to relationship quality. Theoretical considerations suggest that this represents the prevailing direction of causality: trust and commitment are built over time when the OEM experiences the supplier's delivery of high value. This view is also supported by the literature (Eggert, 2004; Ulaga and Eggert, 2006a). An argument could, however, be made for an additional reciprocal causal effect of relationship quality on the OEM's value perception of the branded component. In order to rule out this possibility, the reciprocal effect is also included as a null hypothesis; in other words, I hypothesize that the reciprocal effect does not exist.

3.2.4   Impact of OEMs' Perceptions on Behavioral Outcomes

Another consequence of the OEM's value perception of the branded component concerns the cooperation of supplier and OEM. Cooperation refers to the closeness between the supplier and OEM working together to create value (Anderson and Narus, 1990, p. 45). Resource-advantage theory implies that firms collaborate to join their critical resources in gaining a competitive advantage (Dyer and Singh, 1998). If a supplier firm's resources promise high value to an OEM, the OEM will be interested in intensive cooperation with the supplier in order to reap the best possible benefits from these resources. Thus:

H_6:   The higher the OEM's value perception of the branded component, the closer the cooperation between the supplier and the OEM.

The following two hypotheses pertain to the effect of the OEM's value perception of the branded component on the OEM's behavioral loyalty. While behavioral loyalty has been conceptualized in different ways, share of wallet and future expansion are held to fit a business marketing context best (cf. Eggert, 2004, p. 159; Ulaga, Eggert, and Schultz, 2006, p. 1). Share of wallet represents the actual share of purchases for a product sourced through a particular supplier (Ulaga, Eggert, and Schultz, 2006, p. 10). Correspondingly, future expansion of purchases mirrors a buyer's propensity to enlarge the share of wallet in the future (Sirdeshmukh, Singh, and Sabol, 2002, p. 20).

Customer-perceived value is held to be a key driver of customer loyalty (Parasuraman and Grewal, 2000, p. 168-69). Because companies can be thought of as "value maximizers," they will do more business with suppliers that provide high value (Sirdeshmukh, Singh, and Sabol, 2002, p. 21; Ulaga, Eggert, and Schultz, 2006). With the trend towards supplier base consolidation, the effect of an OEM's value perception of a branded component on share of wallet can be even more decisive: in the case of single sourcing the supplier that provides better value will get 100% of the OEM's business. In dual sourcing situations, the primary supplier and the backup supplier will likely be chosen based on value perceptions. The above discussion suggests that:

H_7:   The higher the OEM's value perception of the branded component, the larger the share of wallet.

H_8:   The higher the OEM's value perception of the branded component, the more likely the OEM will expand its purchases from the supplier in the future.

Trust and commitment, both reflective of relationship quality, are related to cooperation between the supplier and the OEM. As part of their commitment, OEMs may be willing to invest resources in collaborating with suppliers they trust in an effort to make relationships work (Morgan and Hunt, 1994, p. 26). For suppliers, in turn, close cooperation can be a way to respond to the OEM's commitment by signaling their own commitment to the relationship through, for example, specific investments. Trust in suppliers reduces risk perceived by OEMs and will thus also increase the OEM's inclination to engage in close cooperation (Heide and John, 1990, p. 26; Morgan and Hunt, 1994, p. 26). Stated formally:

H_9:   The better the quality of the relationship between the supplier and the OEM, the closer the cooperation between supplier and OEM.

H_{10}:   The better the quality of the relationship between supplier and OEM, the larger the share of wallet.

H_{11}:   The better the quality of the relationship between supplier and OEM, the more likely the OEM will expand its purchases from the supplier in the future.

The next two hypotheses pertain to the effect of cooperation between the supplier and the OEM regarding behavioral loyalty. As the relationship between supplier and OEM gets closer, the two parties will interact more intensively. Close interaction enables the supplier to learn about the OEM's needs and to develop customized products that better serve them (Ramani and Kumar, 2008, p. 27; Srivastava, Shervani, and Fahey, 1999, p. 171). Closer cooperation also means that the supplier will be involved early in new product development, which gives it a better chance to compete for new business (Ulaga and Eggert, 2006b, p. 130). The more customized the products are, the less attractive it will be for the OEM to source through a number of other suppliers, and the greater the loyalty will be as reflected in share of wallet and expansion of purchases. That is:

H_{12}:   The closer the cooperation between supplier and OEM, the larger the share of wallet.

H_{13}:   The closer the cooperation between supplier and OEM, the more likely the OEM will expand its purchases from the supplier in the future.

Hypotheses H_6 to H_{13} formulate a flow of causality from perceptual measures at the OEM level to behavioral outcomes. From a theoretical perspective, this direction of causality is in line with the assumption that buying decisions in business markets are usually based on a careful evaluation of alternatives prior to purchase. The inverse flow of causality, a post-hoc rationalization of decisions following an impulse-driven buying behavior, appears much less plausible in business markets. The hypothesized direction of causality also reflects the predominant view in the literature (Eggert, 2004; Ulaga and Eggert, 2006a) and, in addition, is supported by the meta-analysis by Palmatier et al. (2006). Thus, I also formulate null hypotheses for the inverse effects of the effects formulated in Hypotheses H_6 to H_{13} and subject them to hypotheses testing in Chapter 5.

3.2.5   *Moderating Effects of Situational Context Factors*

Considerable differences exist among business markets, especially with regard to various industry-specific and company-specific situational factors (e.g. Sheth, 1973). It is therefore crucial to determine if the causal linkages formulated in main Hypotheses H_{1-13} are universally valid or contingent upon certain situational factors. In this section, I draw on the resource-based view (RBV) to develop a set of hypotheses concerning how the size of effects in the model is moderated by situational variables. According to RBV, A strong supplier brand is viewed as an intangible, market-based asset that can be leveraged by the supplier to attain a competitive advantage (Srivastava, Fahey, and Christensen, 2001). The marketing strategy literature has highlighted the importance of competitive environment as a moderator of the link between intellectual and relational market based assets (e.g. Bharadwaj, Varadarajan, and Fahy, 1993; Kohli and Jaworski, 1990). I identify four moderating variables pertaining to the competitive environment. First, I introduce two sets of moderating hypotheses analyzing the competitive situation in a specific OEM industry. Then I formulate two sets of hypotheses that suggest how the level of competition among component suppliers moderates effects in the model. OEM brand strength and competitive intensity in the OEM industry, the first two moderators, pertain to the competitive situation in the OEM industry. The level of competition faced by the component supplier is captured by the number of competitors for the component and by the degree of commoditization of the component.

The first set of hypotheses pertains to the *moderating effect of OEM brand strength*, defined as the image and awareness of the OEM corporate brand among its potential customers. According to the resource-based view of the firm, companies cooperate to combine complementary resources (Dyer and Singh, 1998). In this way, the partner companies will be able to compete more effectively than when they operate individually (Dyer and Singh, 1998). Complementarity – in terms of the brand as an intangible, market-based asset – will be high if a strong component supplier brand complements a weaker OEM brand. Thus, OEMs that only have a weak brand of their own stand to gain more in terms of market performance from using a strong component compared to OEMs with a strong brand. The formal testable hypothesis is:

H_{14}: The higher the OEM brand strength, the weaker the relationship between component supplier brand strength and incremental market performance.

At the same time, the higher complementarity that results from combining a strong supplier brand with a weak OEM brand also means that the dependence of the OEM on the component supplier's brand as an asset will grow. The larger the dependence of the OEM on the component supplier brand, the more power the supplier gains and thus the more likely that the supplier will use coercive power. I therefore hypothesize:

H_{15}: The greater the OEM brand strength, the weaker the relationship between the component supplier's brand strength and coercive power use by the supplier.

When using a strong component supplier brand to achieve better market performance for its product, OEMs basically rent access to the brand as a market-based asset. In order to achieve comparable market performance without the component brand, the OEM would have to engage in costly and time-consuming marketing activity, e.g., by launching a market communications campaign. To achieve an increase in market performance equivalent to that gained from using the branded component, OEMs with weak brands would have to invest more time and money because they first need to build awareness of their brand names before they can build a favorable brand image (Kotler, Keller, and Bliemel, 2007, p. 660). OEMs with weak brands will also need to spend additional resources in order to overcome threshold levels of advertising (Kotler, Keller, and Bliemel, 2007, p. 594), and their marketing programs will be less efficient (Keller, 1993, p. 2). When using a strong component supplier brand, OEMs with weak brands will thus save more than OEMs with strong brands and, accordingly, will see higher value in the incremental market performance when buying from this supplier. Stated formally:

H_{16}:   The higher the OEM brand strength, the weaker the relationship between incremental market performance and the OEM's value perception of the branded component.

In the last paragraph, I found that alternative ways to better market performance (other than using the component supplier's brand) will be more costly for OEMs with weak brands. This observation also yields an interesting implication for the effect of coercive power on the OEM's value perception of the branded component. For OEMs with strong brands, engaging in their own marketing activities will represent a viable alternative to using the component supplier brand. For OEMs with weak brands, however, the high cost of achieving comparable market performance by their own means makes this option increasingly unrealistic. Given their lack of alternative options, OEMs with weak brands will therefore be more inclined to overlook the sacrifice of dealing with an OEM who uses coercive power. In contrast, OEMs with strong brands that face a realistic choice between the two options will perceive coercive power use by the supplier as a greater sacrifice when buying from the supplier. The above discussion suggests:

H_{17}:   The higher the OEM brand strength, the stronger the negative relationship between coercive power use by supplier and the OEM's value perception of the branded component.

The second set of hypotheses examines the *moderating effect of competitive intensity in the OEM industry,* which is defined as the level of competition between firms in the OEM's industry (Jaworski and Kohli, 1993, p. 57). In situations of high competitive intensity, it is more difficult for OEMs to achieve and sustain a competitive advantage. OEMs in such an industry will take any possible action to stay ahead of competition. An OEM's competitors will thus readily counter any effort made by the OEM to achieve a competitive edge and will try to neutralize eventual gains in incremental market performance by using a strong supplier brand quickly. This tendency leads to the following hypothesis:

H_{18}:   The higher the competitive intensity in the OEM industry, the weaker the relationship between component supplier brand strength and incremental market performance.

In a highly competitive OEM industry, even small competitive advantages can be decisive for an OEM's success as the different OEMs compete closely. As a consequence, OEMs in those industries can grow more dependent on a strong component supplier brand than they do in less competitive industries. The increase in dependence of the OEM on the supplier leads to a stronger link between component supplier brand strength and coercive power use, leading to the following formally testable hypothesis:

H_{19}:   The higher the competitive intensity in the OEM industry, the stronger the relationship between component supplier brand strength and the supplier's use of coercive power.

Given that the level of competition in a specific OEM industry is high, different competitors in such an industry will be more prone to adapt branded components. Competition thus increases the penetration of branded components within a certain OEM industry. With the low penetration of branded components, the incremental market performance from using a strong component supplier brand helps to differentiate offers from the competition. Conversely, when penetration of branded components is high in an industry, using a branded component no longer represents a differentiator but becomes a necessity in matching competitors' offers. The more the use of branded components has become a necessity, rather than a differentiator, in an OEM industry, the more OEMs will perceive the gain in incremental market performance as a zero-sum game that provides little benefit for their business. Thus:

H_{20}: The higher the competitive intensity in the OEM industry, the weaker the relationship between incremental market performance and the OEM's value perception of the branded component.

Also, as the use of branded components becomes more a necessity than a differentiator in an OEM industry due to intensive competition between OEMs, OEMs perceive the use of coercive power differently. In a situation where a component supplier brand provides differentiation from competitors, coercive power use will primarily be an issue of horizontal competition between the supplier and the OEM. The supplier uses the brand strength to claim a higher share of the value. When the use of branded components, however, provides no significant differentiation from competitors, the use of coercive power will increasingly be perceived as a supplier playing different OEMs off against each other. This perception will not only put the OEM's business performance at risk due to vertical competition, but it will additionally lead to risks from increased horizontal competition. The increase in risk translates into higher perceived sacrifices by the OEM. Stated formally:

H_{21}: The higher the competitive intensity in the OEM industry, the stronger the negative relationship between coercive power use by the supplier and the OEM's value perception of the branded component.

I now examine how competitive pressures in the supplier industry moderate the effects in the model. It has frequently been put forward in the marketing literature that strong brands are market-based assets that enable firms to deal with competition more effectively (cf. Srivastava, Fahey, and Christensen, 2001) by (1) helping to differentiate products from competitors' offers (Park, Jaworski, and MacInnis, 1986), (2) preventing market share erosion during price and promotional wars (Kamakura and Russell, 1993), and (3) preventing market share erosion by giving firms time to respond to competitive threats (Aaker, 1991; Bharadwaj, Varadarajan, and Fahy, 1993). For example, firms with a monopoly in a market might perform well, no matter whether they have a strong brand or not. In contrast, for firms in a highly competitive market, a strong brand can be decisive in differentiating their offers from those of the competition. It can thus be expected that a strong brand would be more effective for a component supplier in an environment of high competitive pressure. I investigate two sources of competitive pressure: the number of competitors for the component and the degree of commoditization of the component.

The third set of hypotheses formulates how the number of competitors for the component – a first indicator of competitive pressure in the suppliers' industry – moderates the relationships in the model. When there are only a couple of competing suppliers for a component, differentiation through the tangible product itself can be easier to achieve. For example, OEMs are likely able to recognize and evaluate tangible product differences for three alternative component choices, but might be less able to do so for twenty choices. However, differentiation is not only more difficult to achieve when facing a high number of competitors, it also becomes more crucial for business performance. When there are many suppliers for a component, OEMs have more choices. Only a well-differentiated product will make sure that they select a certain supplier's component over that of their competitors. Thus, the additional differentiation provided by the incremental market performance associated with buying from a strong component supplier brand will have a larger impact when there are many competitors. The formal hypothesis is:

H_{22}: The higher the number of competitors for the component, the stronger the relationship between incremental market performance and the OEM's value perception of the branded component.

However, the number of competitors for a component will also affect how OEMs think about coercive power use. As mentioned before, a higher number of competitors creates more choices for customers. As a consequence, there will be more potential options for an OEM to move away from a component supplier that uses coercive power. Conversely, if there are few alternative choices, OEMs have few options for switching, and will therefore be more inclined to overlook the sacrifice of dealing with an OEM who uses coercive power. In other words, OEMs with switching options will perceive coercive power as a larger sacrifice than those that do not have such options. This leads to the following testable hypothesis:

H_{23}: The higher the number of competitors for the component, the stronger the negative relationship between the use of coercive power by the supplier and the OEM's value perception of the branded component.

Ultimately, I formulate a fourth set of hypotheses to investigate how the degree of commoditization of the component – a second indicator of competitive pressures in the supplier industry – moderates the main effects in the model. Commoditization is defined as the technical similarity of different supplier's components, i.e., the extent to which a common standard or design is established in a supplier industry. The more technically similar different suppliers' components, the fewer opportunities exist to differentiate the tangible product. This fact, in turn, leads to greater importance of an offer's intangible aspects in differentiating the component. In this situation, the intangible benefit of a strong component supplier brand that provides incremental market performance to an OEM will be weighted more positively by the OEM.

H_{24}:   The higher the degree of commoditization of the component, the stronger the relationship between incremental market performance and the OEM's value perception of the branded component.

At the same time, I also expect that the degree of commoditization of a component affects the relationship between coercive power use and the OEM's value perception of the branded component. The more technically similar and standardized different supplier's components are, the more interchangeable they become, enabling easier switching between different suppliers. Less commoditized products, however, create additional switching costs for OEMs. These additional switching costs add to the sacrifices of switching suppliers and thereby reduce the relative sacrifice of dealing with a supplier's coercive influence. Stated formally:

H_{25}:   The higher the degree of the component's commoditization, the stronger the negative relationship between the coercive power used by supplier and the OEM's value perception of the branded component.

In the next section, I develop the theoretical framework for research question two.

3.3 Research Question Two: Effectiveness of Brand Management Instruments in Building, Sustaining, and Leveraging Component Supplier Brand Strength

In this section, I examine the effectiveness of brand management instruments that managers can use to build, sustain, and leverage component supplier brand strength. As illustrated by Figure 17, the variables in the theoretical framework fall into three blocks: (1) what the component supplier does, i.e., brand management actions, (2) what the OEM's customers think, and (3) what the OEM gets.

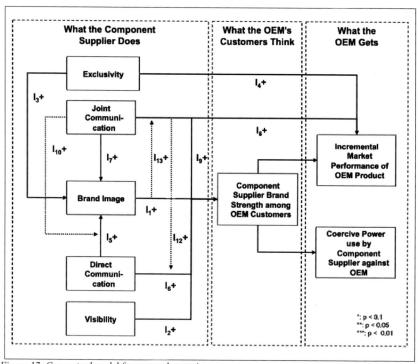

Figure 17: Conceptual model for research question two

First, I discuss how brand image acts as a mediator of the effect of brand management instruments on the outcome variables in section 3.3.1. Then I hypothesize about the effects of visibility and exclusivity in section 3.3.2. Next, I analyze the impact of marketing communications instruments in section 3.3.3. I conclude with the moderation hypotheses on the interactions among marketing communications instruments in section 3.3.4. The hypotheses for research question two are differentiated from those for research question one by using the capital letter I instead of H.

3.3.1   Brand Image as a Mediator

The first hypothesis pertains to the effect of the supplier brand's image upon the OEM's customers. In the model, brand image acts as a mediator of the effect of the brand management instruments on component supplier brand strength. Brand image describes the perceptions about a brand as reflected by the brand associations held in customer memory (Aaker, 1991, p. 15; Farquhar, 1990, p. 7; Keller, 1993, p. 2). From the review of the literature in Chapter 2, I conclude that brand image in business markets exist at different levels of abstraction. In the present study, brand image is conceptualized by higher-level abstractions such as credibility, trustworthiness, skillfulness, and quality. The distinct streams of research on branding research from consumer behavior, information economics theory, and social network theory suggest avenues for analyzing how brand image affects component supplier brand strength. Research on branded ingredients and co-branding in the consumer domain draws on associative network models of the mind to analyze how a partner firm's brand image transfers in terms of a jointly branded product (Desai and Keller, 2002; Park, Jun, and Shocker, 1996; Simonin and Ruth, 1998). This stream of research finds that salient associations linked to an ingredient or co-brand's name in memory will be retrieved automatically upon exposure to a jointly branded product and thereby affect evaluations of the joint product. Empirical studies show that this strategy both works for abstract associations (e.g., attitudes) (Simonin and Ruth, 1998) as well as more specific associations (e.g., product attributes) (Desai and Keller, 2002; Park, Jun, and Shocker, 1996). Rao, Qu, and Ruekert (1999) and Rao and Ruekert (1994) establish an information economics perspective on brand alliances. The authors show that an ingredient brand's or co-brand's reputation can serve as a signal of quality if customers feel that the partner brand would suffer economic losses if the quality claims of the jointly branded product were false. Wuyts et al. (2004) maintain a social network theory perspective to analyze vertical triads consisting of a supplier, a systems provider, and a buyer in markets for complex technical products. Their reasoning is based on the assumption that relationships between companies exist to enable the exchange of valuable resources, especially knowledge. Buyers will consequently infer that those system providers with relationships with reputed suppliers that provide optimal access to crucial resources will be able to provide better value. It is therefore hypothesized that:

I_1:   High and positive brand image of the component supplier leads to increases in component supplier brand strength.

3.3.2   Visibility and Exclusivity as Brand Management Instruments

The next three hypotheses examine the effect of the visibility and exclusivity of the component brand (Caspar, Hecker, and Sabel, 2002, p. 35). Visibility is defined here as the ability of the OEM's customer to identify the supplier brand in the OEM's product. I consider visibility a brand management instrument rather than a property of the component because suppliers can take specific actions to increase the visibility of their components. For example, by painting them in a specific color, the color would then become a brand element. There are two major reasons why visibility is important: first, visibility raises awareness for the component and better enables the OEM's customers to experience the component's contribution to the overall performance of the OEM's product. Second, better visibility of the component can add to the differentiation ability of the component as the OEM's customers learn about the presence of different brands and how to attribute performance differences to the brands. The formal hypothesis is:

I_2:   The better visible the component brand in the OEM's product, the greater the potential of the branded component to add value to the OEM's product.

Next, I analyze the effect of exclusivity on brand image and incremental market performance. Similarly to exclusive distribution in a retailing context (Kotler and Keller, 2005, p. 480), exclusivity is defined here as the extent to which an OEM's customers have access to the branded component. Exclusivity would be low if a supplier chooses to sell to any OEM interested in its component. Conversely, a selective or exclusive strategy involves supplying components only to a selected number of OEMs or to a single OEM, respectively. Selective and exclusive strategies enable the component supplier to collaborate only with reputed OEMs and thereby help to establish quality associations for its brand (Yoo, Donthu, and Lee, 2000, p. 205). Also, just the fact that a component supplier carefully selects OEMs to collaborate with can act as a quality signal for a supplier brand, thereby adding to the brand image. The formal hypothesis is:

I_3:   Exclusivity of the component brand leads to increases in component supplier brand image.

From the perspective of resource-advantage theory (Hunt and Morgan, 1995), the supplier brand represents a valuable resource that provides a competitive advantage to the OEM (Dyer and Singh, 1998). The competitive advantage an OEM gains over competitors and its resulting incremental gain in market performance will depend on the extent to which the OEM's competitors also have access to the supplier's branded component. The more limited the access to the branded component, the greater the potential competitive advantage, and, thus, the greater the incremental market performance. Therefore, it can be expected that:

I_4:   Exclusivity of the component brand will enable higher incremental market performance of the OEM product.

3.3.3   Marketing Communication Instruments

In this section I analyze the contribution of marketing communications to building, sustaining, and leveraging component supplier brand strength. There are two major types of communication instruments available to component suppliers: direct communication and joint communication.

The next two hypotheses pertain to the effects of direct communication, which I define as the marketing communication by the supplier targeted directly at the OEM's customers. The goals of direct communications include informing the OEMs' customers about the brand's positioning and core attributes, about specific benefits of the brand's product, about services for the brand's customers, about technical specifications of the brand's products, etc. In business markets, marketing communication relies less on one-way communication methods, such as advertising. Marketers in business markets rely more heavily on communication through interactive channels in order to better account for the relational nature of buyer-supplier relationships (Bendixen, Bukasa, and Abratt, 2004, p. 379). Possible interactive channels that component manufacturers might use include sales representatives, hotlines and on-call services, training of technical personnel, trade shows, and technical conferences (Abratt, 1986, p. 296; Bendixen, Bukasa, and Abratt, 2004, p. 379; Lynch, 2004, p. 410; Mudambi, Doyle, and Wong, 1997, p. 443). Also, the supplier's website can be an important means of interacting with the OEM's customers, as demonstrated by an exploratory pre-study. Research from consumer markets shows that marketing communication strongly affects brand image (Boulding, Lee, and Staelin, 1994; Simon and Sullivan, 1993; Yoo, Donthu, and Lee, 2000). In line with this observation, I suggest that a direct communication strategy can emphasize the component supplier's unique resources (e.g., skills, experience, and involvement in the OEM customer's industry) to build a positive brand image. Besides its effect on brand image, direct communication can come as direct customer support that directly benefits the OEM's customer, thus directly contributing to the component supplier's brand strength. From the above discussion I conclude:

I_5:   The use of direct communication by the supplier will lead to increases in brand image.

I_6:   The use of direct communication by the supplier will lead to an increase in component supplier brand strength by the supplier brand.

Next, I formulate three hypotheses concerning the effects of joint communication. Joint communication relates to marketing communication aimed at informing the OEM's customers about the cooperation between the supplier and the OEM. Potential avenues for joint communication are partner programs, joint advertising campaigns, and advertising of the supplier brand via OEM information materials as well as on the actual product. Joint communication creates additional exposure to the supplier's brand among the OEM's customers, thus offering opportunities for brand building. For example, Worm and Van Durme (2006) demonstrate how exposure to information about an ingredient branded product strengthens the ingredient brand's brand associations. The formal testable hypothesis is:

I_7:   Joint communication by the component supplier and the OEM will enhance the supplier's brand image.

Another important contribution of joint communication lies in its ability to establish the branded component as a point of differentiation for the OEM brand itself. Even if other OEMs also use the branded component, joint communication can make the OEM's customer base feel that supplier brand and OEM belong together intimately. As a consequence, the component brand may become so strongly linked to the OEM in the customers' minds that they would perceive a discrepancy if the OEM used another component supplier instead. The fact that the OEM's customers would disapprove of the use of another component supplier in turn means that a large share of the OEM's market performance is actually attributable to the component brand. Thus:

I_8:   Joint communication by the component supplier and the OEM will enable higher incremental market performance of the OEM product.

Ultimately, joint communication acts as a signal for the quality of the cooperation between supplier and OEM. As discussed earlier, social network theory implies that customers prefer OEMs that can access valuable resources, especially knowledge, through their partnerships with suppliers (Wuyts, Stremersch, Van Den Bulte, and Franses, 2004). From the fact that both parties engage in joint communication, the OEM's customer can infer that there are strong ties between both parties. This in turn implies that the supplier will actually grant the OEM access to those resources. Therefore, it is hypothesized that:

I_9:   Joint communication by the component supplier and the OEM will lead to an increase in component supplier brand strength by the supplier brand.

Note that the hypotheses in this section capture the intensity of using different communication instruments by a supplier. Yet another question to be answered concerns how effective communication could actually be implemented for each of these instruments. However, this question is beyond the scope of this study.

3.3.4   Interactions among Marketing Communications Instruments

The moderating hypotheses pertain to the interaction of direct communication and joint communication. As discussed earlier, social network theory suggests that customers prefer OEMs whose relationships with suppliers promise access to scarce resources, especially knowledge. The most benefits can be derived if knowledge flows both between supplier and customer (i.e., direct communication) as well as between and supplier and OEM (signaled by joint communication). This perspective implies that the two ways of communication will be mutually reinforcing:

I_{10}:   The positive effect of direct communication on brand image will be stronger the higher the intensity of joint communication.

I_{11}:   The positive effect of joint communication on incremental market performance of OEM product will be stronger for higher levels of direct communication.

I_{12}:   The positive effect of direct communication on component supplier brand strength will be stronger the higher the intensity of joint communication.

The next chapter outlines the methodology used to test the proposed theoretical framework.

4 Methodology

This chapter covers the methodology used in the empirical part of this study. Section 4.1 outlines the actual research design of the study. Subsequently, in Section 4.2, I review the method of structural equations modeling with partial-least-squares (PLS) and covariance-based algorithms.

4.1 Research Design

The following sections outline the research design used in the study. In Section 5.2.1, I discuss the survey procedure and the sample. Section 5.2.2 documents the development and pretest of the measures. Ultimately, the survey instrument is described in Section 5.2.3.

4.1.1 Sampling Procedure

Data is collected using survey methodology in an effort to maximize external validity of the results. A survey, when compared to an experimental design, also enables the inclusion of a much larger set of independent variables. The unit of analysis for the study is the triadic relationship between the OEM firm, a component supplier, and the OEM's customer.

A cross-sectional sample of German original equipment manufacturer (OEM) companies was used to test the hypotheses on a broad empirical basis. The cross-sectional design was chosen for the following three reasons:

- **Generalizability:** For the study to make a substantial contribution to marketing theory and practice, the empirical results have to prove that the conceptual model generalizes across a diverse range of settings. The use of a cross-sectional sample helps to avoid findings that apply only to specific industries.

- **Causality:** A cross-sectional sample enables a more rigid test of causal relationships, thereby increasing the study's internal validity. Because situational variables can be thought of as quasi-randomized across industries and companies, variations in a dependent variable are more likely caused by variations in the independent variable.

- **Variance:** in a cross-sectional sample, variance in the independent and dependent variables, a prerequisite statistical testing of effects in a correlational study, will be greater. Sufficiently high levels of variance in the variables represent an important prerequisite for statistical testing of effects in a correlational study.

The sampling frame for the survey consisted of firms listed in the Database of *ABC der deutschen Wirtschaft*, a major commercial provider of addresses for German businesses. 2200 companies that satisfied the following three criteria were randomly selected:

1. The companies are in the manufacturing industries

2. The firms serve business markets

3. I imposed a quota so that companies of different size (as indicated by their numbers of employees) are equally represented.

Figure 18 displays the survey procedure. Initially, firms were contacted by phone to ask their heads of Marketing/Sales for cooperation and to obtain their personal email address. This solicitation resulted in a primary sample of 989 Marketing and Sales managers. I then used a three-wave mailing approach: the informants were sent an invitation letter and two subsequent reminders by email. In the emails, each informant received a personalized link that allowed him or her to respond to the survey only once. From the primary sample, a total of 241 complete questionnaires were obtained, for an effective response rate of 24%. Despite the length of the survey, the high rank of the managers targeted, and the significant cognitive involvement required by the survey, the response rate well exceeds those of comparable surveys conducted among Marketing, Sales, and General Mangers in Germany, (Homburg, Grozdanovic, and Klarmann, 2007, p. 316; Homburg and Pflesser, 2000).

There is evidence that data obtained from single informants may suffer from validity problems due to common method variance (Van Bruggen, Lilien, and Kacker, 2002). Common method variance is defined as variance attributable to the measurement method rather than to the constructs the measures represent (Podsakoff et al., 2003). It is one of the main sources of measurement error in the social sciences and poses a rival explanation for correlations observed between the measures. To address these validity issues, I collected data from multiple informants in every OEM firm. Towards this goal, respondents in the primary sample were asked to provide the name and email address of a purchasing manager in their respective firms in charge of the procurement of the component that was successful in 83 cases. The remaining 157 companies were then again contacted by phone to identify suitable informants in the purchasing department. Altogether, the secondary sample consisted of 192 potential informants who were sent one invitation and one reminder email for the survey. The managers who had not responded to the reminder received follow-up phone calls and were sent a second reminder email. This procedure resulted in a total of 114 completed questionnaires from the secondary sample for a response rate of 59%.

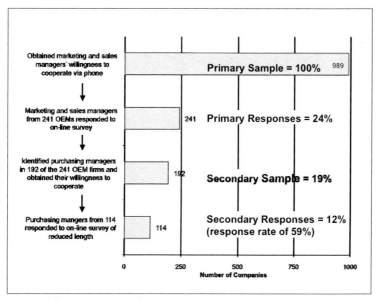

Figure 18: Survey procedure and response rates

Non-response bias was assessed by comparing early and late respondents (Armstrong and Overton, 1977). A Multivariate Analysis of Variance (MANOVA) indicated no individual differences in the measurement items for either of the constructs in the survey. Also, the multivariate statistics showed that the overall MANOVA model was highly insignificant (p > 0.55), thereby implying that no systematic differences exist in the response vectors between early and late respondents. Thus, nonresponse bias was not considered a problem in the present study.

4.1.2   Sample Characteristics

The final sample includes OEM firms in a large variety of manufacturing industries. As shown in Figure 19, firms selling electronics and machinery each make up for 22% of the responses, 16% of the OEMs manufacture metal products, and 8% of the responses are from plastic-product industries. The remaining industries each contribute to 2-5% of the target firms.

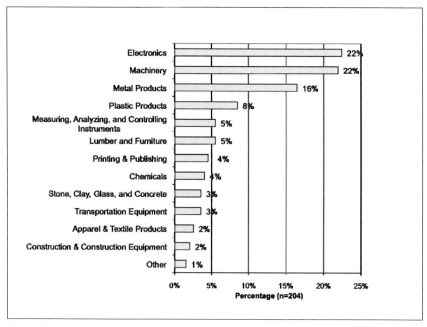

Figure 19: Sample composition by industry

The companies in the sample had an average of 723 employees. Figure 20 demonstrates that companies of different sizes, as indicated by the number of employees, are well represented in the sample. Firms with 100 to 249 employees are the most frequent; they account for 18% of the sample. 9% of the responses are from small companies with less than 20 employees, the smallest group in the sample. The share of the remaining firm sizes range between 13% and 16%. With a difference in size between the largest and smallest group of only 0.5, this makes for a good distribution of company size in the sample.

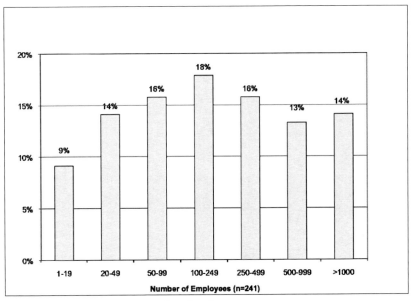

Figure 20: Sample composition by number of employees

Firms in the sample generate an average of 530 million Euros of revenues. The distribution of annual revenues across the companies in the sample can be seen in Figure 21. Companies with annual revenues of a medium range (i.e., between 10 and 100 million Euros) account for almost 50% of the sample. The huge difference between mean and median indicates that the distribution of annual revenues is left-skewed (i.e., some of the companies in the "500 plus" group earn large multiples of the remaining firms' revenues).

In summary, the sample covers a diverse set of companies from different industry backgrounds. Firms ranged from small enterprises with only a few employees to multibillion Euro companies. A majority of the firms cater to an international customer base in European Union countries and worldwide. Thus, the sample characteristics indicate that the sample is truly cross-sectional in nature and therefore satisfies the requirements for valid and generalizable results.

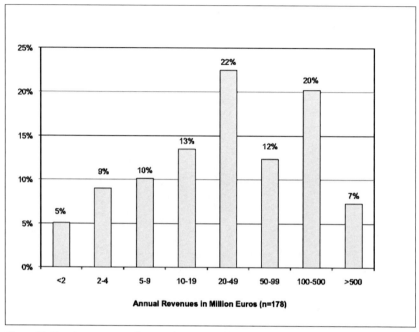

Figure 21: Sample composition by annual revenues of the firm

4.1.3   Informant Characteristics

As discussed earlier, data were collected from multiple informants per OEM firm to obtain more accurate data by taking into account the perspectives of both Marketing/Sales and Purchasing managers. Figure 22 shows that the strategy of obtaining a primary response from Marketing/Sales and a secondary response from Purchasing was largely successful: 78% of the primary respondents had a background in Marketing/Sales while 74% of the secondary responses are from purchasing managers. When looking at the pooled data of the 114 units for which multiple responses were actually obtained, 89% of the primary responses came from Marketing/ Sales and 78% from Purchasing (see Table 10). Most of the remaining responses in the primary sample are from General Management, which makes sense for smaller companies in which the top manager would still be in charge of establishing and maintaining customer relationships. Similarly, most of the non-purchasing respondents in the secondary sample have a background in Technical Management, again making sense for smaller firms without a purchasing department whose technical managers would be responsible for ordering components directly from the supplier. Overall, the survey covered informants from the sample firms who were most likely able to provide accurate measures for the constructs in the study.

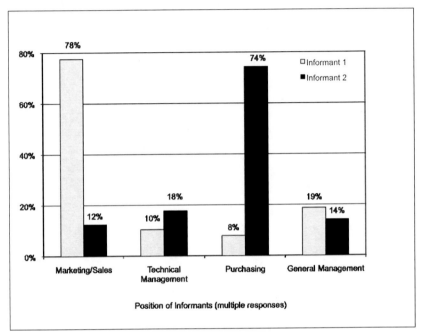

Figure 22: Position of informants

		Informant 1			
		Marketing/ Sales	Technical Management	Purchasing	General Management
Informant 2	Marketing/Sales	10%	1%	0%	2%	**12%**
	Technical Management	12%	2%	0%	4%	**19%**
	Purchasing	61%	6%	0%	11%	**78%**
	General Management	6%	0%	0%	9%	**15%**
		89%	**9%**	**0%**	**26%**	**n=113**

Table 10: Composition of multiple-informant datasets by position of informants

The levels of confidence about answering questions in the survey as reported by informants lent further support to the accuracy of the information they provided. As illustrated in Figure 23, 75% of the informants in the primary sample are at least confident that they provided accurate information about issues relating to their customers' perspectives.

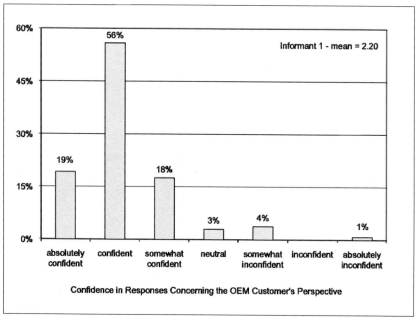

Figure 23: First informant's confidence in responses concerning the OEM customer's perspective

Figure 24 displays the corresponding ratings of their confidence in the ability to accurately envision the OEM's perspective of the relationship with the supplier. As expected, informants in the secondary sample are a more reliable source of information for the OEM's perspective: while 77% of secondary respondents are at least confident, the figure is 63% for primary respondents. When testing for differences in the means of the three confidence distributions, the t-test shows that primary respondents feel in fact significantly more confident about responses about their customers' perspectives as opposed to their own company's perspective ($p<0.01$). Also, secondary respondents feel significantly more confident than primary respondents when it comes to their own company's perspective (p<0.001), thus underscoring the contribution of collecting multiple responses to more accurate data.

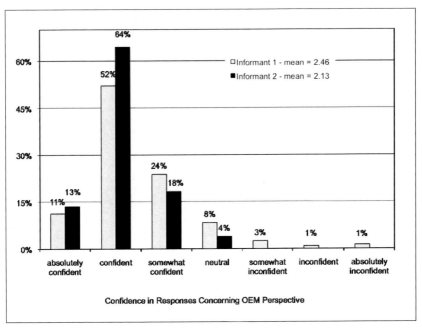

Figure 24: Informant's confidence in responses concerning OEM perspective

Informants in the survey had an average professional experience of eleven years (primary informants) and 12.5 years (secondary informants) in their current industry. The distribution of professional experience in Figure 25 shows that more than 80% of the informants had worked in their industry for at least five years. This high level of seniority provides additional evidence that the managers were indeed reliable informants for the purpose of our study.

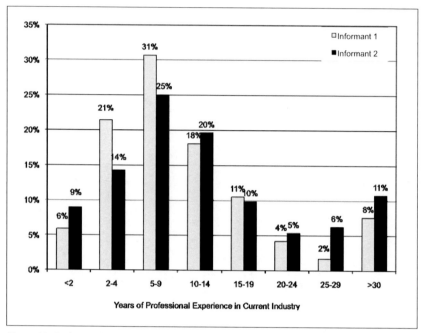

Figure 25: Professional experience of informants

4.1.4   Measure Development and Pretest

In order to ensure the content validity of the measures for the study, I followed a step-wise procedure similar to that suggested by Fassott (2005b) in the development and pretest of the items.

First, I established clear definitions of the latent constructs and decided on the indicator specification (formative vs. reflective) based on the literature review and the underlying theory. Next, an initial set of items was generated for each construct. When available, construct measures from the literature were adapted to the present study's context.

Second, the items for the core constructs were tested and refined in interviews with five experts from Marketing academia and practice. The experts were given a complete but unsorted list of the items. They were then asked (1) to sort the items into self-generated construct categories, (2) to assign a label to each construct category, (3) to provide a brief definition of each construct, and (4) to decide if the construct was formative or reflective in nature (adapted from Moore and Benbasat, 1991). I then presented the experts with the intended item structure and discussed possibilities with them to improve their wording. Some items could be deleted based on the expert interviews. The test also helped to eliminate ambiguous wording in some of the items. At the same time, this procedure provided a strong test of content validity since the experts were largely able to reproduce the intended constructs in most cases.

Third, I tested the revised measures for the core constructs for substantive validity in an item-sorting task. Substantive validity expresses the extent to which a measure is judged to be reflective of, or theoretically linked to, some construct of interest (Anderson and Gerbing, 1991). Substantive validity is therefore a necessary prerequisite for construct validity. The judges were ten marketing academics identified as experts in the fields of branding or industrial marketing. As during the first round of expert interviews, judges received a complete list of the items. In addition, they were provided with a brief definition for each of the constructs. The judges were instructed to assign each item to the "right" construct. I then computed the p_{sa} and c_{sv} index values for each item, following Anderson and Gerbing (1991), to assess their substantive validity:

The proportion of substantive agreement, p_{sa}, indicates the extent to which an item is related to its intended construct. The p_{sa} index reflects the share of respondents who assign a measure to the intended construct. It is calculated as follows (Anderson and Gerbing, 1991):

$$p_{sa} = \frac{n_c}{N}$$

n_c : *number of respondents assigning a measure to its posited construct*

N: *total number of respondents*

Equation 1

The substantive validity coefficient, c_{sv}, indicates the extent to which an item might unintentionally tap other constructs, thereby providing a more accurate estimate of substantive validity (Anderson and Gerbing, 1991):

$$c_{SV} = \frac{n_c - n_o}{N}$$

n_c: number of respondents assigning a measure to its posited construct

n_o: highest number of assignments of the item to any other construct in the set

N: total number of respondents

Equation 2

Table 11 displays the results of the item-sorting task. The p_{sa} and c_{sv} indices exceed the threshold values of 0.7 and 0.5 with only two exceptions, indicating good overall substantive validity of the items. The p_{sv} value for item IMPV2 was not judged critical since it was only slightly below the threshold value. Four of the experts assigned the item COER3, capturing opportunistic behavior, to the trust construct instead of to the construct coercive power use by the supplier. After a follow-up analysis, I concluded that the item tapping the trust construct did not cause this designation. Rather, unclear definitions of the two constructs seem to have caused this error. Since it was still reasonable to expect that the item would load on the coercive power use by the supplier construct in the final study, it was retained.

The final items that resulted from the scale development process are shown in Tables 12 to 29. Table 12 displays the measures for component-level situational context factors along with their means and standard deviations. Following Rossiter's (2002, p. 331) suggestion to measure so-called concrete singular constructs with a single item scale, both constructs are represented by a single item measure. Commoditization of the component is operationalized using a newly developed item. For the number of competitors for the component, the scale used by Cannon and Homburg (2001) was adapted to fit the purpose of this study. For both constructs, the "brand" was selected as the object of reference instead of the "supplier." This way I account for component markets in which suppliers market multiple brands that might even make use of different technologies.

Item	Component Supplier Brand Strength	Brand Image	Brand Visibility	Cooperation of Supplier & OEM	Joint Communication	Exclusivity	Incremental Market Performance	Coercive Power Use by Supplier	OEM's value perception component	Share of Wallet	Relationship Quality	Anticipated Expansion of Purchases	N	n_c	n_o	p_{sa} >0.7	c_{sv} >0.5
VALAD1	8	2	0	0	0	0	0	0	0	0	0	0	8	8	0	1.00	1.00
VALAD2	10	0	0	0	0	0	0	0	0	0	0	0	10	10	0	1.00	1.00
VALAD3	8	0	2	0	0	0	0	0	0	0	0	0	10	8	2	0.80	0.60
VALAD4	9	0	0	0	0	0	0	0	0	0	0	0	9	9	0	1.00	1.00
VALAD5	9	1	0	0	0	0	0	0	0	0	0	0	9	9	0	1.00	1.00
VALAD6	10	0	0	0	0	0	0	0	0	0	0	0	10	10	0	1.00	1.00
IMAG1	0	9	0	0	0	0	0	0	0	0	0	0	9	9	0	1.00	1.00
IMAG2	1	8	0	0	0	0	0	0	0	0	0	0	9	8	0	0.89	0.89
IMAG3	0	9	0	0	0	0	0	0	0	0	0	0	9	9	0	1.00	1.00
IMAG4	2	8	0	0	0	0	0	0	0	0	0	0	10	8	0	0.80	0.80
VISIB	0	0	8	0	0	0	0	0	0	0	0	0	8	8	0	1.00	1.00
COLAB1	0	0	0	10	0	0	0	0	0	0	0	0	10	10	0	1.00	1.00
COLAB2	0	0	0	10	0	0	0	0	0	0	0	0	10	10	0	1.00	1.00
COLAB3	0	0	0	9	0	0	0	1	0	0	0	0	10	9	1	0.90	0.80
COLAB4	0	0	0	10	0	0	0	0	0	0	0	0	10	10	0	1.00	1.00
JCOM1	0	0	0	1	7	1	0	0	0	0	1	0	10	7	1	0.70	0.60
JCOM2	0	0	0	0	10	0	0	0	0	0	0	0	10	10	0	1.00	1.00
JCOM3	0	0	0	1	9	0	0	0	0	0	0	0	10	9	1	0.90	0.80
EXCL	0	0	0	0	0	10	0	0	0	0	0	0	10	10	0	1.00	1.00
IMPV1	0	0	0	0	0	0	7	0	2	0	0	0	9	7	2	0.78	0.56
IMPV2	0	0	0	0	0	1	6	0	1	0	1	0	9	6	1	**0.67**	0.56
IMPV3	0	0	0	0	2	0	7	0	1	0	0	0	10	7	2	0.70	0.50
IMPV4	0	0	0	0	0	0	8	0	1	1	0	0	10	8	1	0.80	0.70
IMPV5	0	0	0	0	0	0	8	0	2	0	0	0	10	8	2	0.80	0.60
COER1	0	0	0	0	0	0	0	10	0	0	0	0	10	10	0	1.00	1.00
COER2	0	0	0	0	0	0	0	9	0	0	1	0	10	9	1	0.90	0.80
COER3	0	0	0	0	0	0	0	6	0	0	4	0	10	6	4	**0.60**	**0.20**
OPV1	0	0	0	0	0	0	0	0	10	0	0	0	10	10	0	1.00	1.00
OPV2	0	0	0	0	0	0	1	0	9	0	0	0	10	9	1	0.90	0.80
OPV3	0	0	0	0	0	0	1	0	9	0	0	0	10	9	1	0.90	0.80
OPV4	0	0	0	0	0	0	0	0	8	0	2	0	10	8	2	0.80	0.60
SHARB	0	0	0	0	0	0	0	0	0	10	0	0	10	10	0	1.00	1.00
COTR1	0	0	0	0	0	0	0	0	0	0	9	1	10	9	1	0.90	0.80
COTR2	0	0	0	1	0	0	0	0	0	0	9	0	10	9	1	0.90	0.80
COTR3	0	0	0	0	0	0	0	0	0	0	10	0	10	10	0	1.00	1.00
XPURCH	0	0	0	0	0	0	0	0	0	1	1	8	10	8	1	0.80	0.70

Table 11: Item sorting task results

Component-Level Situational Context Factors		Code	Mean	SD
Commoditization of Component	♦ **Definition:** *The technical similarity of different suppliers' components in an industry*			
♦ **Based** on: New scale	♦ **Scale:** *7-point Likert Scale (single item)*			
• The competing brands' offers for component [C] differ significantly in technology (Reverse)	• Die unterschiedlichen Komponentenmarken für Komponente [K] unterscheiden sich technisch deutlich (Reverse)	COMC	4.63	1.77
Number of competitors for component	♦ **Definition:** *The number of competing component brands for component [C]*			
♦ **Based** on: Cannon and Homburg (2001)	♦ **Scale:** *7-point Likert Scale (single item)*			
• There is a broad choice of different brands for component [C]	• Es gibt eine Vielzahl von Marken für die Komponente [K]	ALTB	5.08	1.92

Table 12: Measurement of component-level situational context factors

The measures for the supplier's use of brand management instruments are shown in Table 13. Due to the lack of extant scales in this area, all items were generated for the purpose of this study. Again in line with the suggestion by Rossiter (2002, p. 331), visibility and exclusivity are measured with single items. At the same time, formative measures are used for direct and indirect communication because the use of different communication channels is not necessarily correlated – a firm may, for example, provide an extensive website but may make no use of catalogues at all. The formative items for direct communication and joint communication were determined based on an exploratory pre-study of marketing-communications instruments for business markets. I included those instruments that emerged as being most effective in the pre-study. Note that the mean rating of all communication instruments except for "website" is comparatively low, indicating that, on average, component suppliers do not make excessive use of marketing communications as brand-building instruments.

Table 14 reports the measures for the two constructs that capture the perceptions of the component supplier's brand among an OEM's customers, supplier brand image, and component-supplier brand strength. Based on the scales by Erdem and Swait (1998) and Erdem, Swait, and Valenzuela (2006), brand image is measured using a four-item reflective scale format. These items capture the associations that are linked to the component supplier brand in the OEM customer's mind.

For component-supplier brand strength, a new scale was developed incorporating the four interrelated facets of the constructs identified in section 3.2.1: improving perceived quality, reducing perceived risk, reducing information costs, and enabling easier decisions at the buying center. Importantly, the construct was operationalized in a reflective fashion because the causality flows from the latent construct to the items. It is the strength of the brand that causes the items. With mean ratings around the midpoint and a standard deviation of roughly two points, the component supplier brands included in the sample cover a wide range of different brand strengths.

In Table 15 I show the measures for perceptions of what an OEM gets when buying a certain supplier's branded component. For incremental market performance, the market performance scales used by Homburg and Pflesser (2000) Jaworski and Kohli (1993) were adapted to fit the present study's purpose. Even though one could argue that the direction of causality flows from the items to the construct, previous studies and theoretical considerations imply that the measurement items for market performance are heavily correlated. To avoid the problems of formative specification arising from multicollinearity among the items, the construct is specified as formative. Coercive power use by supplier is measured with reflective multi-item scales adapted from the existing literature (Gundlach and Cadotte, 1994; Hunt and Nevin, 1974). OEM's value perception of the branded component was measured using reflective items adapted from Menon, Homburg, and Beutin (2005) and Ulaga and Eggert (2006).

Table 16 displays the measures of variables related to the OEM-supplier relationship, relationship quality and cooperation between the OEM and supplier. Relationship quality is operationalized as being reflected in trust and commitment. The measurement items are similar to or adapted from those in Doney and Cannon (1997), Eggert (2004), Morgan and Hunt (1994). Because previous research has shown that trust and commitment are strongly related (Morgan and Hunt, 1994), they are not incorporated as separate formative dimensions but as reflective items of the relationship quality construct.

Supplier's Use of Brand Management Instruments		Code	Mean	SD
Visibility	♦ **Definition:** *The ability of the OEM's customer to identify the supplier brand in the OEM's product*			
♦ **Based on:** *New scale*	♦ **Scale:** *7-point Likert Scale (single item)*			
• Our customers can easily see it if we use brand [B]'s components in our product.	• Unsere Kunden können es leicht erkennen, wenn in unseren Produkten die Komponentenmarke [B] verwendet wird	VISIB	3.79	2.31
Direct Communication	♦ **Definition:** *Marketing communication by the supplier targeted directly at the OEM's customer*			
♦ **Based on:** *New scale*	♦ **Scale:** *7-point Likert Scale (formative)*			
• On his website, supplier [B] provides a broad array of information targeted specifically at our customers	• Der Hersteller [B] hält auf seiner Internetseite umfangreiche Informationen für unsere Kunden bereit	DCOM1	4.30	2.15
• Supplier [B] regularly provides our customers with catalogues and brochures	• Unsere Kunden erhalten regelmäßig Kataloge und Prospekte von Hersteller [B]	DCOM2	2.54	1.95
• Supplier [B]'s sales force visits our customers on a regular basis	• Der Außendienst von Hersteller [B] besucht unsere Kunden regelmäßig	DCOM3	2.56	2.04
Joint Communication	♦ **Definition:** *Marketing communication aimed at informing the OEM's customers about the cooperation between supplier and OEM*			
♦ **Based on:** *New scale*	♦ **Scale:** *7-point Likert Scale (formative)*			
• Our company is an officially certified partner of supplier [B]	• Wir treten am Markt als zertifiziertes Partnerunternehmen des Herstellers [B] auf	JCOM1	2.09	1.93
• Supplier [B] and our company run joint advertising and communications	• Wir führen gemeinsam mit dem Hersteller [B] Werbemaßnahmen durch	JCOM2	1.95	1.67
• We advertise brand [B]'s logo and/or name on our product or product information	• Wir werben auf unseren Produkten oder in unseren Werbematerialien mit dem Markenlogo/- Namen von [B]	JCOM3	2.48	2.13
Exclusivity	♦ **Definition:** *The extent to which the intermediary's competitors have access to the supplier's branded components*			
♦ **Based on:** *New scale*	♦ **Scale:** *5-point semantic differential scale (single-item)*			
In our industry, supplier [B] collaborates... • exclusively with our company • with selected firms • theoretically with any firm (Reverse)	Der Hersteller [B] arbeitet in unserer Branche bei der Komponente [K] .... • exklusiv mit unserem Unternehmen zusammen • mit ausgewählten Unternehmen zusammen • theoretisch mit jedem Unternehmen zusammen (Reverse)	EXCL	1.76	1.17

Table 13: Measurement of the supplier's use of brand management instruments

OEM's customers' perception of the component supplier brand		Code	Mean	SD
Brand Image of Component Supplier	♦ **Definition:** The image of the supplier brand among the *OEM's* customers			
♦ **Based on:** Erdem and Swait (1998), Erdem, Swait, and Valenzuela (2006)	♦ **Scale:** 7-point Likert Scale (reflective)			
• In the eyes of our customers brand [B] delivers what it promises	• In den Augen unserer Kunden hält die Marke [B], was sie verspricht	IMAGB1	5.21	1.73
• Brand [B] has name that our customers trust	• Unsere Kunden vertrauen der Marke [B]	IMAGB2	5.22	1.70
• Our customers believe in brand [B]'s skills	• Unsere Kunden vertrauen in die Fachkompetenz der Marke [B]	IMAGB3	5.26	1.69
• Among our customers, brand [B] has a reputation for high quality	• Bei unseren Kunden hat die Marke [B] einen Ruf für hohe Qualität	IMAGB4	5.32	1.68
Component Supplier Brand Strength	♦ *Definition: The value that the supplier brand adds to (or distracts from) the OEM's product*			
♦ *Based on: New scale*	♦ *Scale: 7-point Likert Scale* **(reflective)**			
• If we use brand [B]'s components in our product it will better meet quality standards in the eyes of our customers	• Wenn wir Komponenten der Marke [B] in unserem Produkt verwenden, erfüllt unser Produkt in den Augen der Kunden ihre Qualitätsstandards besser	VALAD1	4.75	1.71
• If we use brand [B]'s components in our product our customers perceive it as more reliable	• Wenn wir Komponenten der Marke [B] in unserem Produkt verwenden, nehmen die Kunden unser Produkt als zuverlässiger wahr	VALAD2	4.63	1.76
• If we use brand [B]'s components in our product our customers can more easily understand and evaluate our offer	• Wenn unser Angebot die Komponenten der Marke [B] beinhaltet, ist es für unsere Kunden einfacher, das Angebot zu erfassen und zu bewerten	VALAD3	3.69	1.80
• If we use brand [B]'s components in our product the different parties involved in our customer's buying process will reach agreement on the purchase quicker	• Wenn unser Angebot die Komponenten der Marke [B] beinhaltet, kommen die unterschiedlichen Interessengruppen im Unternehmen des Kunden schneller zur gemeinsamen Entscheidung	VALAD4	3.89	1.71
• If we use brand [B]'s components in our product our customers perceive a lower risk of making a wrong purchase decision	• Wenn unser Angebot die Komponenten der Marke [B] beinhaltet, empfinden unsere Kunden das geringere Risiko eines Fehlkaufs	VALAD5	4.45	1.73
• If we use brand [B]'s components in our product our customers can more easily compare it with competitors' offers	• Wenn unser Angebot die Komponenten der Marke [B] beinhaltet, fällt unseren Kunden der Vergleich mit Konkurrenzangeboten leichter	VALAD6	4.08	1.94

Table 14: Measurement of OEM's customers' perception of the component supplier brand

OEM' Perceptions		Code	Mean	SD
♦ **Incremental Market Performance**	♦ **Definition:** The effectiveness of the supplier brand in driving the market performance of the OEM's product			
♦ **Based on:** Homburg and Pflesser (2000), Jaworski and Kohli (1993)	♦ **Scale:** 7-point Likert Scale (reflective)			
• Brand's [B]'s components increase the customer's satisfaction with our products	• Die Komponenten von [B] steigern die Zufriedenheit der Kunden mit unseren Produkten	IMPV1	4.56	1.76
• Some of our customers will only do business with us if we use brand [B]'s components	• Einige unserer Kunden kaufen nur bei uns, wenn wir Komponenten der Marke [B] einsetzen	IMPV2	2.91	2.06
• Acquiring new customers will be easier if we use brand [B]'s components	• Mit Komponenten der Marke [B] können wir einfacher neue Kunden gewinnen	IMPV3	3.41	1.92
• Some percentage of our market share can be attributed to component brand [B]	• Wir verdanken einen gewissen Prozentsatz unseres Marktanteils der Komponentenmarke [B]	IMPV4	3.30	1.94
• When using brand [B]'s components we can charge higher prices for our products	• Mit Komponenten der Marke [B] können wir für unsere Produkte höhere Preise erzielen	IMPV5	3.32	1.97
Coercive power use by Supplier	♦ **Definition:** The perceived propensity of the supplier to use his brand as a source power over the intermediary			
♦ **Based on:** Gundlach and Cadotte (1994), Hunt and Nevin (1974)	♦ **Scale:** 7-**point** Likert Scale (reflective)			
• Supplier [B] uses his brand's strength to negotiate conditions that are unfavorable for our company	• Der Hersteller [B] nutzt die Stärke seiner Marke als Argument, um für ihn vorteilhafte Vertragskonditionen durchzusetzen	COER1	3.88	1.86
• When negotiating with supplier [B], we will either have to accept their conditions or leave it	• Der Hersteller [B] deutet in Verhandlungssituationen an, uns nicht mehr zu beliefern, wenn wir seine Konditionen nicht akzeptieren	COER2	2.93	1.86
• We are afraid that supplier [B] may take advantage of our dependence on his brand one day	• Es ist möglich, dass der Hersteller [B] unsere Abhängigkeit von seiner Marke eines Tages zu seinen Gunsten ausnutzen wird	COER3	3.35	1.87
OEM's Value Perception of the Branded Component	♦ **Definition:** The OEM's trade-off between the benefits and sacrifices of acquiring the component from the supplier			
♦ **Based on:** Menon, Homburg, and Beutin (2005), Ulaga and Eggert (2006b)	♦ **Scale:** 7-point Likert Scale (**reflective**)			
• Brand [B]'s components are of high value for our company	• Die Komponenten von [B] bieten uns echten Mehrwert für die Kosten	OPV1	4.80	1.43
• The benefits we receive from Brand [B]'s components far outweigh the costs	• Die Vorteile der Komponenten des Herstellers [B] machen die Kosten wett	OPV2	4.64	1.45
• For the costs incurred, we find the benefits offered by brand [B]'s components to be of high value	• Die Nachteile durch die Komponenten von [B] werden durch die Vorteile deutlich aufgewogen	OPV3	5.04	1.27
• Brand [B]'s components create more value for us when comparing all costs and benefits	• Für den Nutzengewinn durch Komponenten von [B] nehmen wir die aktuell bestehenden Nachteile und Kosten gerne in Kauf	OPV4	4.25	1.67

Table 15: Measurement of OEM's perceptions

OEM-Supplier Relationship		Code	Mean	SD
Relationship Quality	♦ *Definition: The overall assessment of the strength of the relationship between OEM and supplier*			
♦ *Based on: Doney and Cannon (1997), Eggert (2004), Morgan and Hunt (1994)*	♦ *Scale: 7-point Likert Scale (reflective)*			
• The relationship with supplier [B] deserves our firm's maximum effort to maintain	• Die Geschäftsbeziehung zu Hersteller [B] ist für uns so wichtig, dass wir sie auf lange Sicht aufrecht erhalten möchten	COTR1	5.64	1.37
• The relationship with supplier [B] is something our firm wants to maintain indefinitely	• Wir messen der Geschäftsbeziehung zu Hersteller [B] einen hohen Stellenwert bei	COTR2	5.65	1.24
• We trust in supplier [B]'s integrity	• Wir vertrauen dem Hersteller [B]	COTR3	5.84	1.20
Cooperation of Supplier & OEM	♦ *Definition: The closeness of the supplier and the OEM working together in the creation of value*			
♦ *Based on: Ulaga and Eggert (2006b)*	♦ *Scale: 7-point Likert Scale (reflective)*			
• We often work together with supplier [B] to improve our products	• Wir arbeiten häufig mit dem Hersteller [B] an Verbesserungen unserer Produkte	COLAB1	4.26	1.90
• Supplier [B] regularly supports us with his know-how	• Der Hersteller [B] hilft uns häufig mit seinem Know-How weiter	COLAB2	4.64	1.74
• Supplier [B] provides us with assistance in integrating their component with our product	• Der Hersteller unterstuetzt uns bei der Integration seiner Komponenten in unsere Produkte	COLAB3	4.65	1.63
• Supplier [B] has made investments in the relationship with us that are of little value with his other customers (e.g. specialized tools, customization of product, adaptation to our business processes, special certification procedures, training of workforce, etc.)	• Der Hersteller [B] hat speziell in die Geschäftsbeziehung zu uns erhebliche Investitionen getätigt, die ihm für andere Kunden wenig nutzen (z.B. für Spezialwerkzeuge, Produktanpassungen, Anpassung an unsere Prozesse, spezielle Zertifizierungen, Mitarbeiterschulungen, etc...)	COLAB5	2.76	1.86

Table 16: Measurement of variables related to the OEM-supplier relationship

Table 17 displays the measures for the behavioral outcomes expansion of purchases and share of wallet. Future expansion of purchases and share of wallet are both operationalized as single item measures (Rossiter, 2002) using measures adapted from Cannon and Homburg (2001) and Ulaga, Eggert, and Schultz (2006), respectively.

Behavioral Outcomes		Code	Mean	SD
Future Expansion of Purchases	♦ *Definition: The OEM's intention to expand business with the supplier in the future.*			
♦ *Based on: Cannon and Homburg (2001), Eggert (2006)*	♦ *Scale: 7-point Likert Scale (single item)*			
• Our firm expects to expand its business done with supplier [B]	• In Zukunft werden wir einen wachsenden Anteil der Komponente von Hersteller [B] beziehen	XPURCH	4.48	1.47
Share of Wallet	♦ *Definition: The share of business for the component done with the supplier*			
♦ *Based on: Ulaga, Eggert, and Schultz (2006)*	♦ *Scale: 5-point labeled scale (single item)*			
• For component [C], you sourced about …% through supplier [B] during the past 12 months. (labels: "<21%", "21-40%", "41-60%", "61-80%", "81-100%")	• Welchen Anteil Ihrer Beschaffungsmenge für die Komponente [K] haben Sie in den vergangenen 12 Monaten von Hersteller [B] bezogen? (labels: "<21%", "21-40%", "41-60%", "61-80%", "81-100%")	SHARB	3.22	1.52

Table 17: Behavioral outcomes

Measures of OEM-level external context factors are provided in Table 18. In order to keep the questionnaire short, OEM-brand strength is measured using a formative two-item scale based on extant research that incorporates both brand awareness and image. I expected that informants from OEM firms with weaker brands who rated the supplier brand as strong earlier in the questionnaire might find it socially undesirable to rate their brand weak. In order to address this potential source of common method variance in the answers, the question was disguised by avoiding the "brand" and making reference only to the OEM "company." Competitive intensity in the OEM's industry is operationalized in a single item measure (Rossiter, 2002) adapted from previous research (Jaworski and Kohli, 1993; Porter, 1985a).

OEM-level Situational Factors		Code	Mean	SD
OEM Brand Strength	♦ *Definition: The strength of the OEM brand among customers*			
♦ *Based on: Keller (1993)*	♦ *Scale: 7-point Likert Scale (formative)*			
• Relative to our main competitors our company has a good reputation among customers	• Im Vergleich zu den wichtigsten Konkurrenten hat unser Unternehmen bei den Kunden einen guten Ruf	OBST1	6.08	0.94
• Relative to our main competitors our is well known among customers	• Im Vergleich zu den wichtigsten Konkurrenten ist unser Unternehmen bei den Kunden bekannt	OBST2	5.64	1.32
OEM's Industry Competitive Intensity	♦ *Definition: The level of competition between firms in the OEM's industry*			
♦ *Based on: Jaworski and Kohli (1993), Porter (1985a)*	♦ *Scale: 7-point Likert Scale (single item)*			
• Competition between firms in our industry is fierce	• Zwischen den Anbietern in unserer Branche herrscht harter Wettbewerb	COIN	6.48	0.84

Table 18: Measurement of OEM-level situational factors

Finally, the scale by van Bruggen, Lilien, and Kacker (2002) is incorporated in the questionnaire to capture the informant's self-assessed accuracy of responses (see Table 19). To enable better comparability of responses between multiple informants from the same unit, a labeled scale is used to provide a precise anchoring of the scale items.

Informant Confidence		Code	Mean	SD
Confidence in Responses	♦ *Definition: The self-assessed accuracy of the responses given by the informant*			
♦ *Based on: van Bruggen, Lilien, and Kacker (2002)*	♦ *Scale: 7-point labeled scale (single item)*			
• Regarding the information on our customer's perspective I am… (endpoints: extremely confident – extremely inconfident)	• Bei den Antworten zum Vertrieb unserer Produkte und zur Sichtweise unserer Kunden bin ich mir… (endpoints: sehr sicher – sehr unsicher)	CONF1	5.85	0.90
• Regarding the information on our company's perspective on supplier [B] I am… (endpoints: extremely confident – extremely inconfident)	• Bei den Antworten zur Bewertung des Hersteller [B] aus Sicht unseres Unternehmens bin ich mir… (endpoints: sehr sicher – sehr unsicher)	CONF2	5.61/ 5.88	0.94/ 0.68

Table 19: Measures of informant confidence

4.1.5   Survey Instrument

The development of the survey instrument focused on maximizing the study's response rate and representativeness while at the same time encouraging thoughtful and accurate responses.

Internet technology provides new opportunities for data collection in business market research (Donath, 2000). While researchers have traditionally relied on mail or telephone surveys to collect data from managers, this study uses a web-based internet questionnaire. Informants for the study were recruited off-line prior to the survey by a call-center. Thus, I expected no sampling bias caused by the survey method.

Table 20 contrasts the advantages and disadvantages of using traditional phone and mail surveys in business market research with those of an internet questionnaire (Donath, 2000; Rangaswamy, 2000). The response rates for the telephone survey will be the highest, but an internet survey will still get a larger share of responses than a mail survey. However, an internet questionnaire is better suited to obtain responses from elusive respondents such as busy mangers. Given the widespread use of mobile internet technologies in the informant group, an internet questionnaire can be answered anywhere and at any time. An internet survey also helps research efficiency by saving time and money; once the survey tool has been set up, the marginal cost per additional respondent is close to zero. Even though managers should be allowed more time than consumers to respond to the survey, the overall duration of the data collection will be significantly shorter. Data collection in the present study was able to be closed three weeks after the initial invitation emails had been sent out. Another advantage of a web-based versus a mail-based questionnaire is the possibility of personalizing the questionnaire: in this case, the component name and supplier brand name provided by the informant were automatically incorporated into the questionnaire by the software. Internet surveys also enable better visualization than phone and mail surveys because they allow for richer content. Compared to alternative survey methods, an internet questionnaire is more convenient to answer because respondents can freely decide when to respond, whether to interrupt the interview and come back later, etc. This flexibility will likely reduce respondent fatigue and thus improve data accuracy. While internet surveys in a consumer environment are still susceptible to nonresponse bias, this is not a likely issue here given the high diffusion of internet technologies among professionals (Chisnall, 2006). To the contrary, an internet survey has less potential for nonresponse bias regarding individuals in positions that involve more work at the office. For the present study, the internet survey technology also offered a convenient way of linking anonymous company-level demographics from the original industry database to the responses.

Criterion	Phone	Mail	Internet
Response Rate	++	+/-	+
Responses from Top Managers	--	+	++
Cost per Response	--	-	++
Duration of Data Collection	-	--	+
Personalization of Questionnaire	++	--	++
Visualization	--	+	++
Informant Convenience	-	+/-	+
Potential Nonresponse Bias	-	+/-	+

--: poor; -: somewhat poor; +/-: neutral; +: good; ++: excellent. Source: Information on this table is compiled from several sources cited in this paragraph

Table 20: Advantages and disadvantages of different survey methods in business market research

The actual implementation of the of the survey instrument and the invitation email were guided by the following motivators identified by Cavusgil & Elvey-Kirk (1998) to encourage both participation and accurate answers:

- **Individual value** reflects the difference between the personal benefits and sacrifices of answering the survey. Both the invitation email and the questionnaire cover page thus emphasized the informant's expert status in their area, their chance to influence the study findings, and the importance of the study in an attempt to enhance the respondents' self image. As a more tangible benefit, informants were offered to receive a brief of the study results and to participate in a prize drawing of *Amazon.com* vouchers. In order to minimize the perceived risk of participating in the survey, the trustworthiness of the institution and the anonymity of responses were highlighted throughout the survey (Diamantopoulos and Schlegelmilch, 1996). Email responses and phone calls from informants confirmed that confidentiality is an important concern in business market research. Each questionnaire page featured the university logo, a link to the department website, and a contact phone number to underscore both the importance and the authenticity of the research (Diamantopoulos and Schlegelmilch, 1996).

- **Societal outcome** relates to the contribution to society made by answering the questionnaire. The study title, invitation email, and the cover page all stressed the relevance and importance of the study for marketing academia and practice (Kanuk and Berenson, 1975). The text made clear that the research and business community needed the informant to generate desperately sought knowledge. Emphasis was also implicitly put on the fact that helping with the completion of doctoral work is considered socially desirable.

- **Commitment** of informants is linked to involvement with a survey. The invitation email therefore reminded informants of their commitment to the survey when they were initially contacted by phone. The start page featured a photo of the researcher and a hand-written signature to reinforce the commitment through a more personal interaction (Diamantopoulos and Schlegelmilch, 1996). Also, because commitment is based on reciprocity, the commitment of substantial resources by the researcher – as demonstrated by a prize drawing – was expected to increase the informant's commitment.

- **Novelty** is present if a study features unusual stimuli or researches a novel topic. The study title was thus phrased to attract the informants' attention.

- **Convenience** reflects the effort needed to complete the survey. In order to minimize the effort, the questionnaire was designed for easy usage, avoiding complicated language, excessive scrolling, or large amounts of text and clutter (Churchill and Iacobucci, 2004). The added convenience of a web-based questionnaire as discussed earlier also contributed to this point.

- **Expertise** mirrors the respondent's perceived ability to supply information that would be useful for the study purpose. The questionnaire therefore started with simple, easy-to-answer questions that needed no great mental effort. In addition, the invitation email and the start page emphasized the unique contribution that each informant could make to the study.

The questionnaire falls into the seven sections displayed in Figure 26. The sequence of the different sections in the questionnaire follows the funnel approach suggested by

Churchill and Iacobucci (2004), starting with general, broad questions and progressively narrowing the scope. Items of different constructs were only intermixed if there was little threat of increasing common method variance (Podsakoff, MacKenzie, Jeong-Yeon, and Podsakoff, 2003). Items for the same construct were randomized. Special care was taken to avoid implicit theory – a potential source of common method variance (Podsakoff, MacKenzie, Jeong-Yeon, and Podsakoff, 2003). Dependent variables were thus sequenced separately from their immediate antecedents and placed earlier in the questionnaire. To increase the psychological separation of the measures (Podsakoff, MacKenzie, Jeong-Yeon, and Podsakoff, 2003), each section was preceded by a brief introductory header preparing the informant to take a different perspective.

Figure 26: Questionnaire structure

The first section, the introduction to the survey, comprises the cover page and the selection of the research stimuli. The cover page served to motivate informants and underscore confidentiality and trustworthiness (Churchill and Iacobucci, 2004). Prior to selecting the stimuli component and the related supplier brand, informants were told that the remainder of the questionnaire would be comprised of specific questions related to the selected stimulus. They were asked to select a component that (1) at least some of their customers knew and (2) was not absolutely irrelevant to their product. To avoid systematic drop-out caused by a perceived lack of expertise, as discussed above, informants were encouraged that their responses served the study purpose well even if their customers did not know the component brand well.

The second section gathered data on the component-related factors. Informants were then asked, in the third section, to take the perspective of their customers when providing measures for the supplier's brand and brand management. The following, fourth section covered the OEM-supplier relationship. In the fifth section, informants were again asked to take their customers' perspective. This section gathered data on the outcomes of co-branding with the supplier brand. Next, the sixth section asked questions about the OEM-related factors. The questionnaire then concluded with measures of informant confidence and informant characteristics. Informants could then indicate if they wanted to participate in the prize drawing.

In addition to the extensive pre-testing when developing the scale items, I pre-tested the internet survey tool in two steps. First, I checked if the questionnaire could be completed in the expected time by asking two graduate students to answer the survey. For the second step, the questionnaire was tested by two marketing/sales managers. Each tester answered the questionnaire on-line while talking to the researcher on the phone. Testers were asked to think aloud and report any problems they had with answering or understanding the questionnaire. The pre-tests revealed no major problems with the questionnaire. However, since the respondents needed a considerable amount of time to initially select their stimuli, the instructions for selecting the stimuli were improved. Also, for two items one word was replaced by a simpler synonym.

4.2   SEM Data Analysis

Both partial least squares (PLS) and covariance-based structural equations modeling (SEM) algorithms are used to analyze the data. This section discusses the methodological aspects of structural equations modeling First, I discuss the differences between PLS and covariance-based SEM and outline how a mixture of both approaches was used to test the hypotheses in section 5.3.1. Second, I describe the process of evaluating the measurement model in section 5.3.2. Third, the procedures used in evaluating the structural model are discussed in section 5.3.3. Finally, I review the approaches employed in testing for moderating and mediating effects in section 5.3.4.

4.2.1 PLS versus Covariance-Based SEM

Latent variable Structural Equations Modeling (SEM) has evolved into a quasi-standard in the analysis of complex phenomena in the management and social sciences (Bliemel et al., 2005, p. 10). SEM models can be classified as second generation multivariate techniques (Fornell, 1987). Second generation models involve generalizations and extensions of first generation multivariate techniques such as principal components analysis, factor analysis, discriminant analysis, or multiple regression (Chin, 1998a). The fundamental advantage of second generation techniques lies in their ability to enable a more flexible interplay between theory and data (Fornell, 1987), a prerequisite for advances in theory development (cf. Zaltmann, LeMasters, and Heffring, 1982). More specifically, SEM enables the researcher to: (1) model relationships among multiple predictor and criterion variables, (2) construct unobservable latent variables, (3) model errors in measurements for observed variables, and (4) perform confirmatory analysis as a test of priori substantive/theoretical and measurement assumptions (Fassott, 2005a).

Figure 27 shows an example of a basic SEM model involving two latent constructs, ξ_1 and ξ_2. The exogenous variable ξ_1 is measured by three formative indicators, x_{11}-x_{13}. The weight of each indicator is represented in the model by π_{11}-π_{13}. Variables x_{21}-x_{23} are reflective measures of the endogenous variable ξ_2 where ε_{21}-ε_{23} represent the measurement error and λ_{21}-λ_{23} mirror the indicator loadings. The structural model consists of the two latent variables and the structural relationship β_{21}, a causal effect of ξ_1 on ξ_2.

There are two basic approaches to estimate SEM models (Bliemel, Eggert, Fassott, and Henseler, 2005, p. 10):

- Covariance-based SEM procedures estimate model parameters as to optimally reproduce the empirically observed covariance matrix (Hulland, 1999, p. 202). Popular software packages that implement covariance-based SEM are LISREL and AMOS.

- Partial-Least-Squares procedures estimate model parameters based on the empirically observed variance structure. The algorithm optimizes the model to best explain the variance observed in the data (Hulland, 1999, p. 202). Currently available software packages such as SmartPLS and PLSgraph allow users to specify both formative and reflective measures.

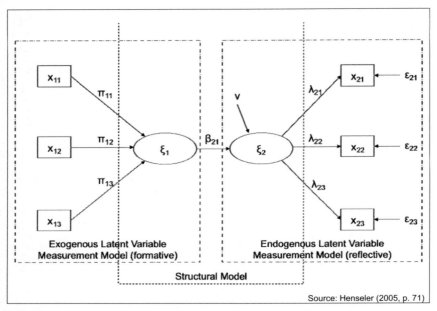

Figure 27: Basic example of an SEM model

Despite the similarity between the two techniques, PLS and the covariance-based method are not just alternative algorithms to perform the same analysis. They should rather be viewed as separate modeling approaches (Bliemel, Eggert, Fassott, and Henseler, 2005, p. 10). Generally speaking, PLS is "primarily intended for causal-predictive analysis in situations of high complexity but low theoretical information" (Joereskog and Wold, 1982, p. 270). The PLS approach should be given preference over the covariance-based method if at least one of the following applies (Chin and Newsted, 1999, p. 336):

- The researcher aims at predicting

- The phenomenon under investigation is relatively novel and no measures exist

- The models are highly complex, with many indicators

- Measures are not multinormally distributed

- The samples are small

- The model contains both formative and reflective measures

In the present study, the second, fifth and sixth criteria apply. Especially the central construct *component supplier brand strength* has never been measured before, to the best of my knowledge, in an empirical study. The sample size for the multiple informant data set only contains 114 responses – far less than the size required for covariance-based analysis. The model contains both formative and reflective indicators.

I consequently opted for the PLS approach as the primary analysis tool because it presented the better procedure for the problem at hand. However, PLS was supplemented by covariance-based SEM using the AMOS software package in order to test the moderating effects of situational context factors in a multi-group analysis, a test that can not be carried out in the PLS algorithm due to the lack of a global fit measure. The test of moderating effects in the model is discussed in more depth in section 4.2.4.

4.2.2   Evaluation of the Measurement Model

Reliable and valid measurements are considered a *conditio sine qua non* of empirical research (Fassott, 2006, p. 69). Validity is the extent to which a set of measured items actually reflect the theoretical construct they intend to measure (Hair et al., 2006, p. 771). A measure is reliable if it is free of measurement error (Hair, Black, Babin, Anderson, and Tatham, 2006, p. 8). The measurement model in the present study is evaluated using the well-established criteria from the SEM literature (Bagozzi and Yi, 1988; Churchill, 1979; Gerbing and Anderson, 1988; Homburg and Giering, 1996) while taking into account the special requirements of both the PLS approach and formative measures (Krafft, Goetz, and Liehr-Goebbers, 2005). Here, I first discuss the procedures used in assessing the reflective measures before I turn to the evaluation of formative measures.

Reflective measures are evaluated based on five criteria: substantive validity, indicator reliability, composite reliability, average variance extracted, and discriminant validity:

- *Substantive validity* is the extent to which the measures for a construct are conceptually linked to the construct's domain (Anderson and Gerbing, 1991). It is assessed by testing for unidimensionality. Confirmatory factor analysis, the traditional test for unidimensionality, cannot be carried out in PLS. Following recommendations in the literature, I consequently performed exploratory factor analysis using the SPSS software to test if the a priori factor pattern represents the actual data (Fassott, 2005b, p. 115). Principal axis factoring is the appropriate method here because it aims at identifying the underlying factors (Hair, Black, Babin, Anderson, and Tatham, 2006, p. 117).

- *Individual item reliability* captures the share of variance in each measurement item explained by the latent variable (Homburg and Giering, 1996). The generally agreed-on threshold value for item reliability is 0.5. In other words, an item should share at least 50% of its variance with the latent variable (Krafft, Goetz, and Liehr-Goebbers, 2005, p. 73). Item reliability can be calculated as the squared factor loading. It is formally defined as follows (Homburg and Giering, 1996, p. 10):

$$rel(x_i) = \frac{\lambda_{ij}^2 \phi_{jj}}{\lambda_{ij}^2 \phi_{jj} + \Theta_{ii}}$$

λ_{ij} : *Factor loading of item x_i*

Φ_{jj}: *Latent variable variance*

Θ_{ii}: *Measurement error variance*

Equation 3

In addition to assessing individual item reliability, the present study tested if t-values for the item loadings were significant at least at *p>0.01* (Fassott, 2005b).

- *Composite reliability (CR)* and average variance extracted (AVE) are indicators of convergent validity. These two criteria measure the extent to which the individual measures of construct are internally consistent or share a high proportion of variance (Hair, Black, Babin, Anderson, and Tatham, 2006, p. 776; Krafft, Goetz, and Liehr-Goebbers, 2005, p. 74). Convergent validity is considered even more crucial than individual item reliability (Homburg and Giering, 1996, p. 10). Composite reliability can be calculated as follows (Homburg and Giering, 1996, p. 10):

$$rel(\xi_j) = \frac{\left(\sum_{i=1}^{k} \lambda_{ij}\right)^2 \phi_{jj}}{\left(\sum_{i=1}^{k} \lambda_{ij}\right)^2 \phi_{jj} + \sum_{i=1}^{k} \Theta_{ii}}$$

λ_{ij} : Factor loading of item x_i

Φ_{jj}: Latent variable variance

Θ_{ii}: Measurement error variance

Equation 4

Composite reliability values should exceed 0.7 (Homburg and Giering, 1996, p. 10). Average variance extracted is defined as (Fornell and Larcker, 1981, p. 46):

$$AVE(\xi_j) = \frac{\sum_{i=1}^{k} \lambda_{ij}^2 \phi_{jj}}{\sum_{i=1}^{k} \lambda_{ij}^2 \phi_{jj} + \sum_{i=1}^{k} \Theta_{ii}}$$

λ_{ij} : Factor loading of item x_i

Φ_{jj}: Latent variable variance

Θ_{ii}: Measurement error variance

Equation 5

AVE values should be greater than the commonly agreed-on threshold level of 0.5 (Fassott, 2005b, p. 116).

- *Discriminant validity* reflects the extent to which a construct is substantially different from other constructs in the same study. A measure shows discriminant validity if it is unique in capturing phenomena other measures do not (Hair, Black, Babin, Anderson, and Tatham, 2006, p. 778). The present study used the criterion suggested by Fornell and Larcker (1981) to test for discriminant validity, and so each pair of AVE for any two variables in the study should be greater than the squared correlation observed between these variables. The rationale behind this approach is that a latent variable should explain its indicator items better than other constructs (Hair, Black, Babin, Anderson, and Tatham, 2006, p. 778).

Formative measures are not necessarily highly correlated, so internal consistency is not a useful criterion (Hair, Black, Babin, Anderson, and Tatham, 2006, p. 788). As a consequence, none of the five criteria commonly used in the evaluation of reflective construct measures can be applied to formative measures (Krafft, Goetz, and Liehr-Goebbers, 2005, p. 76). In the evaluation of the formative measures I rely on two criteria suggested by Krafft et al. (2005) – expert validity and item relevance:

- An item displays *expert validity* if experts agree that it belongs to the domain of the construct. I therefore sought expert judgment on the validity of the measures during the scale development stage (see the detailed discussion earlier this chapter). In an item-sorting task according to Anderson and Gerbing (1991), experts were given a list of the items and brief definitions for each construct. They then sorted each item into one construct category. Two indices were calculated for each item (Anderson and Gerbing, 1991, p. 734): (1) proportion of substantive agreement, p_{sa}, representing the proportion of respondents who correctly assigned an item, and (2) substantive-validity coefficient, c_{sv}, expressing the extent to which an items taps different constructs.

- When examining *item relevance*, the contribution of each item to the construct is assessed based on a comparison of indicator weights (Krafft, Goetz, and Liehr-Goebbers, 2005, p. 78; Sambamurthy and Chin, 1994, p. 231). Unlike reflective item loadings, formative item weights can be both positive and negative. Also, items should not be deleted based on small weights (Krafft, Goetz, and Liehr-Goebbers, 2005, p. 78). Comparing indicator weights only makes sense in situations of low multicollinearity among a construct's formative items. I consequently carried out the standard multicollinearity tests available in the SPSS software for each formative item: Tolerance, Variance Inflation Factor, and Condition Index (cf. Fassott, 2005b).

4.2.3   Evaluating the Structural Model

Unlike covariance-based path modeling, the PLS approach makes no distributional approaches other than predictor specification (Chin, 1998b, p. 316). As a consequence, the evaluation of the structural model relies on non-parametric techniques (Krafft, Goetz, and Liehr-Goebbers, 2005, p. 83).

The prediction-oriented evaluation of the structural model centers on both the coefficient of determination (R Square) for each latent variable and the standardized path coefficients in the model (Krafft, Goetz, and Liehr-Goebbers, 2005, p. 83). R Square values result from the regression of latent variables in the structural model (Henseler, 2005, p. 74). They can thus be interpreted the same way as in a traditional regression (Chin, 1998b, p. 316). R Square is the correlation coefficient squared. It indicates the percentage of total variation in the dependent variable explained by the regression model (Hair, Black, Babin, Anderson, and Tatham, 2006, p. 237). R Square can thus be regarded as a measure of how well the regression model fits the data (Krafft, Goetz, and Liehr-Goebbers, 2005, p. 83). It can take values between 0, indicating no fit, and 1, indicating perfect fit. The standardized path coefficients correspond with regression coefficients in a traditional regression (Chin, 1998b, p. 316). It represents the amount of change in the dependent variable for a one-unit change in the independent variable (Hair, Black, Babin, Anderson, and Tatham, 2006, p. 174). Based on these two parameters, the following criteria are used to evaluate the structural model:

- Standardized path coefficients should be significant at $p < 0.05$ (single-tailed) with T-values calculated through resampling techniques such as bootstrapping (Chin, 1998b, p. 316). Path coefficients should be at least 0.2 and ideally greater than 0.3 for the effect to be a meaningful predictor (Chin, 1998a, p. xiii). The sign of the path coefficient indicates the direction of change induced by the predictor variable.

- The required level for R Square is highly dependent on the nature of the study. When the purpose of the model is to fully explain variance in the dependent variable, an R Square of at least 0.4 is deemed necessary (Fassott, 2005b, p. 118).

- The change in R Square when eliminating or adding a predictor variable can be examined to assess the impact of that particular latent variable on the dependent variable (Chin, 1998b, p. 316). The change in R squared is captured in the effect size f^2 which can be calculated as follows (Cohen, 1988, p. 410f):

$$f^2 = \frac{R^2_{incl.} - R^2_{excl.}}{1 - R^2_{incl.}}$$

$R^2_{incl.}$: R Square of the dependent variable when the predictor is used

$R^2_{excl.}$: R Square of the dependent variable when the predictor is not used

Equation 6

Analogous to Cohen's (1988, p. 413) suggestion for multiple regression, f^2 of 0.02, 0.15, and 0.35 indicate small, medium, and large effect sizes respectively (Chin, 1998b, p. 317).

4.2.4   Testing Moderating and Mediating Effects

The analysis of moderating and mediating effects in a structural model requires other steps than the general procedure for main effects described in the previous section. Before turning to these testing procedures, I briefly review the three different types of effects formulated in this study's hypotheses:

- *Main effects* are present if higher levels of an independent variable X lead to increases in a dependent variable Y. SEM procedures usually assume that the effect is linear in nature.

- A *moderating effect* occurs when a moderator variable M affects the strength or direction of the relationship between the independent variable X and the dependent variable Y (Baron and Kenny, 1986, p. 1174). Figure 28 depicts a model where M has both a direct (b) and a moderating effect (c) on the dependent variable Y.

- *Mediating effects* occur if an independent variable X indirectly affects a dependent variable through an intervening variable C, the mediating variable (Hair, Black, Babin, Anderson, and Tatham, 2006, p. 868).

Moderating and mediating effects are highly relevant in marketing research (Eggert, Fassott, and Helm, 2005, p. 104). Sometimes, main effects in marketing can be somewhat trivial – for example, a positive relationship between customer satisfaction and loyalty is hardly surprising. A much better contribution could be made if research were to show in which situations a main effect is actually strong or weak – i.e., if the contextual or related variables that actually moderate the main effect could be identified (Henseler and Fassott, 2008, p. 2). If mediating effects are not accounted for in an SEM model, it may impose serious limitations on the validity and generalizability of the study's findings (Eggert, Fassott, and Helm, 2005, p. 102-103). Yet despite the broad consensus on the importance of testing for moderating and mediating effects, those relationships are often neglected in SEM models published in scholarly journals (Chin, Marcolin, and Newsted, 2003, p. 193; Henseler and Fassott, 2008, p. 3; Homburg and Giering, 2001, p. 47). Hereafter, I will first discuss the procedures used for testing moderating effects in the current study. I then outline how the mediating effects were analyzed.

Three basic approaches to testing for moderating effects can be found in the literature:

- In a **multigroup analysis**, the sample is split in half or thirds based on the moderator variable score. The model is then estimated separately with the two data sets. Differences in the model parameters between the groups are interpreted as the effect of the moderator (Henseler and Fassott, 2008, p. 7-8). To test for the statistical significance of the moderating effect, the moderated main effect is then constrained to be of equal size across the two groups. If the chi-square global fit measures for the constrained and unconstrained models are significantly different, the moderating hypothesis is supported (Hair, Black, Babin, Anderson, and Tatham, 2006). This approach is frequently used with covariance-based SEM because the alternative procedures are either difficult to implement in these models or cannot be properly implemented (Chin et al. 2003, p. 198).

- According to the **indicator product approach**, the indicator vectors of both the independent (X) and moderator variables (Y) are multiplied to form the indicator matrix of the interaction variable X*Y (Hair, Black, Babin, Anderson, and Tatham, 2006, p. 870-871). Given that the X and Y variables have m and n indicators, respectively, the resulting interaction variable will have m times n indicators. It has been debated if this approach is actually an appropriate test of moderation (cf. Henseler and Fassott, 2008, p. 5). The assumption of uncorrelated error terms strongly limits the applicability of this method to covariance-based SEM (Hair, Black, Babin, Anderson, and Tatham, 2006, p. 870). Because formative indicators are not necessarily correlated, this approach can only be used if both the independent variable and moderator variables are reflective (Eggert, Fassott, and Helm, 2005, p. 108), a problem addressed by the third approach.

- **The variable score product approach** suggested by Henseler and Fassott (2008) (Eggert, Fassott, and Helm, 2005, p. 108) consists of two-stages. The researcher estimates the main effects model in the first stage. The moderator variable M is specified in the main effects model as an antecedent of the dependent variable Y. The latent variable scores calculated in the first stage are saved and used for further analysis. In the second stage, the interaction term M*X of the independent and moderator variables is calculated by simply multiplying their respective latent variable scores obtained from the first stage. Next, both the latent variable scores and the calculated interaction term are entered in a PLS-regression: The latent variable scores are used as single item indicators of their corresponding variable in the model. The interaction term M*X is represented in the model by a single-indicator variable. This approach can accommodate both reflective and formative constructs. Henseler and Fassott (2008, p. 9) report that the results are better or equal compared to those of the indicator product approach.

Both multigroup analysis and the variable score product approach were used to test the different moderating effects in this study:

- **Moderating effects of situational context factors:** Probably due to slight multicollinearity among some of the measures, the variable score product approach using PLS performed unsatisfactorily in estimating the moderating effects of situational context. Because it involves dichotomization of the moderator variable, multigroup analysis was expected to be less sensitive to multicollinearity issues. I therefore implemented the same model using covariance-based SEM in AMOS to test these moderating effects in a multigroup analysis.

- **Interactions among marketing communication instruments:** Due to the formative nature of the marketing communications constructs, the variable score product approach represented the appropriate method to test for interaction effects among those constructs. According to recommendations in the literature (Chin, Marcolin, and Newsted, 2003, p. 199; Eggert, Fassott, and Helm,

2005, p. 108), standardized (mean =1, standard deviation = 1) variable scores were used. As depicted in Figure 28, the test procedure requires the researcher to specify a direct effect of the moderator on the dependent variable even if no main effect is expected. If the interaction term displays a significant effect on the dependent variable, it is up to the researcher's interpretation to decide the nature of the moderating effect – the moderator could have a moderating effect on the main effect of the independent variable and vice versa (Fassott, 2005b, p. 131).

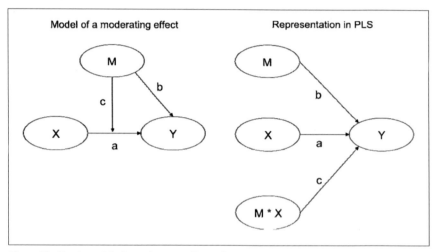

Figure 28: Simple model of a moderating effect and its representation in PLS

Similarly to main effects, mediating effects can be evaluated in PLS via their path coefficients and the changes in the dependent variable's coefficient of determination (R Square):

- A standardized positive path coefficient c from the interaction term M*X to the dependent variable Y indicates that the effect of the independent variable X on Y is stronger for high levels of the moderator variable M. In case of a negative path coefficient, the effect of X on Y is weaker if M increases (Eggert, Fassott, and Helm, 2005, p. 109).

- Path coefficients should be significant at $p < 0.05$ (single-tailed t-test).

- The strength of the moderating effect can be further assessed using a measure of the effect size similar to that discussed in the preceding section (Henseler and Fassott, 2008, p. 19):

$$f^2 = \frac{R^2_{\text{moderated}} - R^2_{\text{main}}}{1 - R^2_{\text{moderated}}}$$

$R^2_{\text{moderated}}$: R Square of the dependent variable when including interaction term

R^2_{main} : R Square of the dependent variable when estimated without the interaction term

Equation 7

Moderating effects displaying effect sizes of 0.02, 0.15, and 0.35 are judged to be small, moderate, and large, respectively (Eggert, Fassott, and Helm, 2005, p. 109). However, as Chin, Marcolin, and Newsted (2003) highlight, "even a small interaction effect can be meaningful under extreme moderating conditions."

Mediation occurs if a causal effect of an independent variable X on a dependent variable Y is explained by a mediator variable Z (Shrout and Bolger, 2002, p. 422). The structural model used to test for mediating effects is depicted in Figure 29 (Eggert, Fassott, and Helm, 2005, p. 111).

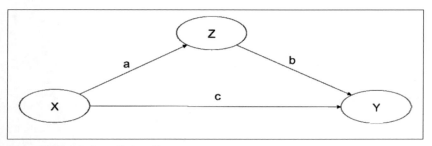

Figure 29: Model of a mediating effect

There are three prerequisites for a mediating effect in a structural model (Fassott, 2005b, p. 132):

- The independent variable X has a significant effect on the mediator Z (path a)

- The mediator Z significantly affects the dependent variable Y (path b)

- The direct effect of X on Y (path c) is stronger if the mediator is omitted. Alternatively, if the direct effect c and the indirect effect a*b have opposite signs and path c is weaker in the unmediated model, a suppressor effect may be present (Shrout and Bolger, 2002, p. 430).

Full mediation is observed if the direct path c is not significant in the mediated model. In cases of partial mediation, which are more likely in social sciences, path c is decreased but still significant, pointing to multiple mediating factors (Baron and Kenny, 1986, p. 1176).

While Baron and Kenny (1986) test for the mediating effect by estimating separate models, Iacobucci and Duhachek (2004) favor an analysis based only on the model in Figure 29. According to their procedure, a mediating effect is present if the indirect effect a*b is significant as demonstrated by the z-statistics developed by Sobel (1982):

$$z = \frac{a \cdot b}{\sqrt{b^2 \cdot s_a^2 + a^2 \cdot s_b^2}}$$

a, b: Path coefficients a and b

s_a, s_b: *Standard deviation of path coefficients a and b*

Equation 8

Once significant mediating effects have been identified, their size can be assessed using the variance accounted for (VAF) measure by Iacobucci and Ducacheck (Iacobucci and Duhachek, 2004). VAF captures the share of the variance explained by the independent variable accounted for by the mediating effect (Eggert, Fassott, and Helm, 2005, p. 106):

$$VAF = \frac{a \cdot b}{a \cdot b + c}$$

a, b, c: Path coefficients a, b, and c

Equation 9

The VAF value is meaningless if a suppressor effect is present. In the case of multiple mediating variables, Worm et al. (2007, p. 4) suggest using the following formula to compute VAF:

$$VAF_i = \frac{a_i \cdot b_i}{c + \sum_{n=1}^{N} a_n \cdot b_n}$$

a_i: Path coefficient from independent variable to mediator variable i

b_i: Path coefficients from mediator variable i to dependent variable

c: Direct path coefficient from independent to dependent variable

Equation 10

4.2.5   Robustness Checks

I conduct several robustness checks to examine the sensitivity of the results obtained for the first research question. The model for the second research question is not included in the analysis because it is perceived as much less susceptible to sensitivity issues due to its relatively reduced complexity.

As discussed earlier, cross-sectional studies are often criticized by their potentially inflated correlations caused by common method variance (CMV). To rule out this probable limitation of the results, I apply the marker-variable technique, a statistical procedure developed by Lindell and Whitney (2001), to test for common method bias in the results. This approach has been used successfully in marketing before by Grayson, Johnson, and Chen (2008) and outperforms the more traditional method suggested by Podsakoff and Todor (1985). Their recommendation to add a method factor in the structural model has been criticized for a large 'partialing out' effect and, therefore, as providing difficult or even impossible interpretations of the results (Kemery and Dunlap, 1986).

I select a measurement item called "technological heterogeneity in the OEM industry," which is conceptually independent to the latent variables in the study, to serve as a proxy for common method variance. I then carry out two independent test procedures.

4.2 SEM Data Analysis 147

As a first step, I use the lowest positive correlation between the marker variable and the latent variables to adjust correlations between the structural variables for common method bias according to Equation 11 (Lindell and Whitney, 2001, p. 116):

$$r_A = \frac{r_U - r_M}{1 - r_M}$$

r_A: Adjusted correlation between two latent variables

r_U: Unadjusted, original correlation between two latent variables

r_M: Smallest positive correlation between marker variable and latent variable in the model

Equation 11

The results for the adjusted correlations are reported in Table 21. A comparison of the original correlations and the adjusted parameters shows only minor differences. Additionally, all correlations maintain their significance levels.

		1	2	3	4	5	6	7	8
Component Supplier Brand Strength	1		0.249***	0.663***	0.177***	0.303***	0.149**	0.184***	0.101*
Coercive Power Use	2	0.252***		0.164***	-0.071	-0.119**	-0.061	-0.074	-0.043
Incremental Market Performance	3	0.665***	0.168***		0.294***	0.501***	0.247***	0.305***	0.169***
Relationship Quality	4	0.180***	-0.068	0.297***		0.598***	0.659***	0.469***	0.189***
OEM's Value Perception of Component	5	0.306***	-0.114**	0.503***	0.600***		0.501***	0.610***	0.340***
Cooperation of Supplier and OEM	6	0.152***	-0.057	0.250***	0.660***	0.503***		0.432***	0.216***
Expansion of Purchases	7	0.187***	-0.070	0.307***	0.471***	0.612***	0.434***		0.211***
Share of Wallet	8	0.105*	-0.039	0.172***	0.192***	0.342***	0.219***	0.214***	

Notes: I report correlations (estimated with AMOS) below the diagonal and correlations adjusted for common method bias using the marker variable technique above the diagonal (Lindell and Whitney, 2001).
*: $p < 0.1$, **: $p < 0.05$, ***: $p < 0.01$

Table 21: Correlations adjusted for common method bias using marker-variable technique

In a second step, I include the marker variable as a common method factor in the structural model as suggested by Podsakoff et al. (2003). In other words, the marker variable was included as a latent variable that directly affects every variable in the model. The resultant model shows a consistent pattern of results. Only marginal changes in path coefficients and no changes in significance levels are observed. Both diagnostics support the assumption that CMV only marginally inflates the correlations of the latent variables in the structural model.

5 Results

In this chapter, I present the results obtained through latent variable structural equations modeling using SmartPLS (Ringle, Wende, and Will, 2005) and covariance-based AMOS 7.0 (Arbuckle, 1983-2006). The PLS model is estimated with reference to three different data sets: (1) the pooled data set of 241 cases consisting of 104 aggregated multiple responses and 137 single responses (referred to as D1), (2) the aggregated multiple responses dataset comprising 104 cases (D2), and (3) the primary responses dataset of 241 single responses (D3). The comparison of the estimates for the three datasets enables an evaluation of the impact of using multiple respondents. The AMOS model was estimated only for the pooled data set (D1) and only for research question one. After briefly describing the data preparation procedure in section 5.1, I evaluate the measurement models for each of the three data sets in section 5.2. Next, in section 5.3, I present the parameter estimates for the structural model that corresponds to research question one. I also examine the differences in estimation results obtained from the three data sets in this section. Ultimately, I present the parameter estimates for research question two in section 5.4.

5.1 Data Preparation

The raw data obtained in the internet-based survey was imported into SPSS for data preparation. Overall, the primary sample consisted of 241 usable datasets. Out of the 114 secondary responses obtained for the survey, ten questionnaires were excluded from further analysis because the secondary informants indicated that they were not sufficiently familiar with the component brand in question. There are no missing values in either of the datasets because informants had to provide a rating for each item in order to complete the survey. For the remaining data, reverse scales were recoded to enable compatibility with the remaining measures. Also, the two measurements of informant confidence were recoded so that a high number represented high confidence. This step was necessary to accommodate the data aggregation procedure for multiple informants.

As the second wave of the survey specifically targeted purchasing managers, measurements from multiple informants are only available for the constructs that fall into the purchasing function's domain: OEM's value perception of the branded component, coercive power use by supplier, relationship quality, cooperation between supplier and OEM, future expansion of purchases, and share of wallet.

Following the procedure suggested by Van Bruggen, Lilien, and Kacker (2002), I aggregated multiple informant data based on the informants' self-assessed confidence in the accuracy of their response estimates. They find evidence that this particular aggregation procedure is superior to the usual approach of just averaging responses in that the resultant data enables more accurate prediction. Consequently, the responses provided by more confident informants are weighted more heavily than those of less confident informants. The weighted confidence-based mean WCMEAN for each measurement item X is computed according to the following formula (Van Bruggen, Lilien, and Kacker, 2002, p. 473):

$$WCMEAN_{xi} = \sum_{j=1}^{n_i} \left[\frac{CONF_{xij}^{\alpha}}{\sum_{j=1}^{n_j} CONF_{xij}^{\alpha}} \cdot X_{ij} \right]$$

i: firm for which multiple responses were obtained

j: index for respondent in firm j

CONF: informant j's self-assessed confidence regarding the relationship with the supplier

α: weighting parameter

Equation 12

The parameter α makes it possible to manipulate the weight assigned to responses from more confident informants, i.e., those that are expected to show less systematic error (Van Bruggen, Lilien, and Kacker, 2002, p. 473). If α is set to zero, WCMEAN will equal the arithmetic mean. If α increases, the responses of more confident informants are weighted more heavily. For the present analysis, α is set to 70, and confident informants' responses receive a much higher weight. This approach makes sense since significant differences in confidence are expected due to informants' different backgrounds. In the following presentation of the analysis' results, items calculated from multiple informants' responses are marked with "w" (e.g., COLAB1_w).

5.2   Measurement Model

The quality of the measurement model is evaluated based on criteria well-established in the SEM literature (Bagozzi and Yi, 1988; Churchill, 1979; Gerbing and Anderson, 1988; Homburg and Giering, 1996) with consideration of the special requirements of the PLS approach (Krafft, Goetz, and Liehr-Goebbers, 2005) as outlined in section 4.3.2. The primary goal of the evaluation is to ascertain that measures for the constructs in the study are valid and reliable. Reflective measures are subjected to factor analysis in section 5.2.1. In section 5.2.2, I examine reflective indicator loadings. An important difference between formative and reflective measurement approaches is that formative constructs cannot be assessed on the internal consistency criteria commonly used with reflective measures (Krafft, Goetz, and Liehr-Goebbers, 2005, p. 76). The formative measures in the study are thus only evaluated, in section 5.2.3, based on their indicator weights. The reliability of reflective measurements is evaluated in section 5.2.4, and then section 5.2.5 concludes with an assessment of discriminant validity for the constructs in the model.

5.2.1   Factor Analysis

Factor analysis is used to ascertain that the reflective indicator data reflect the expected factor structure and to ensure unidimensionality of the measures for each construct. Separate factor analyses were run for each of the three data sets D1-D3. Since a confirmatory factor analysis cannot be carried out in PLS, I performed an exploratory factor analysis using the SPSS software to confirm the factor structure (Fassott, 2005b, p. 115). Table 22 displays the results of the factor analysis for the pooled data set (D1) using principal axis factoring and Varimax rotation. Seven factors emerged based on the Kaiser criterion, thus replicating the a priori factor pattern and confirming the unidimensionality of the constructs. Note that factor loadings smaller than 0.5 are hidden. All items display the highest loadings on their corresponding factors. Altogether, the seven factors explain 66% of the variance in the data. The first factor that emerges is component supplier brand strength (15% variance explained). The brand image items load on a common factor that explains 13% of the variance. The cooperation factor captures 9% of the variance. The item colab4_w is dropped after showing cross loadings with other factors in initial analyses. All items for OEM's value perception of the branded component load on a common factor (9% variance explained). The incremental market performance of OEM product factor accounts for 8% of the variance after removing the item impv_1 due to unfavorable cross loadings. The results for the coer-

cive power use by supplier and relationship quality constructs are also in line with the
hypothesized factor structure (7% and 6% of variance explained).

Construct	Indicator	Factor						
		1	2	3	4	5	6	7
Component Supplier Brand Strength	valad5	0.7798						
	valad2	0.7567						
	valad3	0.7318						
	valad6	0.7162						
	valad4	0.7097						
	valad1	0.7041						
Brand Image	imagb2		0.9323					
	imagb3		0.9013					
	imagb1		0.8563					
	imagb4		0.8512					
Cooperation of Supplier and OEM	colab1_w			0.8280				
	colab2_w			0.6886				
	colab3_w			0.6451				
	colab5_w			0.6047				
OEM's Value Perception of the Branded Component	cpv2_w				0.7838			
	cpv1_w				0.6598			
	cpv3_w				0.6534			
	cpv4_w				0.5569			
Incremental Market Performance of OEM Product	impv4					0.7655		
	impv3					0.7578		
	impv5					0.5559		
	impv2					0.5219		
Coercive Power Use by Supplier	selfi1_w						0.7874	
	selfi3_w						0.7380	
	selfi2_w						0.7266	
Relationship Quality	comit2_w							0.7407
	comit1_w							0.6700
	trust_w							0.5727

Extraction Method: Principal Axis Factoring. Rotation Method: Varimax with Kaiser Normalization Values < 0.5
hidden

Table 22: Rotated factor matrix for pooled dataset (D1)

The results of the factor analysis for the multiple responses data subset (D2) are shown
in Table 23. Similar to the findings for the pooled dataset, seven factors are extracted
based on the Kaiser criterion. Overall, these seven factors explain 71% of the variance.
Except for some marginal differences in the factor loadings, the resulting factor pattern
is the same as that for the pooled data set, thus confirming once again the hypothesized
structure. The comit2_w indicator's loading on the cooperation construct exceeds 0.5,
which is not judged as critical since the indicator still loads higher on relationship
quality.

Construct	Indicator	Factor						
		1	2	3	4	5	6	7
Brand Image	imagb2	0.8989						
	imagb3	0.8943						
	imagb4	0.8819						
	imagb1	0.8381						
Component Supplier Brand Strength	valad5		0.7742					
	valad2		0.7591					
	valad6		0.7044					
	valad1		0.6827					
	valad4		0.6104					
	valad3		0.6023					
Cooperation of Supplier and OEM	colab1_w			0.8036				
	colab3_w			0.7125				
	colab2_w			0.6674				
	colab5_w			0.6477				
Incremental Market Performance of OEM Product	impv4				0.8238			
	impv3				0.7447			
	impv2				0.7160			
	impv5				0.5673			
OEM's value perception of the branded component	cpv1_w					0.8108		
	cpv2_w					0.7976		
	cpv3_w					0.6743		
	cpv4_w					0.5288		
Coercive Power Use by Supplier	selfi1_w						0.9207	
	selfi3_w						0.7472	
	selfi2_w						0.6999	
Relationship Quality	comit1_w							0.7494
	comit2_w		0.5490					0.6980
	trust_w							0.6407

Extraction Method: Principal Axis Factoring. Rotation Method: Varimax with Kaiser Normalization Values < 0.5 hidden

Table 23: Rotated factor matrix for multiple responses data subset (D2)

Table 24 displays the results of the principal axis factor analysis obtained with the primary responses data set (D3). Overall, six factors explaining 70% of the variance are extracted based on the Kaiser criterion. Unlike the results of the other two factor analyses, relationship quality did not emerge as a factor of its own. The relationship quality indicators instead load on the cooperation and OEM's value perception of the branded component constructs. It may be that the marketing and sales managers who prevailed in the primary sample were less knowledgeable about their firm's relationship with the supplier and gave less accurate answers. This finding lends additional support to the use of multiple informants in this study.

In summary, the factor analyses confirm the expected factor structure in the data for D1 and D2 and partly for D3. The criterion of unidimensionality is satisfied.

Construct	Indicator	Factor					
		1	2	3	4	5	6
Component Supplier Brand Strength	valad3	0.7560					
	valad5	0.7481					
	valad2	0.7376					
	valad4	0.7238					
	valad6	0.7219					
	valad1	0.6739					
Brand Image	imagb2		0.9335				
	imagb3		0.8985				
	imagb4		0.8508				
	imagb1		0.8502				
OEM's value perception of the branded component	cpv2			0.6834			
	cpv3			0.6218			
	comit1			0.5873			
	cpv4			0.5759			
	trust			0.5714			
	cpv1			0.5319			
Cooperation of Supplier and OEM	colab1				0.7650		
	colab2				0.6719		
	colab3				0.6569		
	colab5				0.6101		
	comit2				0.5616		
Incremental Market Performance of OEM Product	impv4					0.7379	
	impv3					0.7119	
	impv5					0.5779	
	impv2						
Coercive Power Use by Supplier	selfi2						0.7453
	selfi1						0.7092
	selfi3						0.6756

Extraction Method: Principal Axis Factoring. Rotation Method: Varimax with Kaiser Normalization Values < 0.5 hidden

Table 24: Rotated factor matrix for primary responses dataset (D3)

5.2.2 Reflective Indicator Loadings

Table 25 provides the summary statistics for the formative indicator loadings estimated from the pooled dataset. The third column from the left displays the actual loading for each item. For single-item measures, the loading equals one. All loadings exceed the commonly agreed-on minimum level of 0.7 (Fassott, 2005b, p. 116). Loadings are highest for *brand image* and *relationship quality* but remain reasonably high for the remaining constructs. The next column lists the standard deviation of indicator loadings obtained from the bootstrapping procedure.

While standard deviations for the single item measures are set equal to zero, low standard deviations indicate stability of the estimates for the indicator loadings. The next two columns show the confidence intervals of the loading estimates. There is a 95% chance that the true loading value falls into this interval. Given the low standard deviations, the lower confidence interval limit is clearly larger than zero for all items and even greater than 0.7 for many items. The t-statistic values for multi-item measures obtained from the bootstrapping procedure are shown in the following column. Those t-statistics are all significant (at least at $p < 0.001$) as displayed in the last column. Significance testing does not apply to single item measures.

Table 26 reports the formative indicator loadings obtained from estimating the model with the multiple responses data subset. Similar to the results for the pooled dataset, all loadings are well above the threshold level of 0.7 with brand image and relationship quality showing the highest loadings. Since standard deviations of loading estimates are low, even the confidence intervals for the majority of loadings lie above the threshold of 0.7. Also, all loading estimates are significant at $p < 0.001$.

As can be seen from Table 27, the estimates for the loadings of the formative indicators mostly replicate the results for the other two data sets. Brand image displays the highest loadings, while the estimates for relationship quality, cooperation, and OEM's value perception of the branded component are somewhat lower. This finding may be due to the lack of knowledge of marketing among sales managers about the relationship with the supplier as discussed in the preceding section.

Construct	Indicator	Loading	Standard Deviation	Lower Conf. Interval Limit	Upper Conf. Interval Limit	T-Value	Sig.
Number of Competitors for Component	altbc	1.000	0.000	1.000	1.000	0.0	n/a
Brand Image	imagb1	0.934	0.025	0.885	0.983	37.2	0.000
	imagb2	0.976	0.009	0.959	0.993	114.9	0.000
	imagb3	0.967	0.011	0.945	0.989	87.3	0.000
	imagb4	0.939	0.022	0.895	0.982	42.2	0.000
Brand Visibility	visib	1.000	0.000	1.000	1.000	0.0	n/a
Coercive Power Use by Supplier	selfi1_w	0.814	0.078	0.660	0.967	10.4	0.000
	selfi2_w	0.862	0.041	0.781	0.942	20.9	0.000
	selfi3_w	0.861	0.045	0.773	0.948	19.2	0.000
Cooperation of Supplier & OEM	colab1_w	0.871	0.030	0.813	0.928	29.5	0.000
	colab2_w	0.815	0.047	0.722	0.907	17.2	0.000
	colab3_w	0.821	0.045	0.733	0.910	18.3	0.000
	colab5_w	0.708	0.066	0.579	0.836	10.8	0.000
Share of wallet	sharb_w	1.000	0.000	1.000	1.000	0.0	n/a
Exclusivity	excl	1.000	0.000	1.000	1.000	0.0	n/a
Future Expansion of Purchases	xpurch_w	1.000	0.000	1.000	1.000	0.0	n/a
Incremental Market Performance	impv2	0.726	0.064	0.601	0.851	11.4	0.000
	impv3	0.889	0.023	0.845	0.933	39.3	0.000
	impv4	0.877	0.032	0.815	0.939	27.6	0.000
	impv5	0.811	0.039	0.735	0.887	20.9	0.000
OEM's Value Perception of the Branded Component	cpv1_w	0.805	0.069	0.671	0.940	11.7	0.000
	cpv2_w	0.867	0.032	0.805	0.929	27.4	0.000
	cpv3_w	0.780	0.054	0.674	0.886	14.4	0.000
	cpv4_w	0.754	0.073	0.611	0.897	10.3	0.000
OEM Brand Strength	imagi	1.000	0.000	1.000	1.000	0.0	n/a
Relationship Quality	comit1_w	0.908	0.020	0.870	0.946	46.5	0.000
	comit2_w	0.904	0.029	0.847	0.960	31.1	0.000
	trust_w	0.781	0.070	0.644	0.917	11.2	0.000
Competitive Intensity in OEM Industry	coini	1.000	0.000	1.000	1.000	0.0	n/a
Component Supplier Brand Strength	valad1	0.830	0.042	0.748	0.912	19.8	0.000
	valad2	0.873	0.030	0.814	0.931	29.3	0.000
	valad3	0.835	0.038	0.761	0.909	22.1	0.000
	valad4	0.830	0.044	0.744	0.916	19.0	0.000
	valad5	0.861	0.034	0.794	0.929	25.0	0.000
	valad6	0.791	0.052	0.689	0.894	15.1	0.000

Table 25: Reflective indicator loadings for pooled data set (D1)

Construct	Indicator	Loading	Standard Deviation	Lower Conf. Interval Limit	Upper Conf. Interval Limit	T-Value	Sig.
Number of Competitors for Component	altbc	1.000	0.000	1.000	1.000	0.0	n/a
Brand Image	imagb1	0.948	0.022	0.905	0.991	43.6	0.000
	imagb2	0.974	0.009	0.956	0.993	104.0	0.000
	imagb3	0.971	0.010	0.951	0.990	96.9	0.000
	imagb4	0.956	0.014	0.929	0.983	68.9	0.000
Brand Visibility	visib	1.000	0.000	1.000	1.000	0.0	n/a
Coercive Power Use by Supplier	selfi1_w	0.858	0.035	0.789	0.927	24.4	0.000
	selfi2_w	0.883	0.039	0.807	0.960	22.6	0.000
	selfi3_w	0.823	0.048	0.729	0.918	17.1	0.000
Cooperation of Supplier & OEM	colab1_w	0.875	0.025	0.827	0.923	35.7	0.000
	colab2_w	0.814	0.056	0.704	0.924	14.5	0.000
	colab3_w	0.844	0.039	0.767	0.921	21.5	0.000
	colab5_w	0.730	0.050	0.633	0.828	14.6	0.000
Share of wallet	sharb_w	1.000	0.000	1.000	1.000	0.0	n/a
Exclusivity	excl	1.000	0.000	1.000	1.000	0.0	n/a
Future Expansion of Purchases	xpurch_w	1.000	0.000	1.000	1.000	0.0	n/a
Incremental Market Performance	impv2	0.848	0.032	0.785	0.911	26.5	0.000
	impv3	0.871	0.029	0.815	0.928	30.4	0.000
	impv4	0.864	0.036	0.793	0.935	23.8	0.000
	impv5	0.787	0.052	0.684	0.889	15.0	0.000
OEM's Value Perception of the Branded Component	cpv1_w	0.841	0.060	0.724	0.958	14.1	0.000
	cpv2_w	0.884	0.032	0.821	0.947	27.4	0.000
	cpv3_w	0.790	0.040	0.711	0.869	19.6	0.000
	cpv4_w	0.768	0.078	0.615	0.921	9.9	0.000
OEM Brand Strength	imagi	1.000	0.000	1.000	1.000	0.0	n/a
Relationship Quality	comit1_w	0.922	0.017	0.889	0.956	53.7	0.000
	comit2_w	0.906	0.032	0.843	0.969	28.3	0.000
	trust_w	0.822	0.056	0.712	0.932	14.7	0.000
Competitive Intensity in OEM Industry	coini	1.000	0.000	1.000	1.000	0.0	n/a
Component Supplier Brand Strength	valad1	0.830	0.040	0.752	0.907	21.0	0.000
	valad2	0.864	0.029	0.806	0.921	29.6	0.000
	valad3	0.796	0.040	0.717	0.875	19.8	0.000
	valad4	0.827	0.032	0.764	0.889	26.0	0.000
	valad5	0.846	0.035	0.777	0.915	24.0	0.000
	valad6	0.826	0.041	0.745	0.907	20.0	0.000

Table 26: Reflective indicator loadings for multiple responses data set (D2)

Construct	Indicator	Loading	Standard Deviation	Lower Conf. Interval Limit	Upper Conf. Interval Limit	T-Value	Sig.
Number of Competitors for Component	altbc	1.000	0.000	1.000	1.000	0.0	n/a
Brand Image	imagb1	0.934	0.020	0.895	0.973	46.6	0.000
	imagb2	0.976	0.007	0.962	0.990	139.1	0.000
	imagb3	0.967	0.010	0.947	0.986	98.0	0.000
	imagb4	0.939	0.019	0.902	0.975	50.4	0.000
Brand Visibility	visib	1.000	0.000	1.000	1.000	0.0	n/a
Coercive Power Use by Supplier	selfi1	0.827	0.059	0.711	0.943	14.0	0.000
	selfi2	0.817	0.096	0.629	1.005	8.5	0.000
	selfi3	0.836	0.094	0.652	1.019	8.9	0.000
Cooperation of Supplier & OEM	colab1	0.853	0.033	0.788	0.917	25.9	0.000
	colab2	0.791	0.066	0.662	0.920	12.0	0.000
	colab3	0.817	0.048	0.723	0.910	17.1	0.000
	colab5	0.706	0.060	0.589	0.823	11.8	0.000
Share of wallet	sharb	1.000	0.000	1.000	1.000	0.0	n/a
Exclusivity	excl	1.000	0.000	1.000	1.000	0.0	n/a
Future Expansion of Purchases	xpurch	1.000	0.000	1.000	1.000	0.0	n/a
Incremental Market Performance	impv2	0.723	0.068	0.590	0.855	10.7	0.000
	impv3	0.888	0.022	0.846	0.930	41.4	0.000
	impv4	0.876	0.035	0.808	0.943	25.4	0.000
	impv5	0.815	0.044	0.730	0.901	18.7	0.000
OEM's Value Perception of the Branded Component	cpv1	0.771	0.073	0.628	0.914	10.6	0.000
	cpv2	0.827	0.042	0.744	0.909	19.6	0.000
	cpv3	0.738	0.070	0.600	0.876	10.5	0.000
	cpv4	0.772	0.081	0.614	0.930	9.6	0.000
OEM Brand Strength	imagi	1.000	0.000	1.000	1.000	0.0	n/a
Relationship Quality	comit1	0.890	0.026	0.839	0.941	34.1	0.000
	comit2	0.895	0.027	0.842	0.949	32.9	0.000
	trust	0.779	0.060	0.662	0.897	13.0	0.000
Competitive Intensity in OEM Industry	coini	1.000	0.000	1.000	1.000	0.0	n/a
Component Supplier Brand Strength	valad1	0.831	0.049	0.735	0.926	17.1	0.000
	valad2	0.873	0.023	0.827	0.919	37.3	0.000
	valad3	0.834	0.040	0.756	0.912	21.0	0.000
	valad4	0.829	0.036	0.758	0.900	23.0	0.000
	valad5	0.863	0.038	0.789	0.936	23.0	0.000
	valad6	0.791	0.057	0.679	0.902	13.9	0.000

Table 27: Reflective indicator loadings for primary responses data set (D3)

5.2.3   Formative Indicator Weights

Due to the lack of statistical test procedures, assessment of formative constructs must rely solely on the evaluation of indicator weights. Unlike reflective indicator loadings, formative indicator weights can be both positive and negative. Multicollinearity among the set of indicators for a variable may, however, lead to negative weights even in situations of positive correlation between an item and the construct. Consequently, I tested for multicollinearity among the indicator items for each reflective construct prior to interpreting the indicator weights. Since no multicollinearity tests are implemented in the SmartPLS software, I separately ran linear regression models for each of the four constructs in SPSS using the indicators as independent variables and another randomly selected variable as a dependent variable. Table 28 summarizes the results of the multicollinearity checks provided by SPSS. Tolerance values smaller than 0.1 indicate the presence of multicollinearity. At the same time, VIF (variance inflation factor) values greater than 10 indicate multicollinearity. The condition index should be smaller than 15 to avoid problems of multicollinearity. As can be seen from the results, multicollinearity among the formative indicators is not an issue for any of the constructs. Indicator weights may thus be used in the assessment of the formative measurement model.

Construct	Indicator	Tolerance	VIF	Max. Condition Index
	dcom1	0.743	1.346	9.866
Direct Communication	dcom2	0.519	1.925	
	dcom3	0.530	1.887	
	jcom1	0.534	1.874	11.746
Joint Communication	jcom2	0.565	1.771	
	jcom3	0.688	1.454	

Table 28: Multicollinearity test for formative indicators

The formative indicator weights and their corresponding standard deviations, confidence intervals, and statistical significance tests obtained from the pooled data set are displayed in Table 29.

For direct communication, the first indicator, capturing the extent to which the component manufacturer provides information on his website targeted specifically at the OEM's customers, is assigned the highest weight of 0.7 (p < 0.001). The weight for the second item, measuring the provision of catalogues and brochures to the OEM's customers by the manufacturer, is relatively small (0.17) and is found to be insignificant at p > 0.1. The third formative indicator is the intensity of the visits that the OEM's customers' receive from the manufacturer's sales force. This item is assigned a relatively large weight of 0.33 (p < 0.1). The manufacturer's website thus represents the most effective channel for direct communication, followed by sales force visits. Catalogues and brochures are found to be much less effective means of direct communication.

Construct	Indicator	Weight	Standard Deviation	Lower Conf. Interval Limit	Upper Conf. Interval Limit	T-Value	Sig.
	dcom1	0.687	0.169	0.356	1.018	4.1	0.0000
Direct Communication	dcom2	0.171	0.195	-0.211	0.553	0.9	0.1901
	dcom3	0.329	0.211	-0.085	0.743	1.6	0.0600
	jcom1	-0.015	0.202	-0.411	0.381	0.1	0.4704
Joint Communication	jcom2	0.424	0.198	0.036	0.812	2.1	0.0163
	jcom3	0.735	0.140	0.461	1.008	5.3	0.0000

Table 29: Formative indicator loadings for pooled data set (D1)

The analysis of the formative indicators for *joint communication* reveals that the weight assigned to the first item, which asks if the OEM is an officially certified partner of the component manufacturer, almost equals zero and results insignificant. The second item, capturing the extent to which the manufacturer and the OEM run joint advertising, is weighted by 0.4 and results as significant from the bootstrapping at p < 0.05. Display of the component manufacturer's brand on the OEM's product and product information received the highest weight of 0.7 (p < 0.001). Joint advertising and displaying the manufacturer brand are consequently the most effective means of joint communication. Certification of OEM's showed no effect in the current study but, given that this strategy is extremely uncommon among component manufacturers (mean rating of 1 on a seven-point scale where 7 indicates absolute agreement), caution is warranted when evaluating this result. In line with recommendations in the literature (Krafft, Goetz, and Liehr-Goebbers, 2005, p. 78), formative indicators were retained in the model despite low and insignificant weights.

The analysis of formative indicator weights is repeated for datasets D2-3. Table 30 shows the indicator weights along with their standard deviations, confidence intervals, and statistical significance obtained from the multiple responses data subset (D2).

Findings for the constructs direct communication and joint communication replicate those of the pooled data. The manufacturer's website and sales force visits are the most effective means of direct communication (weights of 0.75 and 0.35, and p < 0.001 and 0.05, respectively). Display of the component manufacturer's brand (0.8, p < 0.001) and joint advertising (0.5, p < 0.05) proved to be the most effective avenues for joint communication.

Construct	Indicator	Weight	Standard Deviation	Lower Conf. Interval Limit	Upper Conf. Interval Limit	T-Value	Sig.
Direct Communication	dcom1	0.746	0.171	0.411	1.082	4.4	0.0000
	dcom2	0.031	0.213	-0.387	0.449	0.1	0.4420
	dcom3	0.368	0.223	-0.069	0.805	1.6	0.0497
Joint Communication	jcom1	-0.155	0.241	-0.628	0.318	0.6	0.2600
	jcom2	0.507	0.220	0.077	0.938	2.3	0.0106
	jcom3	0.780	0.161	0.465	1.096	4.9	0.0000

Table 30: Formative indicator loadings for multiple responses data set (D2)

The indicator weights and their corresponding standard deviations, confidence intervals, and statistical significance tests for the model estimated with the primary responses dataset (D3) are shown in Table 31. The basic results for direct communication and joint communication mirror those obtained for the previous two datasets.

Construct	Indicator	Weight	Standard Deviation	Lower Conf. Interval Limit	Upper Conf. Interval Limit	T-Value	Sig.
Direct Commu-nication	dcom1	0.687	0.166	0.362	1.012	4.1	0.0000
	dcom2	0.170	0.199	-0.219	0.560	0.9	0.1959
	dcom3	0.330	0.217	-0.095	0.754	1.5	0.0642
Joint Commu-nication	jcom1	-0.015	0.190	-0.387	0.357	0.1	0.4681
	jcom2	0.425	0.190	0.053	0.797	2.2	0.0127
	jcom3	0.734	0.141	0.458	1.010	5.2	0.0000

Table 31: Formative indicator loadings for primary responses data set (D3)

5.2.4   Reliability

The reliability statistics for reflective constructs that have been discussed in Chapter 4 are displayed in Table 32. These values are first estimated from the pooled data subset. As mentioned earlier, this analysis is limited to reflective constructs as formative constructs that cannot be evaluated based on their indicators' internal consistency. Reliability is evaluated both at the level of the individual indicator item and at the level of the construct.

The third column in Table 32 shows the reliability calculated for each item by squaring the indicator loadings estimated by the PLS procedure. All item reliabilities exceed the commonly agreed-on threshold level of 0.5 with the majority of items even showing reliabilities greater than 0.6. This result indicates excellent reliability of the individual item measurements.

The AVE (average variance extracted) values displayed in the following column are indicative of a high level of convergence among the indicators for each construct. AVE for all constructs is well above the lower limit of 0.5. The values of composite reliability reported in the next column are all greater than 0.85, thereby well exceeding the threshold level of 0.7. The Cronbach's Alpha values listed in the last column are well above the lower limit and thus further confirm the excellent reliability of measurement at the construct level. Cronbach's Alpha can only be calculated for multi-item measures.

Construct	Indicator	Item Relia-bility	AVE	Composite Reliability	Cronbach's Alpha
Number of Competi-tors for Component	altbc	1.000	1.000	1.000	n/a
Brand Image	imagb1	0.872	0.910	0.976	0.967
	imagb2	0.953			
	imagb3	0.935			
	imagb4	0.881			
Brand Visibility	visib	1.000	1.000	1.000	n/a
Coercive Power Use by Supplier	selfi1_w	0.662	0.715	0.883	0.802
	selfi2_w	0.742			
	selfi3_w	0.741			
Cooperation of Sup-plier & OEM	colab1_w	0.758	0.649	0.880	0.818
	colab2_w	0.663			
	colab3_w	0.675			
	colab5_w	0.501			
Share of wallet	sharb_w	1.000	1.000	1.000	n/a
Exclusivity	excl	1.000	1.000	1.000	n/a
Future Expansion of Purchases	xpurch_w	1.000	1.000	1.000	n/a
Incremental Market Performance	impv2	0.527	0.686	0.897	0.846
	impv3	0.790			
	impv4	0.769			
	impv5	0.657			
OEM's Value Percep-tion of the Branded Component	cpv1_w	0.648	0.644	0.878	0.815
	cpv2_w	0.751			
	cpv3_w	0.608			
	cpv4_w	0.569			
OEM Brand Strength	imagi	1.000	1.000	1.000	n/a
Relationship Quality	comit1_w	0.824	0.750	0.900	0.832
	comit2_w	0.816			
	trust_w	0.609			
Competitive Intensity in OEM Industry	coini	1.000	1.000	1.000	n/a
Component Supplier Brand Strength	valad1	0.689	0.701	0.934	0.914
	valad2	0.761			
	valad3	0.697			
	valad4	0.689			
	valad5	0.741			
	valad6	0.626			

Table 32: Reflective item reliability for pooled data set (D1)

Overall, the results indicate that measurements for all reflective constructs in the study are highly reliable.

Table 33 shows the estimated reflective indicator item reliabilities, AVE-values, com-posite reliabilities, and Cronbach's Alpha values based on the multiple responses data subset. Similar to the results from the pooled dataset, the reflective measures exhibit highly reliable measurement properties at both the item and construct level.

All individual item reliabilities exceed the lower limit of 0.5. Similarly, the measures of reliability at the construct level, AVE, composite reliability, and Cronbach's Alpha, are all well above their respective thresholds of 0.5, 0.7, and 0.7.

The reflective indicator item reliabilities, AVE-values, composite reliabilities, and Cronbach's Alpha values estimated from the primary responses dataset are listed in Table 34. Parallel to the findings obtained from the previous two datasets, all measures satisfy or exceed the required levels for all statistics, thus indicating good reliability of the reflective measurements.

However, a comparison of the actual values for the pooled data subset and for the primary responses dataset reveals that the reliability of measurement was mostly more reliable in the pooled data subset. Although these differences may be judged marginal, since they are not critical to the evaluation of the measurement model, this slight discrepancy indicates that the accuracy of measurement is improved by the use of multiple respondents per unit.

Construct	Indicator	Item Reliability	AVE	Composite Reliability	Cronbach's Alpha
Number of Competitors for Component	altbc	1.000	1.000	1.000	n/a
Brand Image	imagb1	0.899	0.926	0.980	0.973
	imagb2	0.949			
	imagb3	0.942			
	imagb4	0.914			
Brand Visibility	visib	1.000	1.000	1.000	n/a
Coercive Power Use by Supplier	selfi1_w	0.736	0.731	0.891	0.824
	selfi2_w	0.780			
	selfi3_w	0.678			
Cooperation of Supplier & OEM	colab1_w	0.766	0.669	0.889	0.834
	colab2_w	0.663			
	colab3_w	0.712			
	colab5_w	0.533			
Share of wallet	sharb_w	1.000	1.000	1.000	n/a
Exclusivity	excl	1.000	1.000	1.000	n/a
Future Expansion of Purchases	xpurch_w	1.000	1.000	1.000	n/a
Incremental Market Performance	impv2	0.719	0.711	0.908	0.864
	impv3	0.759			
	impv4	0.746			
	impv5	0.619			
OEM's Value Perception of the Branded Component	cpv1_w	0.707	0.676	0.893	0.839
	cpv2_w	0.782			
	cpv3_w	0.624			
	cpv4_w	0.590			
OEM Brand Strength	imagi	1.000	1.000	1.000	n/a
Relationship Quality	comit1_w	0.851	0.782	0.915	0.860
	comit2_w	0.821			
	trust_w	0.676			
Competitive Intensity in OEM Industry	coini	1.000	1.000	1.000	n/a
Component Supplier Brand Strength	valad1	0.688	0.692	0.931	0.911
	valad2	0.746			
	valad3	0.634			
	valad4	0.684			
	valad5	0.715			
	valad6	0.683			

Table 33: Reflective item reliability for multiple responses data set (D2)

Construct	Indicator	Item Relia-bility	AVE	Composite Reliability	Cronbach's Alpha
Number of Competitors for Component	altbc	1.000	1.000	1.000	n/a
Brand Image	imagb1	0.872	0.910	0.976	0.967
	imagb2	0.953			
	imagb3	0.935			
	imagb4	0.881			
Brand Visibility	visib	1.000	1.000	1.000	n/a
Coercive Power Use by Supplier	selfi1	0.684	0.683	0.866	0.769
	selfi2	0.667			
	selfi3	0.698			
Cooperation of Supplier & OEM	colab1	0.727	0.630	0.871	0.803
	colab2	0.626			
	colab3	0.667			
	colab5	0.499			
Share of wallet	sharb	1.000	1.000	1.000	n/a
Exclusivity	excl	1.000	1.000	1.000	n/a
Future Expansion of Purchases	xpurch	1.000	1.000	1.000	n/a
Incremental Market Performance	impv2	0.522	0.686	0.897	0.846
	impv3	0.789			
	impv4	0.767			
	impv5	0.664			
OEM's Value Perception of the Branded Component	cpv1	0.594	0.604	0.859	0.782
	cpv2	0.683			
	cpv3	0.544			
	cpv4	0.596			
OEM Brand Strength	imagi	1.000	1.000	1.000	n/a
Relationship Quality	comit1	0.793	0.734	0.892	0.818
	comit2	0.801			
	trust	0.607			
Competitive Intensity in OEM Industry	coini	1.000	1.000	1.000	n/a
Component Supplier Brand Strength	valad1	0.690	0.701	0.934	0.914
	valad2	0.762			
	valad3	0.695			
	valad4	0.688			
	valad5	0.745			
	valad6	0.625			

Table 34: Reflective item reliability for primary responses data set (D3)

5.2.5   Discriminant Validity

Fornell and Larcker's (1981) criterion is then used to assess discriminant validity –
i.e., the extent to which each of the measured constructs is different from other constructs in the study. Based on the model estimation with the pooled dataset, Table 35

shows a matrix plotting the squared correlations between each pair of constructs in the study. Bold numbers on the diagonal represent the AVE values for each construct. Note that AVE can only be computed for reflective constructs. The table shows that the AVE for each construct by far exceeds the squared correlations of that construct with any other construct in the study. This indicates a satisfactory level of discriminant validity.

Tables 36 and 37 then display the results of Fornell and Larcker's (1981) criterion for the multiple responses data subset and the primary responses dataset, respectively. Except for some minor differences in the squared correlations and AVE values, these tests replicate the findings obtained with the pooled dataset. Overall, it can be concluded that discriminant validity is successfully established for all measurements in the three datasets.

	Number of Competitors for Component (1)	Brand Image (2)	Brand Visibility (3)	Coercive Power Use by Supplier (4)	Cooperation of Supplier & OEM (5)	Share of wallet (6)	Direct Communication (7)	Exclusivity (8)	Future Expansion of Purchases (9)	Incremental Market Performance (10)	OEM's value perception of the branded component (11)	Joint Communication (12)	OEM Brand Strength (13)	Relationship Quality (14)	OEM Competitive Intensity (15)	component supplier brand strength (16)	Max
1	**1.000**																0.000
2	0.011	**0.9103**															0.011
3	0.009	0.189	**1.000**														0.189
4	0.015	0.011	0.006	**0.715**													0.015
5	0.015	0.014	0.018	0.017	**0.649**												0.018
6	0.000	0.002	0.001	0.002	0.039	**1.000**											0.039
7	0.033	0.240	0.067	0.002	0.009	0.005	n/a										0.240
8	0.017	0.002	0.014	0.007	0.174	0.023	0.016	**1.000**									0.174
9	0.001	0.031	0.021	0.001	0.161	0.029	0.016	0.050	**1.000**								0.161
10	0.009	0.143	0.220	0.030	0.082	0.028	0.058	0.068	0.102	**0.686**							0.220
11	0.007	0.030	0.037	0.015	0.174	0.092	0.006	0.056	0.313	0.135	**0.644**						0.313
12	0.003	0.091	0.170	0.008	0.114	0.015	0.098	0.109	0.110	0.272	0.105	n/a					0.272
13	0.005	0.000	0.003	0.001	0.009	0.000	0.000	0.000	0.000	0.020	0.001	0.004	**1.000**				0.020
14	0.013	0.021	0.002	0.003	0.281	0.032	0.027	0.036	0.188	0.047	0.299	0.056	0.001	**0.750**			0.299
15	0.007	0.000	0.000	0.010	0.000	0.003	0.002	0.000	0.011	0.034	0.011	0.009	0.035	0.000	**1.000**		0.035
16	0.016	0.293	0.224	0.042	0.057	0.009	0.185	0.004	0.028	0.360	0.089	0.113	0.005	0.043	0.004	**0.7006**	0.360
Max	0.033	0.293	0.224	0.042	0.281	0.092	0.185	0.109	0.313	0.360	0.299	0.113	0.035	0.043	0.006	0.000	

Note: Bold numbers on the diagonal show AVE. Numbers below the diagonal represent squared correlations

Table 35: Fornell-Larcker test of discrimimant validity for pooled data set (D1)

	1 Number of Competitors for Component	2 Brand Image	3 Brand Visibility	4 Coercive Power Use by Supplier	5 Cooperation of Supplier & OEM	6 Share of wallet	7 Direct Communication	8 Exclusivity	9 Future Expansion of Purchases	10 Incremental Market Performance	11 OEM's value perception of the branded component	12 Joint Communication	13 OEM Brand Strength	14 Relationship Quality	15 OEM Competitive Intensity	16 component supplier brand strength	Max
1	1.000																0.000
2	0.017	0.9103															0.017
3	0.024	0.199	1.000														0.199
4	0.016	0.017	0.004	0.731													0.017
5	0.005	0.028	0.040	0.002	0.669												0.040
6	0.001	0.015	0.025	0.003	0.023	1.000											0.025
7	0.059	0.234	0.054	0.003	0.018	0.000	n/a										0.234
8	0.000	0.003	0.016	0.000	0.045	0.041	0.036	1.000									0.045
9	0.004	0.023	0.012	0.014	0.282	0.044	0.014	0.026	1.000								0.282
10	0.027	0.157	0.206	0.035	0.039	0.049	0.109	0.114	0.026	0.711							0.206
11	0.009	0.013	0.042	0.001	0.212	0.055	0.007	0.056	0.378	0.064	0.676						0.378
12	0.035	0.087	0.111	0.008	0.096	0.072	0.075	0.162	0.093	0.297	0.079	n/a					0.297
13	0.000	0.013	0.006	0.028	0.001	0.001	0.018	0.003	0.005	0.019	0.017	0.035	1.000				0.035
14	0.021	0.009	0.001	0.068	0.342	0.005	0.029	0.019	0.276	0.035	0.284	0.076	0.003	0.782			0.342
15	0.026	0.002	0.010	0.017	0.001	0.015	0.037	0.000	0.027	0.003	0.008	0.003	0.020	0.001	1.000		0.068
16	0.022	0.418	0.244	0.068	0.048	0.000	0.245	0.006	0.016	0.357	0.043	0.070	0.012	0.009	0.001	0.7006	0.418
Max	0.059	0.418	0.244	0.068	0.342	0.072	0.245	0.162	0.378	0.357	0.284	0.076	0.020	0.009	0.024	0.000	

Note: Bold numbers on the diagonal show AVE. Numbers below the diagonal represent squared correlations

Table 36: Fornell-Larcker test of discriminant validity for multiple responses data set (D2)

	1 Number of Competitors for Component	2 Brand Image	3 Brand Visibility	4 Coercive Power Use by Supplier	5 Cooperation of Supplier & OEM	6 Share of wallet	7 Direct Communication	8 Exclusivity	9 Future Expansion of Purchases	10 Incremental Market Performance	11 OEM's value perception of the branded component	12 Joint Communication	13 OEM Brand Strength	14 Relationship Quality	15 OEM Competitive Intensity	16 component supplier brand strength	Max
1	**1.000**																0.000
2	0.011	**0.9103**															0.011
3	0.009	0.189	**1.000**														0.189
4	0.013	0.021	0.016	**0.683**													0.021
5	0.010	0.012	0.017	0.035	**0.630**												0.035
6	0.001	0.000	0.000	0.002	0.044	**1.000**											0.044
7	0.033	0.240	0.067	0.003	0.008	0.015	**0.000**										0.240
8	0.017	0.002	0.014	0.015	0.204	0.004	0.016	**1.000**									0.204
9	0.000	0.043	0.033	0.009	0.145	0.011	0.024	0.069	**1.000**								0.145
10	0.009	0.143	0.220	0.059	0.090	0.013	0.057	0.069	0.143	**0.686**							0.220
11	0.006	0.052	0.060	0.000	0.140	0.040	0.009	0.072	0.279	0.211	**0.604**						0.279
12	0.003	0.091	0.170	0.013	0.132	0.004	0.098	0.109	0.129	0.271	0.112	**n/a**					0.271
13	0.005	0.000	0.003	0.000	0.004	0.002	0.000	0.000	0.000	0.020	0.000	0.004	**1.000**				0.020
14	0.008	0.046	0.006	0.001	0.266	0.040	0.027	0.043	0.162	0.058	0.266	0.067	0.001	**0.734**			0.266
15	0.007	0.000	0.000	0.007	0.001	0.000	0.002	0.000	0.012	0.034	0.010	0.009	0.035	0.000	**1.000**		0.035
16	0.016	0.293	0.224	0.083	0.053	0.004	0.185	0.004	0.047	0.360	0.137	0.113	0.005	0.069	0.004	**0.7006**	0.360
Max	0.033	0.293	0.224	0.083	0.266	0.040	0.185	0.109	0.279	0.360	0.266	0.113	0.035	0.069	0.005	0.000	

Note: Bold numbers on the diagonal show AVE. Numbers below the diagonal represent squared correlations.

Table 37: Fornell-Larcker test of discriminant validity for primary responses data set (D3)

5.3   Structural Model for Research Question One

This section presents structural model parameter estimates for the first research question obtained with SmartPLS (Ringle, Wende, and Will, 2005) and AMOS (Arbuckle, 1983-2006) SEM for each of the three data sets D1-D3 and examines the differences between the three resulting models. In section 5.3.1, I analyze the main effects in the model. Next, the mediating effects are examined in section 5.3.2 before I turn to the moderating effects in section 5.3.3. In section 5.3.4, I conclude with robustness checks.

5.3.1   Main Effects

In this section, I first report results obtained for the main effects between the variables in the core model estimated from the pooled dataset (D1). Next, the results for these main effects are contrasted with those obtained from the multiple response (D2) and primary response (D3) datasets. I then broaden the focus to examine the main effects of the context variables on the core model along with the differences between the results for the different three data sets.

The main effects for the core model estimated with the pooled data set are shown in Table 38. Columns four, five, and six list the path coefficients, the corresponding t-values, and the resulting significance of the estimate. Next follow the R^2 inclusive and R^2 exclusive values in columns seven and eight. R^2 inclusive represents the coefficient of determination for the consequence variable if the main effect is included in the model. R^2 exclusive results if the model is estimated without the main effect in question. Finally, the effect size computed from the R^2 incl. and R^2 excl. values is displayed in the last column of the table.

As expected in Hypothesis H_1, component supplier brand strength has a significant positive effect on incremental market performance of OEM product ($\beta_1 = 0.47$, p < 0.01). The size of this effect is medium ($f^2 = 0.172$). Component supplier brand strength also has a positive significant effect on coercive power use by supplier ($\beta2 = 0.22$, p < 0.05). This effect is small ($f^2 = 0.047$). Thus, H_2 is confirmed.

Support is also found for H_3, which predicted a positive effect of incremental market performance of OEM product on OEM's value perception of the branded component ($\beta_3 = 0.31$, p < 0.01). The effect is of medium size ($f^2 = 0.209$). In line with H_4, coer-

cive power use by supplier has a negative effect of small size on OEM's value perception of the branded component (β_4 = -0.21, p < 0.05, f^2 = 0.05).

Antecedent	Consequence	Hyp.	Path Coeff.	T-Value	Sig.	R^2 Incl.	R^2 Excl.	Effect Size
component sup-plier brand strength	Incremental Market Performance	H_1	0.47	5.40	0.000	0.539	0.459	0.172
	Coercive Power Use by Supplier	H_2	0.22	1.86	0.032	0.186	0.148	0.047
Incremental Mar-ket Performance	OEM's value per-ception of the branded compo-nent	H_3	0.31	2.70	0.003	0.185	0.015	0.209
Coercive Power Use by Supplier	OEM's value per-ception of the branded compo-nent	H_4	-0.21	2.17	0.015	0.185	0.145	0.050
OEM's value perception of the branded compo-nent	Relationship Quali-ty	H_5	0.54	5.80	0.000	0.299	0.056	0.347
	Cooperation of Supplier & OEM	H_6	0.18	1.62	0.052	0.304	0.281	0.033
	Share of wallet	H_7	0.28	2.40	0.008	0.098	0.046	0.057
	Future Expansion of Purchases	H_8	0.43	4.10	0.000	0.354	0.229	0.194
Relationship Quality	Cooperation of Supplier & OEM	H_9	0.43	4.36	0.000	0.304	0.174	0.187
	Share of wallet	H_{10}	-0.02	0.17	0.431	0.098	0.098	0.000
	Future Expansion of Purchases	H_{11}	0.11	1.01	0.156	0.354	0.347	0.012
Cooperation of Supplier & OEM	Share of wallet	H_{12}	0.09	0.88	0.189	0.098	0.092	0.007
	Future Expansion of Purchases	H_{13}	0.16	1.48	0.069	0.354	0.336	0.028

Table 38: Main effect estimates for pooled data set (D1)

H_5 through H_8 pertain to the effect of OEM's value perception of the branded component on the relationship between component supplier and OEM. OEM's value perception of the branded component is found to have a positive effect on relationship quality
($\beta5$ = 0.54, p < 0.01), thus confirming H_5. With an effect size of approx. 0.35, this
finding represents the largest effect in the model. Support is also found for H_6, which
formulates a positive effect of OEM's value perception of the branded component on
cooperation of supplier and OEM ($\beta6$ = 0.18, p < 0.1, f^2 = 0.033). H_7 expects that

OEM's value perception of the branded component positively affects share of wallet. The empirical findings confirm H_7 ($\beta7 = 0.28$, $p < 0.01$, $f^2 = 0.057$). Finally, supporting H_8, OEM's value perception of the branded component is found to have an effect of medium size on future expansion of purchases ($\beta_8 = 0.43$, $p < 0.01$, $f_2 = 0.194$).

H_9 through H_{11} hypothesized the effects of relationship quality on relational outcomes. Strong support was found for H_9, which posited that relationship quality leads to more intense cooperation of supplier and OEM ($\beta_9 = 0.43$, $p < 0.01$, $f^2 = 0.187$). However, no evidence is provided by the data for the positive effects of relationship quality on either share of wallet (H_{10}, $\beta_{10} = -0.02$, $p > 0.1$) or future expansion of purchases (H_{11}, $\beta_{11} = 0.11$, $p > 0.1$).

H_{12} and H_{13} pertain to the impact of cooperation of supplier and OEM on other relational outcomes. The data provides no support for H_{12}, which posits an effect of cooperation of supplier and OEM on share of wallet ($\beta_{12} = 0.09$, $p > 0.1$). H_{13}, however, formulating a positive effect of cooperation of supplier and OEM on future expansion of purchases, is confirmed ($\beta_{13} = 0.16$, $p < 0.1$, $f^2 = 0.028$).

Table 39 compares the main effects for the core model estimated from the pooled dataset (D1) with the corresponding values obtained from the multiple responses data subset (D2) and the primary responses data set (D3).

H_1 is supported by all three data sets with hardly any variation in the path coefficients. At the same time, a significant effect of component supplier brand strength on coercive power use by supplier (H_2) is only present in D1 and D3. H3, again, finds support in all three datasets with path coefficients covering the range of 0.21 (D2) to 0.39 (D3). Evidence for H_4 is also provided by all three data sets. Interestingly, the underlying effect of coercive power use by supplier on OEM's value perception of the branded component is considerably smaller for D3, indicating that less confident informants seem to underestimate the consequences of coercive power use by supplier.

The effects hypothesized by H_5 and H_6 are significant in all three datasets with only small differences in the size of the path coefficients. While it is significant for the datasets D1 and D2, the effect of OEM's value perception of the branded component on share of wallet hypothesized in H_7 does not manifest in the primary responses dataset. This finding again highlights the additional insight provided by the multiple informant data collection strategy.

The effects formulated in H_8 and H_9 yield almost identical significant path coefficients among all data sets. Also, H_{10} is consistently not confirmed. Some divergence can, however, be found for H_{11}, suggesting that relationship quality affects future expansion of purchases. This effect is only significant for the multiple responses data subset (β_{11} = 0.16, p < 0.1), again emphasizing the additional information obtained through multiple informants.

Antecedent	Consequence	Hyp.	Pooled (D1)		Multiple (D2)		Primary (D3)	
			Path Coeff.	Sig.	Path Coeff.	Sig.	Path Coeff.	Sig.
component supplier brand strength	Incremental Market Performance	H_1	0.47	0.000	0.47	0.000	0.48	0.000
	Coercive Power Use by Supplier	H_2	0.22	0.032	0.11	0.171	0.32	0.002
Incremental Market Performance	OEM's value perception of the branded component	H_3	0.31	0.003	0.21	0.039	0.39	0.000
Coercive Power Use by Supplier	OEM's value perception of the branded component	H_4	-0.21	0.015	-0.23	0.017	-0.15	0.064
OEM's value perception of the branded component	Relationship Quality	H_5	0.54	0.000	0.50	0.000	0.52	0.000
	Cooperation of Supplier & OEM	H_6	0.18	0.052	0.21	0.036	0.15	0.082
	Share of wallet	H_7	0.28	0.008	0.25	0.011	0.11	0.183
	Future Expansion of Purchases	H_8	0.43	0.000	0.42	0.000	0.41	0.000
Relationship Quality	Cooperation of Supplier & OEM	H_9	0.43	0.000	0.47	0.000	0.44	0.000
	Share of wallet	H_{10}	-0.02	0.431	-0.14	0.177	0.08	0.275
	Future Expansion of Purchases	H_{11}	0.11	0.156	0.16	0.071	0.10	0.208
Cooperation of Supplier & OEM	Share of wallet	H_{12}	0.09	0.189	0.11	0.185	0.13	0.157
	Future Expansion of Purchases	H_{13}	0.16	0.069	0.25	0.003	0.18	0.048

Table 39: Comparing the main effect estimates for the three data sets

H_{12} is not supported by any of the datasets. At the same time, H_{13} receives support in all three datasets.

In Chapter 4, I also discuss the direction of causality hypothesized for the main effects in H_5 to H_{13}. To test if the direction of causality implied by the theoretical framework is confirmed by the data, I use AMOS 7.0 (Arbuckle, 1983-2006) which allows for the simultaneous modeling of bi-directional main effects between two variables. In other words, the hypothesized antecedent variable (e.g., OEM's value perception of the branded component) would be modeled as affecting the dependent variable (e.g., relationship quality) while the dependent variable would also be modeled as having a main effect on the hypothesized independent variable. The inverse effect of cooperation between supplier and OEM and relationship quality cannot be estimated for model identification issues. The results of the test for the direction of main effects are reported in Table 40. I report the significance of hypothesized main effects above the diagonal and the significance of their inverse counterparts below the diagonal. The table shows that all tested inverse effects are not significant, thus supporting the hypothesized direction of causality for these hypotheses and confirming the null hypotheses formulated for the inverse effects.

Independent Variable	Dependent Variable					Hypotheses
	OEM's value perception of the branded component	Relationship Quality	Cooperation of Supplier & OEM	Future Expansion of Purchases	Share of wallet	
OEM's value perception of the branded component		***	*	***	***	H_5, H_6, H_7, H_8
Relationship Quality	n.s.		***	n.s.	n.s	H_9, H_{10}, H_{11}
Cooperation of Supplier & OEM	n.s.	n/a		**	n.s	H_{12}, H_{13}
Future Expansion of Purchases	n.s.	n.s.	n.s.		n/a	
Share of wallet	n.s.	n.s.	n.s.	n/a		

Notes: significance levels of hypothesized direction of main effect above the diagonal, significance levels for inverse direction of main effect below the diagonal: ***: $p < 0.01$, **: $p < 0.5$, *: $p < 0.1$

Table 40: Test for direction of main effects

5.3.2 Mediating Effects

The hypotheses for main effects in the model establish a chain of effects linking the component supplier brand strength to the outcomes of the OEM firm's relationship with the supplier. Implicit in this chain of effects are a number of hypotheses about mediating effects that must be tested if one is to confirm that the hypothesized model is actually reflected in the underlying data. In this section, I use the procedure by Iacobucci and Ducacheck (2004) to test for those mediating effects that are implicitly stated in the hypotheses. For many relationships, the hypotheses assume partial mediation, i.e., the antecedent variable affects the dependent variable both directly and through the mediator (Baron and Kenny, 1986, p. 1176). In all other cases where only an indirect effect is hypothesized, the test for mediation requires that the direct path is also included in the model. Table 41 shows the PLS path results for those additional non-hypothesized main effects that resulted from the simultaneous estimation of all effects in the model. Except for the direct effect of component supplier brand strength on OEM's value perception of the branded component, which is only significant in the D1 and D3 datasets, none of the direct paths showed as significant in the data, thus lending initial support to the underlying implicit mediation hypotheses.

Antecedent	Consequence	Pooled (D1)		Multiple (D2)		Primary (D3)	
		Path Coeff.	Sig.	Path Coeff.	Sig.	Path Coeff.	Sig.
Coercive Power Use by Supplier	Relationship Quality	0.01	0.475	-0.08	0.196	0.04	0.326
Incremental Market Performance	Relationship Quality	0.02	0.427	0.07	0.196	-0.01	0.468
component supplier brand strength	OEM's value perception of the branded component	0.16	0.086	0.11	0.196	0.18	0.088

Table 41: Non-hypothesized main effects for the three data sets

In Table 42 I conduct the statistical tests to evaluate the mediating effects. The first column lists the mediated relationships. In the second column appear the corresponding mediating variables. I calculate the z-statistics by Sobel (1982) and the VAF measure (Eggert, Fassott, and Helm, 2005, p. 106) for the path estimates obtained from each of the three data sets (see Chapter 4 for a detailed discussion of these statistics). The z-statistics indicates whether the mediated path in the model is significant. As can be seen in Table 42, all mediated relationships in the three models are significant even if the indirect paths themselves are not significant, as evident in the effect of exclusivity on incremental market performance of OEM product, indicating the need for research about more conservative tests of mediation in SEM.

Mediated Relationship	Mediating Variable	Pooled (D1)			Multiple (D2)			Primary (D3)		
		Z-Stat.	Sig.	VAF	Z-Stat.	Sig.	VAF	Z-Stat.	Sig.	VAF
Coercive Power Use by Supplier → Relationship Quality	OEM's value perception of component	124	0.00	n/a	102	0.00	n/a	108	0.00	n/a
Incremental Market Performance → Relationship Quality	OEM's value perception of component	107	0.00	48%	102	0.00	34%	93	0.00	58%
OEM's value perception of component → Cooperation of Supplier & OEM	Relationship Quality	136	0.00	56%	115	0.00	53%	102	0.00	61%
Relationship Quality → Share of wallet	Cooperation of Supplier & OEM	100	0.00	n/a	82	0.00	n/a	73	0.00	n/a
Relationship Quality → Future Expansion of Purchases	Cooperation of Supplier & OEM	105	0.00	38%	114	0.00	42%	89	0.00	44%
OEM's value perception of component → Share of wallet	Cooperation of Supplier & OEM	84	0.00	6%	66	0.00	9%	74	0.00	15%
OEM's value perception of component → Future Expansion of Purchases	Cooperation of Supplier & OEM	88	0.00	6%	91	0.00	11%	90	0.00	6%
component supplier brand strength → OEM's value perception	Incremental Market Performance	93	0.00	n/a	112	0.00	n/a	102	0.00	n/a
component supplier brand strength → OEM's value perception	Coercive Power Use by Supplier	92	0.00	n/a	81	0.00	n/a	93	0.00	n/a

Table 42: Test of mediating effects for the three data sets

The VAF value captures the share of the variance explained by the independent variable accounted for by the mediating effect (Eggert, Fassott, and Helm, 2005, p. 106). VAF cannot be calculated if one of the paths in the mediated relationship is negative. For example, the VAF measures in the second row illustrate that 34-58% of the effect of incremental market performance on relationship quality is mediated by the OEM's value perception of the component.

5.3.3   Moderating Effects

To test the moderating hypotheses of situational context factors, I use multi-group structural equations modeling in AMOS 7 (Arbuckle, 1983-2006). Due to the requirement of large sample size for covariance-based SEM, this test is only performed for the pooled data set (D1). I first conduct a triple split along the values of the moderator variable to create three sub-samples, one with low values of the moderator, one with medium values of the moderator, and one with high values of the moderator. Then I estimate the main effects model for all three sub-samples simultaneously. Table 43 displays the individual path coefficient estimates for the high value of moderator and low value of moderator groups. In a chi-square difference test I then compare the fit for an unconstrained model comprising the low and high groups with a model in which the main effect is constrained to be equal across the two groups. If the free model has a significantly lower chi-square than the constrained model, the moderating hypothesis is confirmed. Table 43 also reports the chi-square differences obtained along with their significance levels. I now discuss the results of the moderation tests for each of the four moderator variables.

The first moderator variable I test is OEM brand strength. As predicted by H_{14} and H_{15}, the effect of component supplier brand strength on incremental market performance and coercive power use, respectively, is stronger when the OEM's brand strength is low ($\Delta\chi2 = 4.6$, $p < 0.05$ and $\Delta\chi2 = 6.6$, $p < 0.05$). H_{16} suggested that incremental market performance affects the OEM's value perception of branded component more strongly for low OEM brand strength. This hypothesis is not confirmed by the data ($\Delta\chi2 = 2.2$, $p > 0.1$). At the same time, I find support for H_{17}, which stated that the negative effect of coercive power use on OEM's value perception of branded component would be stronger for high levels of OEM brand strength ($\Delta\chi2 = 4.5$, $p < 0.05$).

The second moderator variable is competitive intensity in the OEM industry. As H_{18} predicted, the effect of component supplier brand strength on incremental market performance is weaker when competitive intensity in the OEM industry is high ($\Delta\chi2 = 4.5$, $p < 0.05$). H_{19}, however, is not confirmed ($\Delta\chi2 = 0.2$, $p > 0.1$), suggesting that the effect of component supplier brand strength on coercive power use would be positively moderated by the level of competitive intensity in the OEM industry. Also, the data shows no support for the expectation that the effect of incremental market performance on the OEM's value perception of branded component would be smaller in size when competitive intensity in the OEM industry is high ($\Delta\chi2 = 0.1$, $p > 0.1$). Thus, H_{20} is not supported. Partial support is found for H_{21}, which formulated a positive moderating effect of competitive intensity in the OEM industry on the relationship between coercive power use and the OEM's value perception of branded component. Even though the corresponding chi-square difference is not significant ($\Delta\chi2 = 2.2$, $p > 0.1$), the path coefficient switches from not significant in the low group (-0.09, $p > 0.1$) to significant in the high group (-0.26, $p < 0.01$).

The third moderator variable I test is the intensity of the competition faced by the component supplier as indicated by the number of competitors for the component. As suggested by H_{22}, incremental market performance affects the OEM's value perception of the branded component more strongly when facing competition from a high number of competitors ($\Delta\chi2 = 3.2$, $p < 0.1$). At the same time, I find no support for the expected positive moderating effect of the number of competitors on the effect of coercive power use on the OEM's value perception of branded component (H_{23} $\Delta\chi2 = 0.1$, $p > 0.1$).

Ultimately, I test the fourth moderator variable, the commoditization of the component as an indicator for the intensity of competition faced by the component supplier. The data fails to provide support for the expectation in H_{24} that commoditization would moderate the effect of incremental market performance on the OEM's value perception of the branded component ($\Delta\chi2 = 0.9$, $p > 0.1$). I find strong support for the moderating effect formulated in H_{25} in that the effect of coercive power use on the OEM's value perception of branded component is stronger for high levels of commoditization of the component ($\Delta\chi2 = 9.1$, $p < 0.01$).

Mode-rator	Antecedent	Consequence	Δχ²	Sig.	Path Coefficient		Hyp.	Sup-port
					Low Value of Mod.	High Value of Mod.		
OEM Brand Strength	Component Supplier Brand Strength	Incremental Market Performance	4.60	0.03**	0.50***	0.20*	H_{14} -	Yes
		Coercive Power Use	6.60	0.01**	0.39***	-0.04	H_{15} -	Yes
	Incremental Market Performance	OEM's Value Perception of Branded Component	2.20	0.14	0.60***	0.55***	H_{16} -	No
	Coercive Power Use		4.50	0.03**	-0.01	-0.27***	H_{17} +	Yes
Competitive Intensity in OEM Industry	Component Supplier Brand Strength	Incremental Market Performance	4.40	0.04**	0.62**	0.35***	H_{18} -	Yes
		Coercive Power Use	0.20	0.65	0.25*	0.25***	H_{19} +	No
	Incremental Market Performance	OEM's Value Perception of Branded Component	0.10	0.75	0.66***	0.50***	H_{20} -	No
	Coercive Power Use		2.20	0.14	-0.09	-0.26***	H_{21} +	Partly
Number of Competitors for Component	Incremental Market Performance	OEM's Value Perception of Branded Component	3.20	0.07*	0.38***	0.92***	H_{22} +	Yes
	Coercive Power Use		0.10	0.75	-0.16*	-0.26**	H_{23} +	No
Commoditization of Component	Incremental Market Performance	OEM's Value Perception of Branded Component	0.90	0.34	0.39***	0.55***	H_{24} +	No
	Coercive Power Use		9.10	0.0***	0.00	-0.42***	H_{25} +	Yes

Note: Chi-square differences provided for "low" versus "high" group and correspond to a difference in 1 d.f.

Table 43: Moderating effects of situational context factors

5.3.4   Model Fit and Summary

The PLS algorithm does not provide an overall measure of model fit. I therefore report the overall model fit measures obtained when implementing the same model for the D1 dataset in covariance-based AMOS 7.0 (Arbuckle, 1983-2006). Note that the covariance-based algorithm produces a comparable pattern of results for the path coefficients. Given the high complexity of the model and the comparatively small sample size, the global fit of the model is overly satisfactory (C_{min}/d.f. = 1.93, RMSA = 0.06, CFI = 0.91).

Table 44 summarizes the study's PLS main effect estimates that are obtained from the pooled dataset of 241 cases (consisting of 104 aggregated multiple responses and 137 single responses). The columns in the table represent the dependent variables. The first row contains the R^2 values for each dependent variable. For *OEM's value perception of the branded component*, the goal is to introduce new antecedents to supplement other known drivers of value in business markets. Against this context, the R^2 of 0.19 is overly satisfying, as I did not aim to fully explain the variable. In the next rows of Table 44 follow the path coefficients and significance levels for the main effects model along with the result of the corresponding hypothesis test. Figure 30 shows a graphical illustration of these results.

Independent Variable	Incremental Market Performance	Coercive Power Use by Supplier	OEM's value perception of the branded component	Relationship Quality	Cooperation of Supplier & OEM	Future Expansion of Purchases	Share of wallet	Supported	Not Supported
			Dependent Variable (R^2)					Hypotheses	
	(0.19)	(0.19)	(0.19)	(0.30)	(0.30)	(0.35)	(0.10)		
Supplier Brand Strength	0.47***	0.22**	0.16*					H_1, H_2	
Coercive Power Use by Supplier			-0.21**	0.01				H_4	
Incremental Market Performance			0.31***	0.02				H_3	
OEM's value perception of the branded component				0.54***	0.18*	0.43***	0.28***	H_5, H_6, H_7, H_8	
Relationship Quality					0.43***	0.11	-0.02	H_9	H_{10}, H_{11}
Cooperation of Supplier & OEM						0.16**	0.09	H_{12}	H_{13}

Table 44: Summary of hypothesis tests for research question one (Dataset D1)

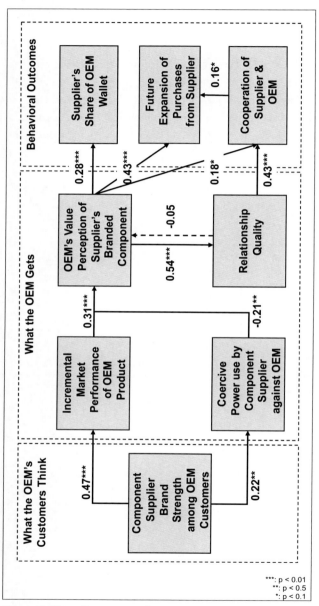

Figure 30: Main effects summary for research question one (Dataset D1)

5.4   Structural Model for Research Question Two

This section reports structural model parameters estimated with SmartPLS SEM (Ringle, Wende, and Will, 2005) for research question two. The structural model estimates reported here are based on the pooled dataset (D1) only because no significant differences are obtained for the other two datasets (D2-D3). Note that main effects, moderating effects, and mediating effects were all simultaneously estimated in a full model. In section 5.4.1, I analyze the main effects in the model. Next, I examine the mediating effects in section 5.4.2 before I turn to the moderating effects in section 5.4.3.

5.4.1   Main Effects

In this section I report estimation results obtained for the main effects model for research question two. The main effects for the core model estimated with the pooled data set are shown in Table 45. Columns four, five and six list the path coefficients, the corresponding t-values, and the resulting significance of the estimate. Next follow the R^2 inclusive and R^2 exclusive values in columns seven and eight. R^2 inclusive represents the coefficient of determination for the consequence variable if the main effect is included in the model. R^2 exclusive results if the model is estimated without the main effect at question. Finally, the effect size computed from the R^2 incl. and R^2 excl. values is displayed in the last column of the table.

I_1 through I_9 hypothesized effects of the brand management instruments that are available to component suppliers.

Brand image has a significant positive effect on component supplier brand strength, thus confirming I_1 ($\beta_1 = 0.32$, $p < 0.01$, $f^2 = 0.114$). In line with I_2, evidence is found that brand visibility positively affects component supplier brand strength ($\beta_2 = 0.23$, $p < 0.01$, $f^2 = 0.064$). Exclusivity has no significant effect on brand image ($\beta_3 = 0.06$, $p > 0.1$), so I_3 is not supported. At the same time, I_4, which expected a positive effect of exclusivity on incremental market performance of OEM product, can be confirmed ($\beta_4 = 0.11$, $p < 0.1$, $f^2 = 0.023$).

I_5 and I_6 pertain to the consequences of direct communication by the component supplier. The data shows a considerable positive effect of direct communication on brand image ($\beta_5 = 0.46$, $p < 0.01$, $f^2 = 0.253$). H_{18} is thus supported. Direct communication also positively affects component supplier brand strength ($\beta_6 = 0.18$, $p < 0.05$, $f^2 = 0.040$), confirming I_6.

Finally, hypotheses I_7 through I_9 posit effects of joint communication by the component supplier. I_7, expecting a positive effect of joint communication on brand image, is supported by the empirical data ($\beta_7 = 0.22$, $p < 0.01$, $f^2 = 0.047$). Joint communication also considerably affects incremental market performance of OEM product ($\beta_8 = 0.31$, $p < 0.01$, $f^2 = 0.127$) (I_8). No evidence is, however, found supporting I_9 for an effect of joint communication on component supplier brand strength ($\beta_9 = 0.08$, $p > 0.1$).

Antecedent	Consequence	Hyp.	Path Coeff.	T-Value	Sig.	R^2 Incl.	R^2 Excl.	Effect Size
Brand Image	component supplier brand strength	I_1	0.32	2.58	0.005	0.459	0.398	0.114
Brand Visibility	component supplier brand strength	I_2	0.23	2.30	0.011	0.459	0.425	0.064
Exclusivity	Brand Image	I_3	0.06	0.59	0.278	0.306	0.303	0.004
	Incremental Market Performance	I_4	0.11	1.46	0.072	0.539	0.528	0.023
Direct Communication	Brand Image	I_5	0.46	5.45	0.000	0.306	0.130	0.253
	component supplier brand strength	I_6	0.18	1.86	0.031	0.459	0.438	0.040
Joint Communication	Brand Image	I_7	0.22	2.44	0.007	0.306	0.273	0.047
	Incremental Market Performance	I_8	0.31	3.41	0.000	0.539	0.480	0.127
	component supplier brand strength	I_9	0.08	0.74	0.231	0.459	0.456	0.006

Table 45: Main effect estimates

5.4.2   Mediating Effects

Implicit in the model are a number of hypotheses about mediating effects that must be tested if one is to confirm that the hypothesized model is actually reflected in the underlying data. In this section, I use the procedure by Iacobucci and Ducacheck (2004) to test for the mediating effects that are implicitly stated in the hypotheses. For many relationships, the hypotheses assume partial mediation – i.e., the antecedent variable affects the dependent variable both directly and through the mediator (Baron and Kenny, 1986, p. 1176). In all other cases in which only an indirect effect is hypothesized, the test for mediation requires that the direct path is also included in the model. Table 46 shows the PLS path results for those additional non-hypothesized main effects as they resulted from the simultaneous estimation of all effects in the model. None of the direct paths shows as significant in the data, thus lending initial support to the underlying implicit mediation hypotheses.

Antecedent	Consequence	Path Coefficient	Significance
Direct Communication	Coercive Power Use by Supplier	-0.05	0.333
	Incremental Market Performance	-0.06	0.283
Exclusivity	Component Supplier Brand Strength	0.05	0.257

Table 46: Non-hypothesized main effects

In Table 47, I conduct the statistical tests to evaluate the mediating effects. The first column lists the mediated relationships. In the second column appear the corresponding mediating variables. I calculate the z-statistics by Sobel (1982) and the VAF measure (Eggert, Fassott, and Helm, 2005, p. 106) for the path estimates obtained from each of the three data sets (see Chapter 4 for details on the statistics). The z-statistics indicate whether the mediated path in the model is significant. As can be seen in Table 47, all mediated relationships in the three models are significant.

The VAF value captures the share of the variance explained by the independent variable accounted for by the mediating effect (Eggert, Fassott, and Helm, 2005, p. 106). VAF cannot be calculated if one of the paths in the mediated relationship is negative. For example, the VAF measures in the third row illustrate that 45% of the effect of direct communication on component supplier brand strength is mediated by brand image.

Mediated Relationship	Mediating Variable	Z-Stat.	Sig.	VAF
Direct Communication → Incremental Market Performance	Component supplier brand strength	111	0.00	n/a
Direct Communication → Coercive Power Use by Supplier	Component supplier brand strength	95	0.00	n/a
Direct Communication → component supplier brand strength	Brand Image	102	0.00	45%
Exclusivity → Incremental Market Performance	Component supplier brand strength	128	0.00	18%
Joint Communication → Incremental Market Performance	Component supplier brand strength	105	0.00	11%
Joint Communication → Component supplier brand strength	Brand Image	83	0.00	48%

Table 47: Test of mediating effects

5.4.3 Moderating Effects

Moderating hypotheses are modeled using the variable score approach suggested by Henseler and Fassott (2008, see also Chapter 4 for a detailed discussion) to accommodate formative and reflective constructs in the analysis. Because the moderating effects are hypothesized as interactions between variables in the main effects model, multigroup analysis was not an option. Table 48 shows the path coefficients, corresponding t-values, and significances of the interaction terms' estimated effect on the consequence variable. Next follow the R^2 inclusive and R^2 exclusive values and the corresponding effect size. These estimates are based on the D1 dataset.

I_{10} through I_{12} pertain to interaction effects of joint communication and direct communication. I_{10} expects that direct communication will more strongly affect brand image in the presence of joint communication. I find strong support for this hypothesis ($\beta_{10} = 0.21$, $p < 0.01$, $f^2 = 0.056$). At the same time, the effect of joint communication on incremental market performance of OEM product is not enhanced by direct communication as stated in I_{11}. Hypothesis I_{12} is supported: joint communication positively moderates the effect of direct communication on component supplier brand strength ($\beta_{12} =$ 0.12, p < 0.1, $f^2 = 0.018$).

Antecedent	Consequence	Hyp.	Path Coeff.	T-Value	Sig.	R^2 Incl.	R^2 Excl.	Effect Size
Direct Communication X Joint Communication	Brand Image	l_{10}	0.21	2.36	0.009	0.306	0.267	0.056
	Incremental Market Performance	l_{11}	0.00	0.01	0.497	0.539	0.539	0.000
	Component supplier brand strength	l_{12}	0.12	1.31	0.095	0.459	0.450	0.018

Table 48: Test of moderating effects

5.4.4 Model Fit and Summary

Table 49 summarizes the results of the hypothesis testing for research question two. The columns in the table represent the dependent variables. The first row contains the R^2 values for each dependent variable. The independent variables explain 46% and 54% of the variance in the variables component supplier brand strength and incremental market performance of OEM product, respectively. The model for research question two could not be implemented in covariance-based SEM in order to calculate global fit measures because of the formative constructs. Thus, only R^2 values are reported. The study aimed at identifying all important antecedents to these two variables. The corresponding requirement of $R^2 > 0.4$ (Homburg and Baumgartner, 1995, p. 172) is thus more than satisfied. In the next rows of Table 49 follow the path coefficients and significance levels for the main effects and moderating effects in the model. Figure 31 shows a graphical illustration of the results.

	Dependent Variable (R^2)				Hypotheses	
Independent Variable	**Brand Image** (0.31)	**Component supplier brand strength** (0.46)	**Incremental Market Performance** (0.54)	**Coercive Power Use** (0.19)	**Supported**	**Not Supported**
Brand Image		0.32***			I_1	
Brand Visibility		0.23**			I_2	
Exclusivity	0.06	0.05	0.11*		I_4	I_3
Direct Communication	0.46***	0.18**	-0.06	-0.05	I_5, I_6,	
Joint Communication	0.22***	0.08	0.31***		I_7, I_8	I_9
Direct Communication X Joint Communication	0.21***	0.12*	0.00		I_{10}, I_{12}	I_{11}

Table 49: Hypothesis test summary for research question two

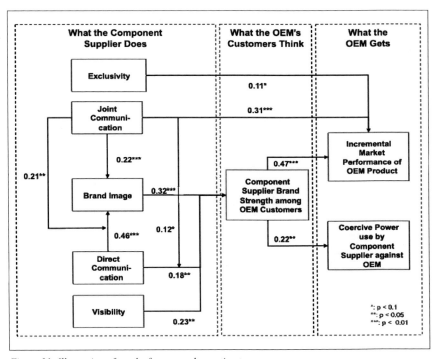

Figure 31: Illustration of results for research question two

The next Chapter discusses the implications of the empirical findings presented in this Chapter.

6 Discussion

This chapter discusses the implications and limitations of the present study's results. In section 6.1, I discuss the implications for theoretical development in the marketing discipline. Subsequently, in section 6.2 I focus on the implications of this research for managerial practice. Section 6.3 then examines the methodological implications that can be derived from the study. I then conclude, in section 6.4, with a discussion of the limitations and avenues for future research.

6.1 Implications for Theoretical Development

This study yields important implications for theoretical development in the marketing discipline. By developing and testing the theoretical framework I address two research questions regarding the performance outcomes and management issues of branded component strategies. In doing so, I give special consideration to the gaps in the literature I identified from reviewing it. In this section, I assess the theoretical contributions of this study by evaluating to what extent my findings advance our theoretical understanding of marketing with respect to the gaps in the literature identified in Chapter 1.

From a theoretical perspective, the motivation for this study arose from the considerable discrepancy between the observed relevance of branding in business markets and the state of theoretical development in this area. Initial support for the relevance of branding for firm performance in business markets comes from anecdotal evidence and a few empirical studies that are mostly exploratory in nature. Yet despite initial evidence, rigorous research on branding in business markets is scarce. When judging from the sheer amount and quality of publications, it seems that research on brands and branding has been almost exclusively focused on the arena of consumer-packaged goods. Most of the few existing empirical studies on branding in business markets are industry-specific and therefore lack generalizability. Another problem with many of those studies is that they merely apply the branding principles from consumer markets to the business-marketing context. Thus, the starting point for my study was the proposition that the theoretical framework of business marketing could more accurately explain firm performance if it incorporated brand-related constructs in addition to the traditional relationship metrics. In the remainder of this section, I discuss in detail how the study's findings contribute to theoretical development by (1) linking a component supplier's brand management activity to the behavioral market performance outcomes of the supplier, (2) identifying the mediating effects of variables related to OEM perceptions (i.e., "what the OEM gets"), and (3) examining the moderating effects of a competitive environment.

First, the most significant theoretical contribution of this study lies in establishing an effect of brand-related metrics on relationship metrics. As illustrated in Figure 32, the theoretical framework establishes a chain of effects that links a component supplier's brand management actions that are directed at OEM's customers to perceptual relationship metrics and to the market performance outcomes of the supplier in relationships with OEMs. Several important implications for thinking about branding in business markets emerge from this finding:

- This finding *refutes the rationality assumption of organizational buying*. This assumption suggests that, due to their high degree of professionalization, organizational buying centers are able to evaluate different offers based on objective information about the products' true value (Gilliland and Johnston, 1997, p. 17). Even though the existence of the concept of "true" objective value is at least questionable, the rationality assumption has very much shaped the way business marketing researchers view branding. Contrary to what this assumption may suggest, the brand as a "non-objective" characteristic of an offer has a considerable effect on component suppliers' business performance, even when the brand building actions are directed at the indirect customer.

- The finding *supports the case for a stronger integration of the buyer-supplier relationship and branding literatures.* Since branding and relationship marketing have evolved as separate streams of research, academics have put forward different market-performance-chains. However, for research on branding in business markets to be relevant to both practice and academia, I initially called for an integrated perspective on how brand management ties in with established findings and practices in relationship marketing. My theoretical framework integrates brand-related constructs and relationship management in buyer-supplier relationships. These two major streams of research have so far merely co-existed. During the past two decades, each of these two streams of research has received considerable attention from marketing academia. The two streams' points of contact, however, have been fairly limited to date. In this study, the value added to an

OEM's product by the supplier brand is introduced as an additional driver of the value an OEM perceives in the supplier's component. This means that, in addition to value creation instruments that have been suggested in the literature (i.e., core offering, sourcing, and operations (Ulaga and Eggert, 2006b)) buyers also take into account the component supplier brand's ability to affect their own business through its brand.

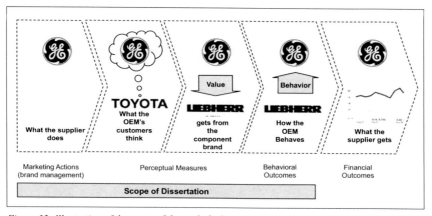

Figure 32: Illustration of the scope of the study findings

- This finding also uncovers the limitations of *the focus on buyer-firm dyads as the unit of analysis* in academic marketing research. Researchers have criticized both the buyer-supplier relationship literature (Anderson, Hakansson, and Johanson, 1994) and the branding literature (Bliemel, 1987, p. 5; Webster, 2000, p. 20) for overly simplifying the networked nature of markets by almost exclusively examining dyadic relationships. It is suggested that future research could gain explanatory power if it also considered triadic relationships (Menon, Homburg, and Beutin, 2005, p. 5; Ulaga and Eggert, 2006b, p. 133). In response to these shortcomings of the literature, this study puts forward a triadic perspective that accounts for the triangular relationship between manufacturer, intermediary (e.g., an OEM), and end customer. Overall, these results support calls that marketing academia could better contribute to an understanding of the broad area of exchange transactions and relations by taking into account the triadic and broader network structures instead of dyadic phenomena (Wuyts, Stremersch, Van Den Bulte, and Franses, 2004, p. 486).

The second most significant finding in this study concerns identifying the key variables that mediate the effect of brand-related metrics on relationship metrics. Importantly, brand management instruments and component supplier brand strength, respectively, may affect the OEM's value perception of the branded component in both positive and negative ways. A benefit for the OEM, resulting in higher perceived value, is created to the extent that component supplier brand strength translates into better market performance of the OEM. Conversely, component supplier brand strength also add to the sacrifices if the supplier chooses to use the brand as a source of coercive power and thus reduce the OEM's value perception of the branded component. The OEM's value perception of the branded component in turn acts as a mediator that links component supplier brand strength to the outcomes of the supplier-OEM relationship. Thus, the positive (or negative) effects of component supplier brand strength are found to increase (decrease) the OEM's share of wallet at the supplier, lead to better (worse) relationship quality and increased (decreased) future purchases, and more (less) intense cooperation between the supplier and the OEM. These findings on mediating effects yield two important implications for theoretical development:

- The finding that coercive power use by the supplier negatively affects the supplier's market performance demonstrates that the traditional view of brands as a general source of power over intermediaries (McCarthy, Shapiro, and Perreault, 1986) is ill-advised because it will lead to a dysfunctional relationship with OEMs and shift business to competitors.

- Another important finding relevant to theory development in the area of relationship management concerns the fact that the OEM's value perception of the branded component has a strong direct effect on the OEM's actual and planned future behavior. Contrary to what is suggested by the literature, the mediating effect of relationship quality is much weaker. The fact that the OEM's value perception of the branded component acts as the main mediator underscores the central importance of value in the business-marketing domain. In the same vein, this finding helps to question the validity of the often proclaimed centrality of the quality of the relationship itself as the universal mediating perceptual metric.

The third most important finding with regard to theoretical development concerns the findings on the *moderating effects of the competitive environment* on the effectiveness of branded component strategies. These findings provide evidence for the role of market-based assets in resisting competitive pressures (Srivastava, Fahey, and Christensen, 2001). The findings also highlight the relevance of including the competitive environment as a moderator in the marketing strategy literature (e.g. Bharadwaj, Varadarajan, and Fahy, 1993; Kohli and Jaworski, 1990). For example, research on buyer-supplier relationships has mainly focused on main effects models and has only to a much lesser extent examined how the benefits of relationships are contingent upon the situation.

In addition to the above mentioned three major contributions, the research findings also emphasize that, in addition to "soft" relational outcomes, theory development in the domain of relationship marketing should include "hard" relationship outcomes of the buyer-supplier relationships, such as share of wallet as an acid test of nomological validity. Notwithstanding the insight provided by linkages between attitudinal constructs, knowledge about the causal relationships between attitudinal variables and actual behavior is even more valuable. Because the goal of theoretical development lies in the explanation and prediction of how subjects behave in the marketplace (Hunt, 2002, p. 116-142), a theoretical framework adds more to knowledge generation in the discipline if it demonstrates its ability to explain and predict behavior.

6.2   Managerial Implications

Besides being theoretically insightful, the study has several important implications for managers. At a very general level, the study's results demonstrate that a branded component strategy can represent an opportunity for component suppliers to better differentiate their products. Using a well-devised branded component strategy, suppliers can move away from purely price-based competition in increasingly commoditized markets and thereby achieve better market performance in their relationships with OEMs.

It turns out that the pivotal point in the design of a branded component strategy would be to create a brand that adds value to the OEM's product. Only if the brand creates additional value will there be potential for it to improve the market performance of the OEM's product and thereby add to the value of the component from the OEM's perspective. Thus, the question that component suppliers need to ask is not whether to put a brand name or logo on their product. They will rather need to decide whether they want to devote considerable resources to building a brand. The findings also imply that the supplier-OEM relationship is not supported by brand building efforts at the level of the OEM's customers unless OEMs become aware of the value added to their product and the incremental market performance of their product. Suppliers may thus want to illustrate those gains to the OEM to reap the maximum benefits from the strategy.

The supplier should usually caution against the use of coercive strategies (the exception to this is discussed later in this section). If the brand is used as a source of power to make the OEM accept unreasonable conditions, the perceived value gains for the OEM may be reduced or offset. It may even make sense for suppliers to credibly reassure OEMs that they will not make use of coercive power in the future. The finding that use of coercive power by the supplier is not a beneficial outcome of a branded component strategy shows that the traditional view of brands as a means of power over intermediaries implied by the push-pull concept is counterproductive, thus confirming Webster's (2000, p. 18) assertion.

The study shows that a successful branded component strategy will indirectly lead to better outcomes of the supplier-OEM relationship by improving relationship quality and by intensifying cooperation between the supplier and the OEM. At a behavioral level, the OEM does a larger share of the business for the component with the supplier and is more likely to expand purchases from the supplier if the component branding strategy works. The use of share of wallet as a "hard" outcome and the corresponding path coefficient provide a tangible proof of a branded component strategy's potential benefits for business performance and thereby enable easier justification of brand investments at the top management level.

The study also provides guidance to managers regarding the implementation of marketing programs to build, nurture, and leverage component brands. Four major instruments are identified: direct communication, joint communication, exclusivity, and visibility. Additionally, brand image is included to represent the OEM's past experiences with the supplier. Direct communication turns out to be a powerful tool in building an image for a component brand and for the building of component supplier brand strength. Direct communication through interactive channels, such as internet and sales force visits, is more effective than one-way communication through catalogues. Supplier firms who use the latter as their primary communications tool should rethink their communications strategy. Joint communication in turn both helps with building and leveraging a component brand. Joint communication (1) makes direct communication more effective in building brand image and building component supplier brand strength and (2) increases the market performance of the OEM product. Making the branded component available only exclusively or selectively improves the incremental market performance to some extent. Visibility of the component brand in the product is also crucial as it enables the building of component supplier brand strength.

The analysis of the moderating effects of situational context factors also reveals that the effectiveness of a branded component strategy is contingent upon situational context factors. The competitive environment of both the component supplier and OEMs must be taken into account when evaluating or implementing of a branded component strategy for a certain firm. With regard to the OEMs' competitive environment, OEM brand strength and the competitive intensity in the OEM industry represent the key situational context factors that managers must consider. When it comes to the competitive environment of the component supplier, the number of competitors for the component and commoditization of the component are decisive.

Table 50 shows how managers can decide on a branded component strategy based on the findings for moderating effects of situational context factors. The columns in the table capture the brand strength of OEMs with which a component supplier does business. The degree of commoditization of the component appears in the rows. For component suppliers in situation (1), selling non-commoditized components to OEMs with low brand strength, a branded component strategy can be highly effective. Due to the switching barriers, these suppliers even face few negative consequences from coercive power use. Suppliers in situation (2), selling commodity components to OEMs with low brand strength, can also reap considerable benefits from a branded component strategy. However, they should refrain from using coercive power. Component suppliers who find themselves in situation (3), selling commodity components to OEMs with high brand strength, may want to stay away from a branded component strategy in the interest of their businesses. Not only is the strategy generally less effective in this situation, the adverse effects of coercive power use are also especially strong. Component suppliers who find themselves in situation (4), i.e., who are selling non-commoditized components to OEMs with high brand strength, should carefully evaluate if a branded component strategy will be for the benefit of their businesses. In this situation the strategy may be less effective, and caution is also warranted with regard to using coercive power.

Situational Context Factors		OEM Brand Strength	
		Low	High
Commoditization of Component	Low	(1) Branded component strategy highly effective, coercive power use not problematic	(4) Branded component strategy less effective, coercive power use *not* recommended
	High	(2) Branded component strategy highly effective, coercive power use *not* recommended	(3) Branded component strategy less effective, coercive power use *not* recommended at all

Table 50: Assessing the potential of a branded component strategy based on situational context factors

While this study focuses on branding in a pure business marketing environment, the integration of branding and relationship management also yields managerial implications for firms in consumer packaged goods markets. As retail organizations become increasingly powerful (Shocker, Srivastava, and Ruekert, 1994, p. 152-53), the isolated treatment of branding and key-account management diminishes the power of existing theories in those areas. Manufacturers of consumer-packaged goods should thus consider their brands' value to the retailer's business in their brand-building activities as a key success factor and account for this interdependence in their management organization (Webster, 2000).

6.3   Methodological Implications

Based on the expectation that use of single informants may lead to informant bias in the data (Homburg and Pflesser, 2000, p. 458), the present study relied on multiple informant data from a subset of 104 firms to eliminate measurement error. Unlike previous organizational marketing research that used multiple responses (Homburg, Grozdanovic, and Klarmann, 2007; Jaworski and Kohli, 1993), multiple responses are not just averaged to form a score for each company. Instead, an aggregation approach using weights based on the informant's self-assessed confidence in the accuracy of responses is used (Van Bruggen, Lilien, and Kacker, 2002). Consequently, responses from confident informants within a firm are weighted much more strongly than those from less confident informants.

Based on the results, a strong argument can be made that the use of multiple informants increases the accuracy of the results. Since data were collected from both marketing/sales managers and the purchasing function inside the OEM, it can be demonstrated that a branded component strategy is not only relevant to an OEM's customer-facing personnel, but that it will result in tangible performance outcomes in the OEM's relationship with the supplier. Interestingly, the comparison of model estimates obtained from the single and multiple informant data confirms speculations in the literature that method error could not only cause the researcher to overestimate but also underestimate certain relationships between variables: A halo effect can result in estimates of a stronger relationship while random error caused by less knowledgeable informants can disguise a true effect. The latter seems to be the case with the effect of the OEM's value perception of the branded component on share of wallet. This effect is significant when including the multiple informant data but does not show in the single response set. Thus, the important link between a branded component strategy and share of wallet could only be confirmed using the multiple informant approach. Overall, those findings indicate that organizational marketing research could achieve substantial validity gains from the more accurate measurement of variables. More research to advance our knowledge of the methodological aspects of multiple informant survey design and analysis is therefore urgently needed.

6.4   Limitations and Future Research Directions

Notwithstanding the insights it provides, there are certain limitations to this study. Also, numerous questions for future research can be identified.

One limitation of the study lies in the national character of the sample. As many component suppliers sell to OEMs worldwide, the present study needs to be extended to an international context. Besides ensuring the validity of the findings in the global arena, an international comparison may provide further interesting insight. One question that may be investigated is how branded component strategies provide protection from so-called white-box competition and the unlicensed use of patent rights in emerging markets countries. Another interesting question would be if OEMs in emerging markets are especially prone to use branded components as a means to establish better perceptions of their products.

The choice of the study design represents another limitation. The present survey takes a one-shot correlational approach while some scholars have called for the use of more longitudinal designs in business market research. Future studies may take a longitudinal approach to learn about the actual stepwise process of building a component brand. Also, compared to experiments, the correlational approach does not provide a strong test of causal direction. However, given the strong theoretical base for the direction of causality in my study, causal direction is not judged to be a big issue. In addition, tests for directionality of effects conducted with covariance-based SEM support the causal directions hypothesized in the study. Also, evolutionary economics theory suggests that even correlational approaches provide a test of causality with cross-sectional samples. Future studies may, however, use experimental designs to subject single relationships in the model to even more rigorously test for direction of causality.

Yet another potential limitation of the research design lies in obtaining the measure for the OEM's customer's perspective indirectly through the OEM's marketing and sales manager. This limitation was imposed by the fact that obtaining access to a larger number of OEM customers must be judged as close to impossible. Given that buyer-supplier relationships in business markets involve close interactions between suppliers and OEMs, it can be assumed, however, that informants were able to provide an accurate estimate for those measures. Support for the validity of these measures also comes from tests of nomological validity as no inconsitencies are observed in the measures' relationships with other constructs. Thus, it can be expected that the measurement of these variables does not limit the results.

My research examines only a limited set of outcome variables for the supplier-OEM relationship. It may be interesting to extend the set of those variables to see how the adoption of innovations by the OEM and the OEM's willingness to pay is affected by a branded component strategy. In addition, the relationship performance variables may be linked to measures of the OEM's financial performance in future studies. Similarly, the conceptual basis of the incremental market performance construct could be broadened to include other aspects of the OEM's market and financial performance.

Also, the present study does not examine how the different parties within the OEM's buying center are influenced by a branded component strategy. Common wisdom may suggest that marketing and sales managers within the OEM's organization value branded components higher than the purchasing function. It may thus be worth taking a closer look at how decisions are made within the OEM's organization. In this respect, knowledge about ways to strengthen the sales and marketing managers' position in convincing their colleagues in purchasing about the value of the branded component could be valuable.

References

Aaker, D. A. (1991), Managing Brand Equity: Capitalizing on the Value of a Brand Name. New York: Free Press.

Aaker, D. A. (1996), Building Strong Brands. New York.

Aaker, D. A. and Jacobson, R. (1994), "The Financial Information Content of Perceived Quality," Journal of Marketing Research (JMR), 31 (2), 191-201.

Aaker, D. A. and Jacobson, R. (2001), "The Value Relevance of Brand Attitude in High-Technology Markets," Journal of Marketing Research (JMR), 38 (4), 485-93.

Aaker, D. A. and Joachimsthaler, E. (2000a), Brand Leadership. New York.

Aaker, D. A. and Joachimsthaler, E. (2000b), "The Brand Relationship Spectrum: The Key to the Brand Architecture Challenge," California Management Review, 42 (4), 8-23.

Aaker, D. A. and Keller, K. L. (1990), "Consumer Evaluations of Brand Extensions," Journal of Marketing, 54 (1), 27-41.

Aaker, J. L. (1997), "Dimensions of Brand Personality," Journal of Marketing Research (JMR), 34 (3), 347.

Abratt, R. (1986), "Industrial Buying in High-Tech Markets," Industrial Marketing Management, 15 (4), 293-98.

Achrol, R. S. (1991), "Evolution of the Marketing Organization: New Forms for Turbulent Environments," Journal of Marketing, 55 (4), 77.

Agrawal, D. (1996), "Effect of Brand Loyalty on Advertising and Trade Promotions: A Game Theoretic Analysis with Empirical Evidence," Marketing Science, 15 (1), 86.

Ailawadi, K. L., Lehmann, D. R., and Neslin, S. A. (2002), "A Product-Market-Based Measure of Brand Equity," in Working Paper. Cambridge, MA: Marketing Science Institute.

Ailawadi, K. L., Neslin, S. A., and Lehmann, D. R. (2003), "Revenue Premium as an Outcome Measure of Brand Equity," Journal of Marketing, 67 (4), 1-17.

Akerlof, G. A. (1970), "The Market For "Lemons": Quality Uncertainty and the Market Mechanism," Quarterly Journal of Economics, 84 (3), 488-500.

Alba, J. W. and Hutchinson, J. W. (1987), "Dimensions of Consumer Expertise," Journal of Consumer Research, 13 (4), 411-54.

Anderson, E. and Weitz, B. (1989), "Determinants of Continuity in Conventional Industrial Channel Dyads," Marketing Science, 8 (4), 310.

Anderson, E. and Weitz, B. (1992), "The Use of Pledges to Build and Sustain Commitment in Distribution Channels," Journal of Marketing Research (JMR), 29 (1), 18-34.

Anderson, E. W. and Mittal, V. (2000), "Strengthening the Satisfaction-Profit Chain," Journal of Service Research, 3 (2), 107.

Anderson, J. C. and Gerbing, D. W. (1991), "Predicting the Performance of Measures in a Confirmatory Factor Analysis with a Pretest Assessment of Their Substantive Validities," in Journal of Applied Psychology Vol. 76: American Psychological Association.

Anderson, J. C., Hakansson, H., and Johanson, J. (1994), "Dyadic Business Relationships within a Business Network Context," Journal of Marketing, 58 (4), 1.

Anderson, J. C. and Narus, J. A. (1990), "A Model of Distributor Firm and Manufacturer Firm Working Partnerships," Journal of Marketing, 54 (1), 42-58.

Anderson, J. C. and Narus, J. A. (2004), Business Market Management – Understanding, Creating and Delivering Value. Upper Saddle River, New Jersey: Prentice Hall.

Arbuckle, J. L. (1983-2006), "Amos 7.0." Spring House, PA.

Armstrong, J. S. and Overton, T. S. (1977), "Estimating Nonresponse Bias in Mail Surveys," Journal of Marketing Research (JMR), 14 (3), 396-402.

Baker, W. H., Hutchinson, J. W., Moore, D., and Nedungadi, P. (1986), "Brand Familiarity and Advertising: Effects on the Evoked Set and Brand Preference," Advances in Consumer Research, 13 (1), 637-42.

Barney, J. (1991), "Firm Resources and Sustained Competitive Advantage," Journal of Management, 17 (1), 99.

Baron, R. M. and Kenny, D. A. (1986), "The Moderator-Mediator Variable Distinction in Social Psychological Research: Conceptual, Strategic, and Statistical Considerations," Journal of Personality and Social Psychology, 51 (6) (December), 1173–82.

Barwise, P. (1993), "Introduction to the Special Issue on Brand Equity," International Journal of Research in Marketing, 10 (1), 3-8.

Bendixen, M., Bukasa, K. A., and Abratt, R. (2004), "Brand Equity in the Business-to-Business Market," Industrial Marketing Management, 33 (5), 371-80.

Berens, G., van Riel, C. B. M., and van Bruggen, G. H. (2005), "Corporate Associations and Consumer Product Responses: The Moderating Role of Corporate Brand Dominance," Journal of Marketing, 69 (3), 35-18.

Berry, L. L. (1996), "Retailers with a Future," Marketing Management, 5 (1), 38-46.

Berry, L. L. (2000), "Cultivating Service Brand Equity," Journal of the Academy of Marketing Science, 28 (1), 128.

Bharadwaj, S. (2008), "Marketing Strategy Course Materials," Emory University, Atlanta.

Bharadwaj, S. G., Varadarajan, P. R., and Fahy, J. (1993), "Sustainable Competitive Advantage in Service Industries: A Conceptual Model and Research," Journal of Marketing, 57 (4), 83.

Bliemel, F. W. (1984), "Price-Quality Evaluations of Brands," in ASAC Conference Proceedings. Montreal.

Bliemel, F. W. (1987), "The Push-Pull Concept and Marketing Strategy. Contributions to Strategic Management," in Annual Conference of the Administrative Sciences Association of Canada Vol. 8. University of Toronto.

Bliemel, F. W., Eggert, A., Fassott, G., and Henseler, J. (2005), "Die Pls-Pfadmodellierung: Mehr Als Eine Alternative Zur Kovarianzstrukturanalyse," in Handbuch Pls-Pfadmodellierung: Methode, Anwendung, Praxisbeispiele, Bliemel, Friedhelm W. and Eggert, Andreas and Fassott, Georg and Henseler, Joerg, Eds. Stuttgart: Schaefer-Poeschl.

Boulding, W., Lee, E., and Staelin, R. (1994), "Mastering the Mix: Do Advertising, Promotion, and Sales Force Activities Lead to Differentiation?," Journal of Marketing Research (JMR), 31 (2), 159-72.

Box, G. E. P. (1976), "Science and Statistics," Journal of the American Statistical Association, 71 (356), 791.

Brodie, R. J., Glynn, M. S., and Van Durme, J. (2002), "Towards a Theory of Marketplace Equity: Integrating Branding and Relationship Thinking with Financial Thinking," Marketing Theory, 2 (1), 5-28.

Buchanan, L., Simmons, C. J., and Bickart, B. A. (1999), "Brand Equity Dilution: Retailer Display and Context Brand Effects," Journal of Marketing Research (JMR), 36 (3), 345-55.

Burgess, S. M. and Steenkamp, J.-B. E. M. (2006), "Marketing Renaissance: How Research in Emerging Markets Advances Marketing Science and Practice," International Journal of Research in Marketing, 23 (4), 337-56.

Cannon, J. P. and Homburg, C. (2001), "Buyer-Supplier Relationships and Customer Firm Costs," Journal of Marketing, 65 (1), 29-43.

Capraro, A. J. and Srivastava, R. K. (1997), "Has the Influence of Financial Performance on Reputation Measures Been Overstated?," Corporate Reputation Review, 1 (1), 86-93.

Carpenter, G. S., Glazer, R., and Nakamoto, K. (1994), "Meaningful Brands from Meaningless Differentiation: The Dependence on Irrelevant Attributes," Journal of Marketing Research (JMR), 31 (3), 339-50.

Caspar, M., Hecker, A., and Sabel, T. (2002), "Markenrelevanz in Der Unternehmensführung – Messung, Erklärung Und Empirische Befunde Für B2b-Märkte," in McKinsey/MCM working paper series, Backhaus, Klaus and Meffert, Heribert and Meffert, Jürgen and Perrey, Jesko and Schröder, Jürgen (Eds.): Marketing Centrum Münster.

Cavusgil, S. T. and Elvey-Kirk, L. A. (1998), "Mail Survey Response Behavior," European Journal of Marketing, 32 (11/12), 939-1192.

Chaudhuri, A. and Holbrook, M. B. (2001), "The Chain of Effects from Brand Trust and Brand Affect to Brand Performance: The Role of Brand Loyalty," Journal of Marketing, 65 (2), 81-93.

Chin, W. W. (1998a), "Issues and Opinion on Structural Equation Modeling," in MIS Quarterly. 22 ed.

Chin, W. W. (1998b), "The Partial Least Squares Approach to Structural Equation Modelling," in Modern Business Research Methods, Marcoulides, G.A., Ed. Mahwah, NJ: Lawrence Erlbaum Associates.

Chin, W. W., Marcolin, B. L., and Newsted, P. R. (2003), "A Partial Least Squares Latent Variable Modeling Approach for Measuring Interaction Effects: Results from a Monte Carlo Simulation Study and an Electronic-Mail Emotion/Adoption Study," Information Systems Research, 14 (2), 189-217.

Chin, W. W. and Newsted, P. R. (1999), "Structural Equations Modelling Analysis with Samples Using Partial Least Squares," in Statistical Strategies for Small Sample Research, Hoyle, R.H., Ed. Thousand Oaks, CA.

Chisnall, P. M. (2006), "Mail and Internet Surveys: The Tailored Design Method," International Journal of Market Research, 48 (6), 762-63.

Churchill, G. A. and Iacobucci, D. (2004), Marketing Research: Methodological Foundations (9 ed.): Cengage Learning Services.

Churchill Jr, G. A. and Iacobucci, D. (2004), Marketing Research: Methodological Foundations (9 ed.): Cengage Learning Services.

Cohen, J. (1988), Statistical Power Analysis for the Behavioral Sciences. Hillsdale, NJ: Lawrence Erlbaum Associates.

Collins, L. (1977), "A Name to Conjure With," European Journal of Marketing, 11 (4/5), 337.

Conner, K. R. (1991), "A Historical Comparison of Resource-Based Theory and Five Schools of Thought within Industrial Organization Economics: Do We Have a New Theory of the Firm?," Journal of Management, 17 (1), 121.

Court, D., French, T. D., and Knudsen, T. R. (2007), "Confronting Proliferation: A Conversation with Four Senior Marketers," McKinsey Quarterly (3), 18-27.

Cretu, A. E. and Brodie, R. J. (2007), "The Influence of Brand Image and Company Reputation Where Manufacturers Market to Small Firms: A Customer Value Perspective," Industrial Marketing Management, 36 (2), 230-40.

Crosby, L. A., Evans, K. A., and Cowles, D. (1990), "Relationship Quality in Services Selling: An Interpersonal Influence Perspective," Journal of Marketing, 54 (3), 68.

Day, G. S. and Wensley, R. (1988), "Assessing Advantage: A Framework for Diagnosing Competitive Superiority," Journal of Marketing, 52 (2), 1.

De Wulf, K., Odekerken-Schröder, G., and Iacobucci, D. (2001), "Investments in Consumer Relationships: A Cross-Country and Cross-Industry Exploration," in Journal of Marketing Vol. 65: American Marketing Association.

Desai, K. K. and Keller, K. L. (2002), "The Effects of Ingredient Branding Strategies on Host Brand Extendibility," Journal of Marketing, 66 (1), 73-93.

Diamantopoulos, A. and Schlegelmilch, B. B. (1996), "Determinants of Industrial Mail Survey Response: A Survey-on-Surveys Analysis of Researchers' and Managers' Views," Journal of Marketing Management, 12 (6), 505-31.

Dobni, D. and Zinkhan, G. M. (1990), "In Search of Brand Image: A Foundation Analysis," Advances in Consumer Research, 17 (1), 110-19.

Dodds, W. B., Monroe, K. B., and Grewal, D. (1991), "Effects of Price, Brand, and Store Information on Buyers' Product Evaluations," Journal of Marketing Research (JMR), 28 (3), 307-19.

Donath, B. (1999), "Mastering Business Brand Evolution – Key Point Summary from the Initial Meeting," in ISBM Business Marketing Brand Consortium. Chicago.

Donath, B. (2000), "Gathering Primary Data on the Web: How to Research Your Markets Quickly and Efficiently Via the Internet." Philadelphia, Pennsylvania: ISBM Business Market Research Consortium.

Doney, P. M. and Cannon, J. P. (1997), "An Examination of the Nature of Trust in Buyer-Seller Relationships," in Journal of Marketing Vol. 61: American Marketing Association.

Doyle, P. (2000), "Value-Based Marketing," Journal of Strategic Marketing, 8 (4), 299-311.

Dwyer, F. R., Schurr, P. H., and Oh, S. (1987), "Developing Buyer-Seller Relationships," Journal of Marketing, 51 (2).

Dyer, J. H. and Singh, H. (1998), "The Relational View: Cooperative Strategy and Sources of Interorganizational Competitive Advantage," Academy of Management Review, 23 (4), 660-79.

Eggert, A. (2004), Wertorientiertes Beziehungsmarketing in Kunden-Lieferantenbeziehungen: Habilitationsschrift, TU Kaiserslautern.

Eggert, A., Fassott, G., and Helm, S. (2005), "Identifizierung Und Quantifizierung Mediierender Und Moderierender Effekte in Komplexen Kausalstrukturen," in Handbuch Pls-Pfadmodellierung: Methode, Anwendung, Praxisbeispiele, Bliemel, Friedhelm W. and Eggert, Andreas and Fassott, Georg and Henseler, Joerg, Eds. Stuttgart: Schaefer-Poeschl.

Eggert, A. and Ulaga, W. (2000), "Customer-Perceived Value: A Substitute for Satisfaction in Business Markets?," in AMA Winter Educators' Conference Proceedings Vol. 11.

Eggert, A., Ulaga, W., and Schultz, F. (2006), "Value Creation in the Relationship Life Cycle: A Quasi-Longitudinal Analysis," Industrial Marketing Management, 35 (1), 20-27.

Eisenstein, P. (2000), "Vertically Challenged," Professional Engineering, 13 (9), 28.

El-Ansary, A. I. and Stern, L. W. (1972), "Power Measurement in the Distribution Channel," in Journal of Marketing Research (JMR) Vol. 9: American Marketing Association.

Erdem, T. l. and Swait, J. (1998), "Brand Equity as a Signaling Phenomenon," Journal of Consumer Psychology, 7 (2), 131.

Erdem, T. l., Swait, J., and Valenzuela, A. (2006), "Brands as Signals: A Cross-Country Validation Study," Journal of Marketing, 70 (1), 34-49.

Esch, F. R. (2001), Markenpositionierung Als Grundlage Der Markenfuehrung (3 ed.). Wiesbaden.

Esch, F. R. (2003), Strategie Und Technik Der Markenfuehrung. Muenchen.

Esch, F. R. (2004), "Umsetzung Von Markenidentitaeten," in Handbuch Markenfuehrung, Bruhn, M., Ed. 2 ed. Vol. 1. Wiesbaden.

Eysenck, M. W. (1999), Principles of Cognitive Psychology. Hove, east Sussex: Psychology Press.

Fang, E., Palmatier, R. W., and Steenkamp, J.-B. E. M. (2008), "Effect of Service Transition Strategies on Firm Value," Journal of Marketing, 72 (5), 1-14.

Farquhar, P. H. (1990), "Managing Brand Equity," Journal of Advertising Research, 30 (4), RC-7-RC-12.

Fassott, G. (2005a), "Die Pls-Pfadmodellierung: Entwicklungsrichtungen, Moeglichkeiten, Grenzen," in Handbuch Pls-Pfadmodellierung: Methode, Anwendung, Praxisbeispiele, Bliemel, Friedhelm W. and Eggert, Andreas and Fassott, Georg and Henseler, Joerg, Eds. Stuttgart: Schaefer-Poeschl.

Fassott, G. (2005b), Nutzung Auslaendischer Internetshops: Modellierung Und Test Auf Basis Des Pls-Strukturgleichungsansatzes: Habilitationsschrift, Technische Universitaet Kaiserslautern.

Fassott, G. (2006), "Operationalisierung Latenter Variablen in Strukturgleichungsmodellen: Eine Standortbestimmung," Zeitschrift fuer betriebswirtschaftliche Forschung, 58 (February), 67-88.

Flint, D. J., Woodruff, R. B., and Gardial, S. F. (1997), "Customer Value Change in Industrial Marketing Relationships: A Call for New Strategies and Research," Industrial Marketing Management, 26 (2), 163-75.

Fornell, C. (1987), "A Second Generation of Multivariate Analysis: Classification of Methods and Implications for Marketing Research" in Review of Marketing, Houston, M.S., Ed. Chicago, IL: American Marketing Association.

Fornell, C. and Larcker, D. F. (1981), "Evaluating Structural Equation Models with Unobservable Variables and Measurement Error," Journal of Marketing Research (JMR), 18 (1), 39-50.

Fournier, S. (1998), "Consumers and Their Brands: Developing Relationship Theory in Consumer Research," Journal of Consumer Research, 24 (4), 343.

Frazier, G. L. and Rody, R. C. (1991), "The Use of Influence Strategies in Interfirm Relationships in Industrial Product Channels," in Journal of Marketing Vol. 55: American Marketing Association.

Frels, J. K., Shervani, T., and Srivastava, R. K. (2003), "The Integrated Networks Model: Explaining Resource Allocations in Network Markets," Journal of Marketing, 67 (1), 29-45.

Gadde, L.-E. and Snehota, I. (1999), "Developing Effective Supply Strategy – Is Outsourcing, Single Sourcing and Patenting with Suppliers the Only Solution?," in 15th Annual IMP Conference, McLoughlin, Damian and Horan, C. (Eds.). Dublin, Ireland.

Ganesan, S. (1994), "Determinants of Long-Term Orientation in Buyer-Seller Relationships," Journal of Marketing, 58 (2), 1.

Gardner, B. B. and Levy, S. J. (1955), "The Product and the Brand," Harvard Business Review, 33 (2), 33-39.

Gaski, J. F. (1984), "The Theory of Power and Conflict in Channels of Distribution," Journal of Marketing, 48 (3), 9-29.

Ghosh, M. and John, G. (forthcoming), "When Should Original Equipment Manufacturers Use Branded Component Contracts with Suppliers?," Journal of Marketing Research.

Gilliland, D. I. and Johnston, W. I. (1997), "Toward a Model of Business-to-Business Marketing Communications Effects," Industrial Marketing Management, 26 (1), 15-29.

Glynn, M. S., Motion, J., and Brodie, R. J. (2007), "Sources of Brand Benefits in Manufacturer-Reseller B2b Relationships," Journal of Business & Industrial Marketing, 22 (6), 400-09.

Golder, P. N. (2000), "Historical Method in Marketing Research with New Evidence on Long-Term Market Share Stability," Journal of Marketing Research (JMR), 37 (2), 156-72.

Gordon, G. L., Calantone, R. J., and di Benedetto, C. A. (1993), "Brand Equity in the Business-to-Business Sector," Journal of Product & Brand Management, 2 (3), 13.

Grayson, K., Johnson, D., and Chen, D.-F. R. (2008), "Is Firm Trust Essential in a Trusted Environment? How Trust in the Business Context Influences Customers," Journal of Marketing Research (JMR), 45 (2), 241-56.

Grönroos, C. (1997), "Value-Driven Relational Marketing: From Products to Resources and Competencies," Journal of Marketing Management, 13 (5), 407-19.

Gundlach, G. T. and Cadotte, E. R. (1994), "Exchange Interdependence and Interfirm Interaction: Research in a Simulated Channel Setting," in Journal of Marketing Research (JMR) Vol. 31: American Marketing Association.

Gupta, S. and Zeithaml, V. (2006), "Customer Metrics and Their Impact on Financial Performance," Marketing Science, 25 (6), 718-39.

Hair, J. F., Black, W. C., Babin, B. J., Anderson, R. E., and Tatham, R. L. (2006), Multivariate Data Analysis (6 ed.): Pearson Education.

Heide, J. B. and John, G. (1990), "Alliances in Industrial Purchasing: The Determinants Of," in Journal of Marketing Research (JMR) Vol. 27: American Marketing Association.

Hempel, C. G. (1970), "Fundamentals of Concept Formation in Empirical Science," in Foundations of the Unity of Science, Neurath, Otto and Carnap, Rudolph and Morris, Charles, Eds. Vol. II.

Hennig-Thurau, T., Gwinner, K. P., and Gremler, D. D. (2002), "Understanding Relationship Marketing Outcomes: An Integration of Relational Benefits and Relationship Quality," Journal of Service Research, 4 (3), 230.

Henseler, J. (2005), "Einfuehrung in Die Pls-Pfadmodellierung," Wirtschaftswissenschaftliches Studium (2), 70-75.

Henseler, J. and Fassott, G. (2008), "Testing Moderating Effects in Pls Path Models: An Illustration of Available Procedures," in Handbook of Partial Least Squares: Concepts, Methods, and Applications in Marketing and Related Areas, Vincenzo, Esposito Vinzi and Chin, Wynne W. and Henseler, Joerg and Wang, Huiwen, Eds. Heidelberg: Springer.

Heskett, J. L., Jones, T. O., Loveman, G. W., Sasser Jr, W. E., and Schlesinger, L. A. (1994), "Putting the Service-Profit Chain to Work," Harvard Business Review, 72 (2), 164-70.

Hibbard, J. D., Kumar, N., and Stern, L. W. (2001), "Examining the Impact of Destructive Acts in Marketing Channel Relationships," Journal of Marketing Research (JMR), 38 (1), 45-61.

Homburg, C. (2003), "Marken Sind Auch Für Industriegüteranbieter Ein Thema," in Frankfurter Allgemeine Vol. 184.

Homburg, C. and Baumgartner, H. (1995), "Beurteilung Von Kausalmodellen: Bestandsaufnahme Und Anwendungsempfehlungen," Marketing ZFP, 17 (3), 162-76.

Homburg, C. and Giering, A. (1996), "Konzeptualisierung Und Operationalisierung Komplexer Konstrukte," Marketing ZFP (1), 5-23.

Homburg, C. and Giering, A. (2001), "Personal Characteristics as Moderators of the Relationship between Customer Satisfaction and Loyalty--an Empirical Analysis," Psychology & Marketing, 18 (1), 43-66.

Homburg, C., Grozdanovic, M., and Klarmann, M. (2007), "Responsiveness to Customers and Competitors:The Role of Affective and Cognitive Organizational Systems," Journal of Marketing, 71 (3), 18-38.

Homburg, C., Jensen, O., and Richter, M. (2006), "Die Kaufverhaltensrelevanz Von Marken Im Industriegueterbereich," Die Unternehmung, 60 (4), 281-96.

Homburg, C., Klarmann, M., and Schmitt, J. (2008), "Do B2b Brands Make a Difference? An Empirical Investigation of the Performance Implications of Branding in B2b Environments," in Proceedings of the 2008 AMA Winter Educator's Conference. Austin, TX.

Homburg, C., Kuester, S., Beutin, N., and Menon, A. (2005), "Determinants of Customer Benefits in Business-to-Business Markets: A Cross-Cultural Comparison," Journal of International Marketing, 13 (3), 1-31.

Homburg, C. and Pflesser, C. (2000), "A Multiple-Layer Model of Market-Oriented Organizational Culture: Measurement Issues and Performance Outcomes," in Journal of Marketing Research (JMR) Vol. 37: American Marketing Association.

Homburg, C. and Schneider, J. (2001), "Industriegütermarketing," in Branchenspezifisches Marketing, Tscheulin, Dieter K. and Helmig, Bernd, Eds. Wiesbaden: Gabler.

Hougaard, S. and Bjerre, M. (2003), Strategic Relationship Marketing: Springer.

Hoyer, W. D. and Brown, S. P. (1990), "Effects of Brand Awareness on Choice for a Common, Repeat-Purchase Product," Journal of Consumer Research, 17 (2), 141-48.

Hulland, J. (1999), "Use of Partial Least Squares (Pls) in Strategic Management Research: A Review of Four Recent," Strategic Management Journal, 20 (2), 195.

Hunt, S. D. (2002), Foundations of Marketing Theory: Toward a General Theory of Marketing. New York: M.E. Sharpe Inc.

Hunt, S. D. and Morgan, R. M. (1995), "The Comparative Advantage Theory of Competition," Journal of Marketing, 59 (2), 1.

Hunt, S. D. and Nevin, J. R. (1974), "Power in a Channel of Distribution: Sources and Consequences," Journal of Marketing Research (JMR), 11 (2), 186-93.

Hutton, J. G. (1997), "A Study of Brand Equity in an Organizational-Buying Context," Journal of Product & Brand Management, 6 (6), 428.

Iacobucci, D. and Duhachek, A. (2004), "Mediation Analysis," Advances in Consumer Research, 31 (1), 395-95.

Interbrand (2005), "Global Brands," Business Week (August), 86-88.

ISBM/BMA (2005), "Summary of Roundtable Discussion: Isbm/Bma Business Marketing Brand Consortium." Chicago: Institute for the Study of Business Markets.

Jacoby, J., Olson, J. C., and Haddock, R. A. (1971), "Price, Brand Name, and Product Composition Characteristics as Determinants of Perceived Quality," Journal of Applied Psychology, 55 (6), 570-79.

Janiszewski, C. and Van Osselaer, S. M. J. (2000), "A Connectionist Model of Brand-Quality Associations," Journal of Marketing Research (JMR), 37 (3), 331-50.

Jap, S. D. and Ganesan, S. (2000), "Control Mechanisms and the Relationship Life Cycle: Implications for Safeguarding Specific Investments and Developing Commitment," Journal of Marketing Research (JMR), 37 (2), 227-45.

Jaworski, B. J. and Kohli, A. K. (1993), "Market Orientation: Antecedents and Consequences," Journal of Marketing, 57 (3), 53.

Joachimsthaler, E. and Pfeiffer, M. (2004), "Strategie Und Architektur Von Markenportfolios," in Handbuch Markenfuehrung, Bruhn, M., Ed. 2 ed. Vol. 1. Wiesbaden.

Joereskog, K. G. and Wold, K. G. (1982), "The Ml and Pls Techniques for Modelling with Latent Variables – Historical and Comparative Aspects," in Systems under Observation, Part 1, Joreskog, Karl G. and Wold, K.G., Eds. Amsterdam/New York/Oxford.

Johansson, J. E., Krishnamurthy, C., and Schlissberg, H. E. (2003), "Solving the Solutions Problem," McKinsey Quarterly (3), 116-25.

Johnston, W. J. and Lewin, J. E. (1996), "Organizational Buying Behavior: Toward an Integrative Framework," Journal of Business Research, 35 (1), 1-15.

Jones, T. O. and Sasser, E. W. J. (1995), "Why Satisfied Customers Defect," Harvard Business Review, 73 (6), 88-91.

Kamakura, W. A. and Russell, G. J. (1993), "Measuring Brand Value with Scanner Data," International Journal of Research in Marketing, 10 (1), 9-22.

Kanuk, L. and Berenson, C. (1975), "Mail Surveys and Response Rates: A Literature Review," Journal of Marketing Research (JMR), 12 (4), 440-53.

Keller, K. L. (1993), "Conceptualizing, Measuring, Managing Customer-Based Brand Equity," Journal of Marketing, 57 (1), 1.

Keller, K. L. (1999), "Brand Mantras: Rationale, Criteria and Examples," Journal of Marketing Management, 15 (1-3), 43-51.

Keller, K. L. (2001), "Building Customer-Based Brand Equity: A Blueprint for Creating Strong Brands," in Working Paper. Cambridge, MA: Marketing Science Institute.

Keller, K. L. (2003), "Brand Synthesis: The Multidimensionality of Brand Knowledge," Journal of Consumer Research, 29 (4), 595-600.

Keller, K. L. (2008), Strategic Brand Management: Building, Measuring, and Managing Brand Equity: Pearson Education.

Keller, K. L. and Lehmann, D. R. (2003), "How Do Brands Create Value?," Marketing Management, 12 (3), 26-31.

Keller, K. L. and Lehmann, D. R. (2006), "Brands and Branding: Research Findings and Future Priorities," Marketing Science, 25 (6), 740-59.

Keller, K. L., Sternthal, B., and Tybout, A. (2002), "Three Questions You Need to Ask About Your Brand," Harvard Business Review, 80 (9), 80-86.

Kemery, E. R. and Dunlap, W. P. (1986), "Partialling Factor Scores Does Not Control Method Variance: A Reply to Podsakoff and Todor," Journal of Management, 12 (4), 525.

Kim, N., Mahajan, V., and Srivastava, R. K. (1995), "Determining the Going Value of a Business in an Emerging Information Technology Industry: The Case for Cellular Communications Industry," Technological Forecasting and Social Change, 49 (July), 257-79.

Kirmani, A. and Rao, A. R. (2000), "No Pain, No Gain: A Critical Review of the Literature on Signaling Unobservable Product Quality," in Journal of Marketing Vol. 64: American Marketing Association.

Kohli, A. K. and Jaworski, B. J. (1990), "Market Orientation: The Construct, Research Propositions, and Managerial Implications," Journal of Marketing, 54 (2), 1-18.

Kohli, C. and LaBahn, D. W. (1997), "Observations: Creating Effective Brand Names: A Study of the Naming Process," Journal of Advertising Research, 37 (1), 67-75.

Kotler, P. and Keller, K. L. (2005), Marketing Management (12th ed.). Upper Saddle River, New Jersey: Pearson/Prentice Hall.

Kotler, P. and Keller, K. L. (2006), Marketing Management (12th ed.). Upper Saddle River, New Jersey: Pearson/Prentice Hall.

Kotler, P., Keller, K. L., and Bliemel, F. W. (2007), Marketing-Management – Strategien Fuer Wertschaffendes Handeln (12 ed.). Munich: Peason Education.

Krafft, M., Goetz, O., and Liehr-Goebbers, K. (2005), "Die Validierung Von Strukturgleichungsmodellen Mit Hilfe Des Partial-Least-Squares (Pls)-Ansatzes," in Handbuch Pls-Pfadmodellierung: Methode, Anwendung, Praxisbeispiele, Bliemel, Friedhelm W. and Eggert, Andreas and Fassott, Georg and Henseler, Joerg, Eds. Stuttgart: Schaefer-Poeschl.

Krishnamurthi, L. and Raj, S. P. (1991), "An Empirical Analysis of the Relationship between Brand Loyalty and Consumer Price Elasticity," Marketing Science, 10 (2), 172.

Kuhn, K.-A. L., Frank, A., and Pope, N. K. L. (2008), "An Application of Keller's Brand Equity Model in a B2b Context," Qualitative Market Research: An International Journal, 11 (1), 40-58.

Kumar, N., Scheer, L. K., and Steenkamp, J.-B. E. M. (1995), "The Effects of Supplier Fairness on Vulnerable Resellers," Journal of Marketing Research (JMR), 32 (1), 54-65.

Laforet, S. and Saunders, J. (1999), "Managing Brand Portfolios: Why Leaders Do What They Do," Journal of Advertising Research, 39 (1), 51-66.

Laforet, S. and Saunders, J. (2005), "Managing Brand Portfolios: How Strategies Have Changed," Journal of Advertising Research, 45 (3), 314-27.

Lai, A. W. (1995), "Consumer Values, Product Benefits and Customer Value: A Consumption Behavior Approach," Advances in Consumer Research, 22 (1), 381-88.

Lehmann, D. R. and O'Shaughnessy, J. (1974), "Difference in Attribute Importance for Different Industrial Products," Journal of Marketing, 38 (2).

Leone, R. P., Rao, V. R., Keller, K. L., Luo, A. M., McAlister, L., and Srivastava, R. (2006), "Linking Brand Equity to Customer Equity," Journal of Service Research, 9 (2), 125-38.

Levin, A. M. and Davis, J. C. (1996), "Theoretical and Empirical Linkages between Consumers' Responses to Different Branding Strategies," Advances in Consumer Research, 23 (1), 296-300.

Lindell, M. K. and Whitney, D. J. (2001), "Accounting for Common Method Variance in Cross-Selectional Research Designs," in Journal of Applied Psychology Vol. 86: American Psychological Association.

Lusch, R. F. and Vargo, S. L. (2006), "Service-Dominant Logic: Reactions, Reflections and Refinements," Marketing Theory, 6 (3), 281-88.

Lynch, J. (2004), "The Power of Emotion: Brand Communication in Business-to-Business Markets," Journal of Brand Management, 11 (5), 403-19.

Madden, T. J., Fehle, F., and Fournier, S. (2006), "Brands Matter: An Empirical Demonstration of the Creation of Shareholder Value through Branding," Journal of the Academy of Marketing Science, 34 (2), 224-35.

Mahajan, V., Rao, V. R., and Srivastava, R. K. (1994), "An Approach to Assess the Importance of Brand Equity in Acquisition Decisions," Journal of Product Innovation Management, 11 (3), 221-35.

McAlister, L. (2005), "Introduction to the Research Overview," in Special Report No. 05-200.

McCarthy, E. J., Shapiro, S. J., and Perreault, W. D. J. (1986), Basic Marketing. Homewood, Illinois: Irwin.

Meffert, H. and Buhrmann, C. (2002), "Managementkonzept Der Identitaetsorientierten Markenfuehrung," in Markenmanagement: Grundlagen Der Identitaetsorientierten Markenfuehrung, Meffert, Heribert and Buhrmann, Christian and Koers, M., Eds. Wiesbaden.

Menon, A., Homburg, C., and Beutin, N. (2005), "Understanding Customer Value in Business-to-Business Relationships," Journal of Business-to-Business Marketing, 12 (2), 1-35.

Michell, P., King, J., and Reast, J. (2001), "Brand Values Related to Industrial Products," Industrial Marketing Management, 30 (5), 415-25.

Mohr, J. J., Fisher, R. J., and Nevin, J. R. (1996), "Collaborative Communication in Interfirm Relationships: Moderating Effects of Integration And," Journal of Marketing, 60 (3), 103.

Montgomery, C. A. and Wernerfelt, B. (1992), "Risk Reduction and Umbrella Branding," Journal of Business, 65 (1), 31.

Moore, G. C. and Benbasat, I. (1991), "Development of an Instrument to Measure the Perceptions of Adopting an Information Technology Innovation," in Information Systems Research Vol. 2: INFORMS: Institute for Operations Research.

Moorman, C., Zaltman, G., and Deshpande, R. (1992), "Relationships between Providers and Users of Market Research: The Dynamics of Trust within and between Organizations," Journal of Marketing Research (JMR), 29 (3), 314-28.

Morgan, R. M. and Hunt, S. D. (1994), "The Commitment-Trust Theory of Relationship Marketing," in Journal of Marketing Vol. 58: American Marketing Association.

MSI (1999), "Value of the Brand," in workshop at Marketing Science Institute Conference on Marketing Metrics. Washington, DC.

MSI (2007), "Top Five Msi Working Papers Downloaded in 2007," Vol. 2008: Marketing Science Institute.

Mudambi, S. M., Doyle, P., and Wong, V. (1997), "An Exploration of Branding in Industrial Markets," Industrial Marketing Management, 26 (5), 433-46.

Nagashima, A. (1970), "A Comparison of Japanese and U.S. Attitudes toward Foreign Products," Journal of Marketing, 34 (1), 68-74.

Nagashima, A. (1977), "A Comparative "Made In" Product Image Survey among Japanese Businessmen," Journal of Marketing, 41 (3), 95-100.

Noordewier, T. G., John, G., and Nevin, J. R. (1990), "Performance Outcomes of Purchasing Arrangements in Industrial Buyer-Vendor Relationships," Journal of Marketing, 54 (4), 80-93.

Oliva, R. A. (2005), "Business Marketing 'Straight up': Understanding, Creating, and Profitably Delivering Competitively Superior Value to Business Buyers," Institute for the Study of Business Markets, Pennsylvania State University.

Olson, J. C. and Jacobi, J. (1972), "Cue Utilization in the Quality Perception Process," in Proceedings of the Third Annual Conference of the Association for Consumer Research. Iowa City.

Palmatier, R. W., Dant, R. P., Grewal, D., and Evans, K. R. (2006), "Factors Influencing the Effectiveness of Relationship Marketing: A Meta-Analysis," Journal of Marketing, 70 (4), 136-53.

Panigyrakis, G. G. and Veloutsou, C. A. (2000), "Problems and Future of the Brand Management Structure in the Fast Moving Consumer Goods Industry: The Viewpoint of Brand Managers in Greece," Journal of Marketing Management, 16 (1-3), 165-84.

Parasuraman, A. (1997), "Reflections on Gaining Competitive Advantage through Customer Value," Journal of the Academy of Marketing Science, 25 (2), 154.

Parasuraman, A. and Grewal, D. (2000), "The Impact of Technology on the Quality-Value-Loyalty Chain: A Research Agenda," Journal of the Academy of Marketing Science, 28 (1), 168.

Park, C. S. and Srinivasan, V. (1994), "A Survey-Based Method for Measuring and Understanding Brand Equity and Its Extendibility," Journal of Marketing Research (JMR), 31 (2), 271.

Park, C. W., Jaworski, B. J., and MacInnis, D. J. (1986), "Strategic Brand Concept-Image Management," Journal of Marketing, 50 (4).

Park, C. W., Jun, S. Y., and Shocker, A. D. (1996), "Composite Branding Alliances: An Investigation of Extension and Feedback Effects," in Journal of Marketing Research (JMR) Vol. 33: American Marketing Association.

Payne, A. and Frow, P. (2005), "A Strategic Framework for Customer Relationship Management," Journal of Marketing, 69 (4), 167-76.

Penrose, E. T. (1959), The Theory of the Growth of the Firm. Oxford.

Podsakoff, P. M., MacKenzie, S. B., Jeong-Yeon, L., and Podsakoff, N. P. (2003), "Common Method Biases in Behavioral Research: A Critical Review of the Literature and Recommended Remedies," Journal of Applied Psychology, 88 (5), 879.

Podsakoff, P. M. and Todor, W. D. (1985), "Relationships between Leader Reward and Punishment Behavior and Group Processes and Productivity," Journal of Management, 11 (1), 55.

Porter, M. E. (1980), Competitive Strategy. New York.

Porter, M. E. (1985a), The Competitive Advantage: Creating and Sustaining Superior Performance. New York: Simon & Schuster.

Porter, M. E. (1985b), Competitive Strategy. New York.

Prahalad, C. K. and Ramaswamy, V. (2000), "Co-Opting Customer Competence," Harvard Business Review, 78 (1), 79-87.

Prahalad, C. K. and Ramaswamy, V. (2004), "Co-Creating Unique Value with Customers," Strategy & Leadership, 32 (3), 4-9.

Raj, S. P. (1982), "The Effects of Advertising on High and Low Loyalty Consumer Segments," Journal of Consumer Research, 9 (1), 77-89.

Ramani, G. and Kumar, V. (2008), "Interaction Orientation and Firm Performance," Journal of Marketing, 72 (1), 27-45.

Rangan, V. K. and Bowman, G. T. (1992), "Beating the Commodity Magnet," Industrial Marketing Management, 21 (3), 215-24.

Rangaswamy, A. (2000), "Rethinking Marketing Research for the Digital Environment." University Park, Pennsylvania: The Pennsylvania State University.

Rao, A. R. and Monroe, K. B. (1989), "The Effect of Price, Brand Name, and Store Name on Buyers' Perceptions of Product Quality : An Integrative Review," Journal of Marketing Research (JMR), 26 (3), 351-57.

Rao, A. R., Qu, L., and Ruekert, R. (1999), "Signaling Unobservable Product Quality through a Brand Ally," in Journal of Marketing Research (JMR) Vol. 36: American Marketing Association.

Rao, A. R. and Ruekert, R. W. (1994), "Brand Alliances as Signals of Product Quality," Sloan Management Review, 36 (1), 87-97.

Rao, V. R., Agarwal, M. K., and Dahlhoff, D. (2004), "How Is Manifest Branding Strategy Related to the Intangible Value of a Corporation?," Journal of Marketing, 68 (4), 126-41.

Rappaport, A. (1983), "Corporate Performance Standards and Shareholder Value," Journal of Business Strategy, 3 (4), 28.

Ravald, A. and Grönroos, C. (1996), "The Value Concept and Relationship Marketing," European Journal of Marketing, 30 (2), 19-30.

Reinartz, W. and Ulaga, W. (2008), "How to Sell Services More Profitably," Harvard Business Review, 86 (5), 90-96.

Reynolds, K. E. and Beatty, S. E. (1999), "Customer Benefits and Company Consequences of Customer-Salesperson Relationships in Retailing," Journal of Retailing, 75 (1), 11-32.

Richter, M. (2007), Markenbedeutung Und -Management Im Industriegueterbereich. Wiesbaden.

Ringle, C. M., Wende, S., and Will, S. (2005), "Smartpls 2.0 (M3) Beta." Hamburg.

Robertson, K. (1989), "Strategically Desirable Brand Name Characteristics," Journal of Consumer Marketing, 6 (4), 61.

Rossiter, J. R. (2002), "The C-Oar-Se Procedure for Scale Development in Marketing," International Journal of Research in Marketing, 19 (4), 305.

Russell-Bennett, R., McColl-Kennedy, J. R., and Coote, L. V. (2007), "Involvement, Satisfaction, and Brand Loyalty in a Small Business Services Setting," Journal of Business Research, 60 (12), 1253-60.

Rust, R. T., Ambler, T., Carpenter, G. S., Kumar, V., and Srivastava, R. K. (2004), "Measuring Marketing Productivity: Current Knowledge and Future Directions," Journal of Marketing, 68 (4), 76-89.

Rust, R. T. and Chung, T. S. (2006), "Marketing Models of Service and Relationships," Marketing Science, 25 (6), 560-80.

Sambamurthy, V. and Chin, W. W. (1994), "The Effects of Group Attitudes toward Alternative Gdss Designs on the Decision-Making Performance of Computer-Supported Groups," Decision Sciences, 25 (2), 215-41.

Samu, S., Krishnan, S., and Smith, R. E. (1999), "Using Advertising Alliances for New Product Introduction: Interactions between Product Complementarity and Promotional Strategies," Journal of Marketing, 63 (1), 57-74.

Schumpeter, J. H. (1934), The Theory of Economic Growth Development. Cambridge.

Seno, D. and Lukas, B. A. (2007), "The Equity Effect of Product Endorsement by Celebrities a Conceptual Framework from a Co-Branding Perspective," European Journal of Marketing, 41 (1/2), 121-34.

Shapiro, C. (1982), "Consumer Information, Product Quality, and Seller Reputation," Bell Journal of Economics, 13 (1), 20-35.

Shapiro, C. (1983), "Premiums for High Quality Products as Returns to Reputations," Quarterly Journal of Economics, 98 (4), 659-79.

Shaw, J., Giglierano, J., and Kallis, J. (1989), "Marketing Complex Technical Products: The Importance of Intangible Attributes," Industrial Marketing Management, 18 (1), 45-53.

Sheth, J. N. (1973), "A Model of Industrial Buyer Behavior," Journal of Marketing, 37 (4), 50-56.

Shipley, D. and Howard, P. (1993), "Brand-Naming Industrial Products," Industrial Marketing Management, 22 (1), 59-66.

Shocker, A. D., Srivastava, R. K., and Ruekert, R. W. (1994), "Challenges and Opportunities Facing Brand Management: An Introduction to the Special Issue," Journal of Marketing Research (JMR), 31 (2), 149.

Shrout, P. E. and Bolger, N. (2002), "Mediation in Experimental and Nonexperimental Studies: New Procedures and Recommendations," Psychological Methods, 7 (4), 13.

Simon, C. J. and Sullivan, M. W. (1993), "The Measurement and Determinants of Brand Equity: A Financial Approach," Marketing Science, 12 (1), 28.

Simon, H. (1979), "Dynamics of Price Elasticity and Brand Life Cycles: An Empirical Study," Journal of Marketing Research (JMR), 16 (4), 439-52.

Simonin, B. L. and Ruth, J. A. (1998), "Is a Company Known by the Company It Keeps? Assessing the Spillover Effects of Brand Alliances on Consumer Brand Attitudes," Journal of Marketing Research (JMR), 35 (1), 30-42.

Sirdeshmukh, D., Singh, J., and Sabol, B. (2002), "Consumer Trust, Value, and Loyalty in Relational Exchanges," in Journal of Marketing Vol. 66: American Marketing Association.

Sivakumar, K. and Raj, S. P. (1997), "Quality Tier Competition: How Price Change Influences Brand Choice and Category Choice," Journal of Marketing, 61 (3), 71-84.

Sobel, M. E. (1982), "Asymptotic Confidence Intervals for Indirect Effects in Structural Equation Models," in Sociological Marketing, Leinhardt, S., Ed. San Francisco, CA: Jossey-Bass.

Srinivasan, V., Chan Su, P., and Dae Ryun, C. (2005), "An Approach to the Measurement, Analysis, and Prediction of Brand Equity and Its Sources," in Management Science Vol. 51: INFORMS: Institute for Operations Research.

Srivastava, R. K. (2006), "Branding Challenges and Opportunuties in B2b and Technology Intensive Markets," in AMA Winter Educator's Conference. Tampa, FL.

Srivastava, R. K., Fahey, L., and Christensen, H. K. (2001), "The Resource-Based View and Marketing: The Role of Market-Based Assets in Gaining Competitive Advantage," Journal of Management, 27 (6), 777.

Srivastava, R. K. and Reibstein, D. J. (2005), "Metrics for Linking Marketing to Financial Performance," in MSI Special Report 05-200: Marketing Science Institute.

Srivastava, R. K., Shervani, T. A., and Fahey, L. (1998), "Market-Based Assets and Shareholder Value: A Framework for Analysis," Journal of Marketing, 62 (1), 2-18.

Srivastava, R. K., Shervani, T. A., and Fahey, L. (1999), "Marketing, Business Processes, and Shareholder Value: An Organizationally Embedded View of Marketing Activities and the Discipline of Marketing," Journal of Marketing, 63 (4), 168-79.

Stanley, J. E. and Wojcik, P. J. (2005), "Better B2b Selling," McKinsey Quarterly (3), 15-15.

Stern, B. B. (2006), "What Does Brand Mean? Historical-Analysis Method and Construct Definition," Journal of the Academy of Marketing Science, 34 (2), 216-23.

Tuli, K. R., Kohli, A. K., and Bharadwaj, S. G. (2007), "Rethinking Customer Solutions: From Product Bundles to Relational Processes," in Journal of Marketing Vol. 71: American Marketing Association.

Ulaga, W. and Chacour, S. (2001), "Measuring Customer-Perceived Value in Business Markets," Industrial Marketing Management, 30 (6), 525-40.

Ulaga, W. and Eggert, A. (2005), "Relationship Value in Business Markets: The Construct and Its Dimensions," Journal of Business-to-Business Marketing, 12 (1), 73-99.

Ulaga, W. and Eggert, A. (2006a), "Relationship Value and Relationship Quality," European Journal of Marketing, 40 (3/4), 311-27.

Ulaga, W. and Eggert, A. (2006b), "Value-Based Differentiation in Business Relationships: Gaining and Sustaining Key Supplier Status," Journal of Marketing, 70 (1), 119-36.

Ulaga, W., Eggert, A., and Schultz, F. (2006), "Relationship Value as a Driver of Customer Share," in 2006 EMAC Conference. Athens, Greece.

Van Bruggen, G. H., Lilien, G. L., and Kacker, M. (2002), "Informants in Organizational Marketing Research: Why Use Multiple Informants and How to Aggregate Responses," in Journal of Marketing Research (JMR) Vol. 39: American Marketing Association.

van Riel, A. C. R., Mortanges, C. P. d., and Streukens, S. (2005), "Marketing Antecedents of Industrial Brand Equity: An Empirical Investigation in Specialty Chemicals," Industrial Marketing Management, 34 (8), 841-47.

Varadarajan, R., DeFanti, M. P., and Busch, P. S. (2006), "Brand Portfolio, Corporate Image, and Reputation: Managing Brand Deletions," Journal of the Academy of Marketing Science, 34 (2), 195-205.

Vargo, S. L. and Lusch, R. F. (2004), "Evolving to a New Dominant Logic for Marketing," Journal of Marketing, 68 (1), 1-17.

Voelckner, F. and Sattler, H. (2006), "Drivers of Brand Extension Success," Journal of Marketing, 70 (2), 18-34.

Webster, F. E. J. (1991), Industrial Marketing Strategy (3 ed.). New York: John Wiley&Sons.

Webster, F. E. J. (2000), "Understanding the Relationships among Brands, Consumers, and Resellers," Journal of the Academy of Marketing Science, 28 (1), 17.

Webster, J. F. E. and Keller, K. L. (2004), "A Roadmap for Branding in Industrial Markets," Journal of Brand Management, 11 (5), 388-402.

Webster Jr, F. E. (2004), "A Roadmap for Branding in Industrial Markets," Journal of Brand Management, 11 (5), 388-402.

Wernerfelt, B. (1984), "A Resource-Based View of the Firm," Strategic Management Journal, 5 (2), 171-80.

Wernerfelt, B. (1988), "Umbrella Branding as a Signal of New Product Quality: An Example of Signalling by Posting a Bond," RAND Journal of Economics, 19 (3), 458-66.

Woodruff, R. B. (1997), "Customer Value: The Next Source for Competitive Advantage," Journal of the Academy of Marketing Science, 25 (2), 139.

Woratschek, H. and Roth, S. (2004), "Informationsökonomischer Erklärungsansatz Der Markenpolitik," in Handbuch Markenführung, Bruhn, M., Ed. 2 ed. Vol. 1. Wiesbaden.

Worm, S., Hansen, F., Peters, P., and Zitzlsperger, D. (2007), "How Brand Equity Affects Channel Equity in B2b Retailing: A Structural Model," in 36th EMAC Conference 2007. Reykjavik, Iceland.

Worm, S. and Srivastava, R. K. (2009), "Brand Strength of Component Suppliers as a Driver of Their Market Performance," Proceedings of 2009 AMA Winter Marketing Educator's Conference in Tampa, Florida.

Worm, S. and Van Durme, J. (2006), "An Empirical Study of the Consequences of Co-Branding on Perceptions of the Ingredient Brand," in Proceedings of the 35th EMAC Conference 2006. Athens, Greece.

Wuyts, S., Stremersch, S., Van Den Bulte, C., and Franses, P. H. (2004), "Vertical Marketing Systems for Complex Products: A Triadic Perspective," in Journal of Marketing Research (JMR) Vol. 41: American Marketing Association.

Yoo, B., Donthu, N., and Lee, S. (2000), "An Examination of Selected Marketing Mix Elements and Brand Equity," Journal of the Academy of Marketing Science, 28 (2), 195-211.

Zaltmann, G., LeMasters, K., and Heffring, M. (1982), Theory Construction in Marketing: Some Thoughts on Thinking. New York, NY: Wiley & Sons.

Zarantonello, L., Schmitt, B. H., and Brakus, J. J. (2007), "Development of the Brand Experience Scale," in Advances in Consumer Research – North American Conference Proceedings Vol. 34: Association for Consumer Research.

Zeithaml, V. A. (1988), "Consumer Perceptions of Price, Quality, and Value: A Means-End Model and Synthesis of Evidence," in Journal of Marketing Vol. 52: American Marketing Association.